Leaving Home

A conducted tour of twentieth-century music
with Simon Rattle

by the same author
Harrison Birtwistle (Robson, 1984)

Leaving Home

A conducted tour of twentieth-century music
with Simon Rattle

Michael Hall

faber and faber

First published in 1996
by Faber and Faber Limited
3 Queen Square London WC1N 3AU

Typeset by Faber and Faber Ltd
Printed in Great Britain by BPC Consumer Books Ltd
A member of the British Printing Company Ltd

A CIP record for this book
is available from the British Library

ISBN 0–571–17877–4

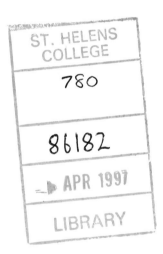
10 9 8 7 6 5 4 3 2 1

Contents

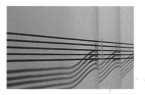

Preface

This book is based on the television series *Leaving Home*, introduced by Sir Simon Rattle and produced by London Weekend Television for Channel Four. It has the same form and focuses largely on the music featured in the series, but introduces where possible composers and works that the 'hard-argued choices' mentioned in Simon Rattle's Foreword forced out.

In the first three programmes Simon Rattle discusses and illustrates three of the basic elements of music – the crisis in tonality in the early years of the century, the radical rethinking of rhythm, and the expansion in conceptions of orchestral colour. In the next two, he looks at the way music has fared in two areas not previously regarded as centres of Classical music, Eastern Europe – focusing on the three major composers of the middle of the century, Bartók, Shostakovich and Lutosławski – and the United States. The last two programmes cover a variety of music composed since the Second World War; both the initial radical responses to that catastrophe, and the broadening out of issues and sound worlds since then.

The book follows these movements, placing them in a broader musical and cultural context than that allowed for even in almost seven hours of television. But it begins with an overview of the century's music and the social conditions that have influenced it.

The extracts in bold in the margins of the book are from the series.

Leaving Home, the book, would not have been possible without the assistance of all the production team at London Weekend Television and Channel Four, especially the series producers, Sue Knussen and Hilary Chadwick. As well as allowing the author to attend recording sessions, they have been supportive and encouraging in many ways. The publishers would like to acknowledge Jenny Borthwick's invaluable work researching pictures, and Sarah Hull's practical help.

The author would like to thank his wife Brenda for being so helpful and so patient, and Michael Durnin for asking him to write the book.

The author and publishers would like to thank the following music publishers for the loan of scores and tapes: Boosey and Hawkes, Chester Music, Editions Salabert, Faber Music, Peters Edition, Schott (London), Universal Edition, United Music Publishers.

Foreword

by Sir Simon Rattle

The genesis of *Leaving Home* stemmed from my desire to bring the music of our wonderful, infuriating century to a wider public, to attempt to piece together some of the connections without which this artistic journey can seem bewildering. At least this is how it all looks in retrospect. At the time I was first approached, fear dominated all my responses. How could this unruly beast be tamed, let alone explained? How could we hope to find a coherent thread through such a rich but tangled store of works? At first, I hardly dared to ask myself the obvious question of what to choose, struck as I was by the essential problem of music on TV, which is that it must take place in time. The great art documentaries, of which Kenneth Clark's *Civilisation* and Robert Hughes' *The Shock of the New* have been particularly influential and memorable, had the enormous advantage of presenting a wide swathe of work rapidly. In an hour, it is perfectly possible to present fifty or sixty works of art – even a few seconds can make a point. Music, however, cannot be taken in at a glance – that is simultaneously its blessing and its curse – and any one programme could only deal with, say, half a dozen pieces without taking on the character of some purgatorial spot-the-masterpiece quiz. It became apparent very quickly that the series could not attempt to be comprehensive, either historically or in viewpoint, and that we had to concentrate on music that somehow drove the century forward. Inevitably, much has been omitted, including a great deal of my favourite music: no Szymanowski or Prokofiev, no Sibelius, Nielsen, Janáček, Elgar, Tippett; the list is painful, but is the result of hard-argued choice. This book has the possibility to cast its net wider, more generously, and for that I am profoundly grateful, as I am for its thoughtful and revealing analysis of the main musical trends of our time.

But this is enough explanation of what the series is *not* – I make no apologies for the music that we *have* been able to choose, or for the fact that they are all, without exception, pieces that I love. As I said in the introduction to my last programme, it has been like compiling a taster menu that people will come back to for more, exploring tastes and textures that might initially seem strange or foreign. The music of our century is an inexhaustible gold mine. I hope that our series encourages people to dig out their own nuggets, and that they will use Michael Hall's informative book as their guide to ever richer seams.

Chapter 1
A View of the Century

For music lovers in Birmingham, the first year of the century was marked by the première of Edward Elgar's oratorio *The Dream of Gerontius*. It was not a success. The choirmaster, a staunch nonconformist, had been openly critical of Cardinal Newman's poem, on which the work is based, as well as Elgar's music, and had not allowed enough time for preparation. Even Hans Richter, the conductor, was puzzled by Elgar's 'novel idiom'. After his first rehearsal with the choir, he spent half the night pacing up and down his bedroom with the score propped open on the mantlepiece trying to master and memorize it. At the première, some of the chorus refused to take the music seriously and one or two of the basses were accused of behaving like buffoons. After the performance, one eminent musician said that the work was 'antagonistic to his inherent Protestantism', another that it 'stank of incense'. Within a year or two, however, the oratorio was being proclaimed a masterpiece. At a reception after a highly successful performance at Düsseldorf in 1902, Richard Strauss raised his glass to 'the first English progressive musician, Meister Elgar'.

Beginnings can be deceptive. The twentieth century has been the most violent in human history, yet it began in a state of relative calm. The culture was still bourgeois, the musical style Romantic, as it had been for eighty-six comparatively peaceful years. The economy had entered a boom period; industry and technology were expanding at an unprecedented rate, trade and business flourished, and the middle classes prospered. For the French it was 'la belle époque'. The advent of the motor car, aeroplane, telephone, wireless telegraph, vacuum cleaner, cinema and gramophone record created optimism, a sense that a bright new future was opening up. But it also brought uncertainty, a feeling of loss. The old, much loved, way of life was disappearing.

The expansiveness and nobility of Elgar's music contains within it an insecurity that seems to be public as well as private. The characteristic feature of *The Dream of Gerontius* is the contrast between the

It has been a century of emigration and exile, both voluntary and forced. But 'leaving home' is also the dominant metaphor for a time in which all the certainties, social, political and artistic have migrated.

The City of Birmingham Symphony Orchestra and Chorus.

assurance that Cardinal Newman conveys in his account of the Soul's journey through judgment to purgatory, and the anxious nature of Elgar's chromaticisms. This dichotomy is also present in Elgar's symphonies, the first movement of the second (1911) in particular. Elgar never took any part in the folksong revival that led composers such as Delius and Vaughan Williams to evoke the English countryside as a 'land of lost content', but in the Violin Concerto (1910) and especially the Cello Concerto (1919), he was able to express a sense of loss by recalling earlier material as if it were a memory to be lingered over.

These Elgarian characteristics are shared by Mahler, although in his music they are taken to extremes. The sense of assurance and optimism pervading the second and concluding movement of his Eighth Symphony, 'the Symphony of a Thousand' (1906), a setting of the last scene in Goethe's *Faust*, is without parallel in music. In Mahler's hands it becomes a celebration of God the creator and of the creative spirit of man, a sustained affirmation of divine and human love. The Ninth Symphony (1909), on the other hand, looks into the abyss. The whole work, from the muted horn call at the beginning to the drawn-out cadence on muted strings at the end, is an unsuccessful attempt to find something that does not mock or dissolve into doubts and uncertainties. Mahler also shared Elgar's sense of loss, the feeling that the world he loved was slipping away. However, in 'Der Abschied', the huge symphonic song that brings *Das Lied von der Erde* (1909) to a close, he says farewell to it in a spirit not of regret but of wonderment. He looks back at 'the dear earth' as if he had never before seen how beautiful it is, how radiant.

For Elgar and Mahler it is clear that 'la belle époque' was not what it seemed to be on the surface. The contradictions in their music point to the fact that all the old certainties were evaporating. In physics, for example, Max Planck's 'quantum hypothesis' (1900), Albert Einstein's 'special theory of relativity' (1905) and Niels Bohr's model of the atom (1913) undermined Newton's theory that the world was stable and mechanically ordered. In psychology, Sigmund Freud and Carl Jung were showing that the mind was also not as stable or as rational as had previously been thought. The bizarre and irrational nature of the unconscious mind appeared to be as important in human behaviour as the conscious mind.

It was the awareness that behind the rational world lie unexplored worlds significant to our lives that prompted most, if not all, the new movements which arose in the arts between 1900 and 1914. The first such development was the advent of Cubism in 1906. Its significance was the discovery of a new way to represent three-dimensional volumes on a two-dimensional surface. This too undermined what had hitherto been considered stable. Instead of depicting an object from one perspective, which had been the norm ever since the Renaissance, the Cubists presented it from different perspectives, so that it could be seen from (say) the back and the sides as well as the front simultaneously. The result was an image that defied the laws of reason and made the real world appear as bizarre as the worlds encountered in dreams.

The wish to explore worlds lying outside normal experience was undoubtedly the reason Schoenberg took the radical step of abandoning the tonal system in 1909, and why, in *The Rite of Spring* (1912), Stravinsky gave such unprecedented importance to rhythm. The tonal system emerged during the Renaissance to reflect the humanist philosophy of the time. People still wanted to be in harmony with themselves and the world, while at the same time being expressive and dynamically purposeful. Although it took nearly two centuries to become firmly established, tonality, the system in which everything is related to the principal chord of a selected key, provided the necessary stable framework for this individualistic yet rational philosophy. It served the differing needs of Baroque, Classical and Romantic composers, and is still in use. But the tonal system has not proved suitable for those who want to look at human experience from another perspective. The distraught inner world of the woman searching for her lover in Schoenberg's dramatic monologue *Erwartung* (1909) needed music that was constantly in flux, that moved from one event to another without any apparent logic, and had no stable harmonic framework to underpin its network of fragmentary and seemingly unrelated melodic cells. The barbaric, pagan world Stravinsky wanted to recreate in *The Rite of Spring* needed music that eschewed civilized values and evoked 'mystic terror'. To do this he had to produce music in which most of the interest lies in the apparently irrational behaviour of the rhythms.

Despite these radical innovations, the watershed between the nineteenth and twentieth centuries was actually the First World War. It brought to an end Romanticism and the dominance of the bourgeoisie in European politics. Those composers who were in their fifties or sixties when the war ended continued to produce Romantic scores, but with considerably less enthusiasm. The operas Richard Strauss produced were mere shadows of the pre-war *Der Rosenkavalier* and *Ariadne auf Naxos*. Elgar wrote virtually nothing after the Cello Concerto. Sibelius, who lived on until 1957, dried up after he completed *Tapiola* in 1926. Puccini, who had wanted to 'strike out on new paths' after the war, left *Turandot* uncompleted when he died the same year. The only composer of that generation who blossomed in the twenties was Janáček, who produced four major operas (*Katya Kabanova*, *The Cunning Little Vixen*, *The Makropulos Affair* and *From the House of the Dead*) as well as some outstanding vocal and instrumental music. Not only did he gain a new lease of life in his sixties, but the style he had evolved in his opera *Jenůfa* (1904) still sounded novel. Melodically it was based on the speech inflections of the Czech language, harmonically, rhythmically and structurally on the folk music of his native Moravia. It was therefore closer to the modal tradition than the tonal, and it gave him the flexibility to explore areas of experience his contemporaries avoided. It is difficult to imagine Puccini or Strauss wanting to write an opera about life in a prison camp, for instance.

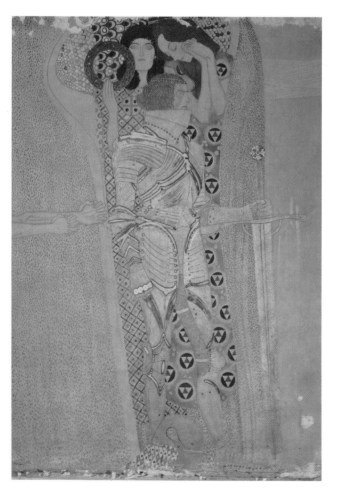

Gustav Klimt, *Beethoven Frieze*. 'The Knight', said to be a portrait of Gustav Mahler.

Although Janáček's late harvest of scores was outstanding, his music was not truly representative of the underlying mood of the twenties. None of his young contemporaries would have been prepared to write music as emotional as that provided for Katya Kabanova. They rejected Romanticism totally. Emotions had to be distanced, and when they were expressed they tended to be derided. Even those who had not experienced life in the trenches knew that in those conditions it was necessary to assume a mask and keep emotions at bay. The only composer who had been overtly anti-Romantic in the period leading up to the war was Erik Satie. His music consisted mainly of short piano pieces with droll or ironic titles, modal harmony, simple rhythms and mosaic-like structures. When Jean Cocteau heard him play in 1915 he proclaimed him to be the anti-Romantic *par excellence*. Within a short while Satie and Cocteau were collaborating on *Parade*, a ballet about a parade of circus turns, which, when it was produced in 1917, was hailed as the model which every composer ought to adopt after the war.

But the music that made the biggest impact in 1917 was jazz, for it was then that the Original Dixieland Jazz Band's recordings of *Livery Stable Blues* and *Dixie Jass Band One Step* were issued. (It had not been decided whether to call the new music jazz or jass.) *Livery Stable Blues*, a jocular number featuring instrumental 'neighing', became a runaway hit. It illustrates the fact that the attraction of jazz in its early days lay not only in its rhythmic freedom and improvisatory character but also its sense of humour and capacity to deride. This is true even when Ma Rainey or Bessie Smith sang slow specimens of the blues. Bessie Smith's 1925 recording of the *St Louis Blues* is probably the most famous example of urban blues. She sings it straight, her simple phrasing and beauty of tone adding dignity to the sadness of the tune and words. Accompanying her are Fred Longshaw on harmonium and Louis Armstrong on cornet, the one providing a church-like ambience, the other a gentle but constant hint of mockery. Armstrong's inherent sense of humour never allows Smith's emotion to predominate.

1917 was also the year when six young French composers (Georges Auric, Louis Durey, Arthur Honegger, Darius Milhaud, Francis Poulenc and Germaine Tailleferre), calling themselves 'Les Nouveaux Jeunes', started giving concerts together in Paris. Later they became known as 'Les Six'. What united them was their enthusiasm for Cocteau's call for a new, anti-Romantic spirit to take over from 'Wagnerian fog', Debussy's 'mists' and Stravinsky's 'theatrical mysticisms'. 'Enough of clouds, waves, aquariums, waterspirits, and nocturnal scents,' he said; 'what we need is a music of the earth, every-day music.' He recommended that the new generation of composers should take as their models Satie and the popular music of the day. In 1920, when Milhaud was asked to write music for Cocteau's ballet *Le*

Pablo Picasso, *Violin* (1911–12).

Claude Debussy with Erik Satie, Paris, 1910.

boeuf sur le toit ('The ox on the roof'), in which the hilarious mime was performed by a celebrated troupe of clowns, he came up with a string of popular dances from Brazil. The following year five of Les Six collaborated in writing music for a ballet by Cocteau called *Les mariés de la tour Eiffel* ('The newly-weds of the Eiffel Tower'), a satire on the bourgeoisie. The wittiest feature was Cocteau's inventive use of gramophones to deliver the cliché-ridden dialogue of the newly-weds. Durey refused to take part on the grounds that the music of his colleagues was becoming too flippant, an opinion that Honegger was also beginning to share.

Thereafter the members of Les Six went their own ways, but their use of popular music exerted an influence on the twenty-one-year-old William Walton when in 1922 he collaborated with Edith Sitwell on their 'drawing-room entertainment', *Façade*. Like Cocteau, Sitwell also set out to shock middle-class philistinism and stodginess, but in her case from an aristocratic stance. Walton described the collaboration as the product of their 'skittish youth'. By combining parodies of popular music and highly unconventional poetry, their intention was to outrage those who expect serious fare when they go to chamber music concerts. The original version of *Façade* consisted of an overture, sixteen poems and an interlude. Later some of these items were dropped and others added. Basically, the poems are witty caricatures oscillating between Symbolism and nonsense verse. Sitwell called them 'patterns in sound, virtuoso exercises of an extreme difficulty'. At the first performance, the six musicians needed for Walton's music sat in front of a screen on which was painted a mask. Behind the mouth of this mask, Sitwell had fitted an elaborate megaphone, so that the sound of her voice reciting the verse must have resembled the disembodied voices coming from the gramophones in Cocteau's ballet. Since she and Walton had decided before the verse was composed what kind of popular music they would draw on, the poetry and the music fitted like hand in glove. At the first public performance, the audience's 'contempt and rage' was exactly what they hoped for. Sitwell had to wait until the audience had dispersed before daring to leave the hall. In her memoirs, she claimed that when she did she was 'nearly lynched by the inevitable old woman, symbol of the enemy, who had waited, umbrella raised, to smite [her]'.

As all the composers who made use of popular music in the early twenties were aware, pieces such as the foxtrot and tango–pasodoble are not suitable for movements lasting more than a few minutes. This is why one of the most adaptable of the objective styles that was adopted after the war was neo-classicism. Sergei Prokofiev led the way with his *Classical Symphony* (1917), a work that could have been written by a Haydn who 'lived in our own day [and] retained his own style while accepting something of the new at the same time'. The work proved to be extremely popular, but Prokofiev failed to follow it up. As his Third Piano Concerto (1917–21) and the grotesque and satirical qualities of his opera *The Love for Three Oranges* (1919) bear witness, he was still experimenting with other styles. By the time he settled in Paris in 1922 and composed his Fifth Piano Sonata (1923), Quintet for oboe, clarinet, violin, viola and double bass (1924) and Second Symphony (1925), classical grace had been replaced by mechanistic harshness.

Prokofiev was not alone in his desire to write music reflecting the characteristics of the new machine age. Honegger's *Pacific 231* (1923) evoked the noises of a locomotive crossing the United States, while Alexandr Mosolov's 'mighty hymn to machine work', *The Iron Foundry* (1928), one of the most notorious works of the decade, echoed the din of a factory. The importance attached to the factory worker in Russia following the Revolution found expression in an art movement known as Constructivism, the sole purpose of which was to establish a rapport between painting and machine production. In 1927, when Prokofiev came to write his ballet *Le pas d'acier* ('The steel step') for the Russian Ballet, which had also settled in France, the set and costumes were based on a Constructivist design by Georgy Yakoulov. The ballet had two tableaux representing scenes from contemporary Russian life: one of peasants in the countryside, the other of workmen in their factories. The one and only set, however, was dominated by symbols of the new age – wheels, levers and pistons.

Neo-classicism did not take root until 1919, when Stravinsky was asked to score some pieces by Pergolesi which Serge Diaghilev, the founder of the Russian Ballet, had come across. Diaghilev's intention was to follow up the success of *The Good-Humoured Ladies* (1917), for which pieces by Domenico Scarlatti had been arranged and orchestrated by Vincenzo Tommasini, with another ballet set in eighteenth-century Italy. This time, it was finally decided, it would be about Pulcinella. Instead of merely orchestrating the pieces, however, Stravinsky made them his own. He retained Pergolesi's melodies and bass lines, but broke up the formal symmetry of the music, supplied his own logical but rather dissonant inner parts, and scored one of the pieces as a duet for solo double bass and trombone.

For a time it looked as if, like Prokofiev, Stravinsky would fail to follow up what he had achieved, because for two years he returned to composing in his earlier Russian style. It was not until 1922, when he began writing his Octet for wind instruments, that he embraced neo-classicism wholeheartedly. The Octet, however, relates to the Classical style of Haydn, Mozart and Beethoven only in terms of the forms Stravinsky uses (sonata form, a set of variations, and a rondo). But the cut of the melodies and the contrapuntal textures are closer to Bach than to Haydn. In fact, when composing the finale, Stravinsky said that he had Bach's Two-Part Inventions in mind. Being a product of the age of reason, the Baroque style was more suitable than the Classical for the emotional distancing required in the twenties. 'My Octet is a musical object,' wrote Stravinsky in 1924. 'It is not an "emotive" work but a musical composition based on objective elements which are sufficient in themselves.' Yet the work would not sound modern had it been based solely on eighteenth-century principles. So as well as including dissonances, Stravinsky also made use of one or two features from his Russian period. The theme of the slow movement is built from the eight-note ('octatonic') scale he inherited from Rimsky-Korsakov, while the introduction to the first movement has almost as many time signatures as some sections of *The Rite of Spring*. The most up-to-date feature, however, is reserved for the coda of the finale, where Stravinsky takes a syncopated rhythmic figure he had been using, and wittily turns it into a stately rumba.

Paris, The Louvre from I. M. Pei's pyramid.

The German composer Paul Hindemith, in his first neo-classical work, *Kammermusik* ('Chamber music') no. 1 (1922), also included a modern dance in the score. But in his case it was a well-known foxtrot of the day. He also included a part for a siren, and requested that the players should be invisible. Hindemith's capacity to shock had been established in 1919 when he wrote a short one-act opera based on Oskar Kokoschka's expressionist play *Mörder Hoffnung der Frauen* ('Murder, the hope of women'), a macabre piece about a woman who stabs her lover and throws him into a cage after he has ruthlessly had her branded. His one-act marionette opera, *Das Nusch-Nuschi* (1921), revolves around a dance contest judged by the Emperor of Burma, and mockingly parodies King Mark's monologue in Wagner's *Tristan and Isolde* when the emperor discovers that his favourite general has seduced all four of his wives. *Kammermusik* no.2 (1924), a concerto for obbligato piano and ten instruments, includes a movement Hindemith calls a 'little potpourri'. His first movement is based on a rhythmic figure from the first movement of Bach's D minor Harpsichord Concerto, his second movement on the elaborate ornamentations found in the Adagio of the same concerto. The 'Kleines Potpourri', which comes third, parodies these characteristics. Rhythmic figures are repeated automatically, as if stuck in a groove, ornamentations are reduced to flutter-tongued trills on the brass instruments, melodies may be in one rhythm, accompaniments in another.

Hindemith was not always as amusing as this. He is much more serious in the other five works he called 'Kammermusik' – the concertos for cello, violin, viola, viola d'amore and organ. Later, however, when *Zeitopern* ('topical operas') became fashionable in Germany, he let his penchant for parody come to the fore again. The most famous of these topical operas was Ernst Krenek's *Jonny spielt auf* ('Jonny plays on', 1925–6), a jazz opera about the emotional entanglements of a black bandleader who steals a Stradivari violin and gets everyone dancing in a fashionable hotel. In Hindemith's *Neues vom Tage* ('News of the day', 1929), all the standard operatic numbers are

Self Portrait, Oskar Kokoschka, painter and playwright of *Morder Hoffnung der Frauen*.

9

reversed. The love duet becomes a hate duet, with husband and wife throwing the breakfast dishes at each other, the wedding march a divorce ensemble. In one scene the rhythm is hammered out by twelve typists working in an office; in another the heroine sings an aria sitting naked in her bath, surrounded by her lover, the hotel manager and all his staff.

1929 was the year in which Bertolt Brecht asked Hindemith to contribute music for two of his didactic plays to be given at the Baden-Baden Music Week: *Das Badener Lehrstück vom Einverständnis* ('The didactic play of Baden on consent') and *Der Lindberghflug* ('Lindbergh's flight'). The *Lehrstück* is a 'short oratorio with an interlude for clowning', and has a substantial role for the audience. It concerns the fate of four airmen who have been trying to cross the Atlantic but have crashed and are now asking mankind for help. The audience debates the question 'Does man help man?', the words and music supplied for them being projected by a magic lattern on a large screen. The conclusion is that man does not help man – the four airmen will have to die. The pilot rebels against his fate and is annihilated; the mechanics consent to die in the cause of human progress and are redeemed. The other play is about a real airman, the aviator who crossed the Atlantic single-handed in 1927. But Brecht considered that Charles Lindbergh's achievement should not be seen as his alone. It swept God from the sky and represented mankind's victory over the forces of nature, so the role is cast for a whole choir of Lindberghs.

The music for *Der Lindberghflug* was written jointly by Hindemith and Kurt Weill, the most successful of Brecht's collaborators. Weill's belief that music should awaken social and political consciousness became apparent in his First Symphony (1921), composed when he was still a student. The original subtitle of the work was 'Workers, Peasants, Soldiers – a People's Awakening to God', the slogan in a play by the communist writer Johannes Becher. Two years later, when the payment of reparations produced hyperinflation in Germany and the French occupation of the Ruhr prevented any chance of economic recovery, Weill composed a twenty-minute motet for choir and children's voices based on verses from the Lamentations of Jeremiah: 'Remember, O Lord, what has befallen us; look, and see how we are scorned.' The work is called *Recordare* ('Remember') and illustrates that by this time Weill had adopted a form of neo-classicism that embraced polyphony but eschewed parody.

Weill's most important work in the neo-classical style was his opera *Der Protagonist* (1926), based on a play by Georg Kaiser. Here the need to awaken social consciousness through music is cast in the form of an indictment of those who cling to illusions and have no sense of reality. The 'protagonist' is an actor who lives in his stage world and identifies himself with whatever role he happens to be playing. He comes in contact with reality only through his sister; it is she who enables him to find his way back to himself. When she tells him she is engaged to be married, however, his part is changed to that of a jealous man, and, carried away by this role, he kills her, thus separating himself from reality completely. By the time Weill met Brecht shortly after the first performance of *Der Protagonist*, both men were keen to create a form of theatre in which illusions were banished. The following year Brecht was calling it 'epic theatre'. 'The essential point of the epic theatre', he wrote, 'is perhaps that it appeals less to the feelings than to the spectator's reason. Instead of sharing an experience the spectator must come to grips with things'.

The first example of epic theatre was *The Threepenny Opera*, a new version of John Gay's *The Beggar's Opera* (1728). Gay had parodied Italian *opera seria* and its concern with the moral behaviour of princes by making his hero a highwayman who is saved from execution only on the grounds that an opera must end happily. Brecht's version is a bitter satire on the bourgeois society of post-war Germany, and Weill based his music on the song style he had developed in *Mahagonny – Songspiel* (1927), a setting of poems in Brecht's *Die Hauspostille* collection. The style had as its model the popular songs of Irving Berlin, George Gershwin and Cole Porter, but in Weill's music forms and rhythms are freer, his harmonies more dissonant, his tone more caustic. Although many of his songs proved to be as popular as his models, they reflect a world that lacks a sense of security and have none of the bonhomie of the American prototypes. In 1929 Brecht and Weill turned the *Mahagonny–Songspiel* into a full-length opera, *Aufstieg und Fall der Stadt Mahagonny* ('Rise and fall of the town of Mahagonny'). In the town of Mahagonny, all restrictions are abolished and the only crime is lack of money. It became a powerful symbol of the helplessness experienced in the late twenties and early thirties by those caught up in the great economic crisis.

The opera had its first performance in March 1930, and by that time the effects of the Wall Street crash of 29 October 1929 were being felt throughout the world. The American financial situation was so serious that banks were forced to close and the government recalled all US overseas investments. The result was a decline in internal sales and exports in industrialized countries, factory closures and massive unemployment. In these circumstances, no composer wanted to shock or to parody any more. Undoubtedly the conversion to seriousness would have come about of its own accord, but it might not have occurred so abruptly or so decisively had it not been for the Great Depression. Walton's progression from *Façade* to the symphony he completed in 1935 took him from 'skittishness' to the most weighty statement he was ever to pen. His Viola Concerto (1928–9), with its jazzy scherzo and Romantically inclined outer movements, was one step in this direction; the grimness and dramatic intensity of his oratorio *Belshazzar's Feast* (1931) another. Some of Belshazzar's mood spills over into the First Symphony, most noticeably in the finale, the writing of which caused Walton a great deal of trouble. He completed it a year after the other three movements had their première in 1934. Traditionally, symphonic finales were either joyous or triumphant, and Walton's hesitation probably stemmed from his doubts as to whether these moods would make a suitable conclusion for the serious, Sibelius-like first movement, the savage scherzo and the probing slow movement. In the event, the movement he produced does culminate in an exultant peroration. Most people now accept it as being an appropriate ending for the work, but in 1935 it was not considered to ring true.

The work that was closer to the spirit of the day, it was felt, was the Fourth Symphony of Ralph Vaughan Williams, which had its première six months before the first complete performance of the Walton. Those who thought that Vaughan Williams would produce something in the vein of his pastoral Third Symphony (1921) were greatly surprised, for the new symphony turned out to be a hard-hitting work in the 'black' key of F minor, from which the English pastoral tradition and folksongs were conspicuously absent. The symphony is based on a vehemently presented four-note motif (F–E–G♭–F) which dominates the first and third movements and returns with devastating effect at the end of the fourth to leave the listener in no doubt that F minor is indeed 'black'.

Hindemith's music also became serious during the thirties. The Wall Street crash had its greatest effect on the German economy.

After 1929 industrial production halved and unemployment trebled from 2 to 6 million. It was this situation that led to the election of Hitler and his Nazi party in 1933. And it was against this background that Hindemith wrote the libretto and music of what is generally considered to be his masterpiece, the opera *Mathis der Maler* ('Matthias the painter'). The issue is the role of the artist in society, especially in periods of political and social uncertainty and conflict. Should he take an active part in affairs or stand aloof and devote himself to his art? Hindemith's conclusion is that the artist will be of more use to society if he does the latter. The story concerns the Renaissance painter Matthias Grünewald, who interrupts work on his great altarpiece in the monastery church of St Anthony at Isenheim to fight on the side of the Lutheran peasants in their revolt against their Catholic overlords. Eventually, when he is forced to accept that as a man of action he is a failure, Grünewald returns to the monastery to complete the altarpiece. The opera was scheduled for production at the Berlin Opera in the autumn of 1933, but the Nazis interpreted one or two of the scenes – notably when books are burned in public – as an indict-

Fireworks at the Brandenburg Gate, Berlin, New Year's Eve, 1989.

ment of themselves, and proscribed the work. Early the next year Furtwängler defied Hitler by conducting a performance of the symphony Hindemith had made out of three incidents in the opera, an event which led to Furtwängler's resignation from the Berlin Philharmonic. Hindemith had already been labelled a 'cultural bolshevik' by the Nazis, and in 1937 was dismissed from his teaching post in Berlin. The following year he left Germany forever.

The control of the state over all artistic matters is a phenomenon peculiar to the twentieth century. The only German composer of stature who did not leave Germany during the Nazi regime was Richard Strauss, but his close association with one or two Jews meant that he too was frowned on. The Soviet Union also imposed severe restrictions on composers in the thirties. When Stalin attained full power in 1932, he put an end to the comparative freedom artists had enjoyed in the twenties. A period of repression and absolute conformity to Soviet ideals was inaugurated. And yet it was in that year, when he was on a concert tour of the Soviet Union, that Prokofiev decided to return to Russia, a decision he finally put into effect in 1936. His main problem was that the Soviet authorities considered the music he had written in France formalist and decadent. They attached these labels even to his ballet *The Prodigal Son* (1929), a much gentler work than the Second Symphony or *The Steel Step*. Prokofiev had therefore to show by what he said and composed that he was prepared to fall in line with Soviet demands. He publicly stated that the music the modern Soviet composer needed to write to reach the new mass audiences had to be clear, simple, and primarily melodious. And he gave proof that this was what he intended to do in his orchestral suite *Lieutenant Kijé* (1934) and his Second Violin Concerto (1935).

The desire to find a simpler style was not confined to Russia. In the United States, Aaron Copland was also calling on composers to be clear and direct. Following President Roosevelt's promise of a 'New Deal' in 1933, most Americans knew that to recover from the Great Depression they would have to forget their differences and pull together. Serious composers began writing in a more popular style; popular musicians adopted some of the characteristics of serious music. 1935 was the year when the swing era came into being and George Gershwin produced his opera *Porgy and Bess*. All jazz should 'swing', but the term specifically refers to the music played by highly disciplined big bands swinging across a very firmly articulated beat. Benny Goodman's was the first to win acclaim and the arrangements he used in 1935 were those of Fletcher Henderson. Goodman set out to have his band play these extremely skilful scores in a manner that would do credit to the precision and tuning of the finest 'classical' ensemble. The repertory of the big bands was based largely on the songs of Tin Pan Alley, many of them by Gershwin, whose tunes lent themselves easily to jazz. But in *Porgy and Bess*, Gershwin transformed his songs into recitatives, arias, duets, choruses and ensembles, the formal procedures of classical opera. The story, set in a black tenement on the waterfront of Charleston, South Carolina, could be considered a modern version of *Carmen*. Certainly no other opera in the twentieth century has been as successful in bridging the gap between classical and popular musical culture as *Porgy and Bess*.

The most influential composer in the thirties was Stravinsky, but although he was still committed to neo-classicalism his models were by now less overtly Baroque. Indeed by the end of the decade he had moved over to that most Classical of all structures, the symphony. The *Symphony of Psalms* (1930) is a symphony only in name, however. His purpose, Stravinsky said, was to 'create an organic whole without conforming to the various models adopted by custom, but still retaining the periodic order by which the symphony is distinguished from the suite'. But by 1938, when he began work on his Symphony in C, Stravinsky's antipathy to the traditional form of the symphony had been overcome. While composing the first two movements he had scores of symphonies by Haydn and Beethoven, and also Tchaikovsky's First, on his desk. The influence of the two Classical composers is most noticeable in the transition and development sections of the first movement, that of Tchaikovsky in the slow movement perhaps. The end of the work, however, recalls Brahms, a composer for whom Stravinsky had little or no sympathy. But Brahms's Third is the only other symphony in the repertory that ends with slow, stately, chorale-like chords on the wind.

Stravinsky's influence on Benjamin Britten, Elliott Carter, Olivier Messiaen and Michael Tippett, the four rising stars of the thirties, showed itself in different ways. Britten came closest to him in his Variations on a Theme of Frank Bridge for strings (1937), except that, instead of parodying the style of a particular period, he parodies certain genres, among which are an Italian aria, a bourrée, a Viennese waltz and a funeral march. The wit lies in the way he exaggerates their characteristic features. At the end, however, when he returns to Bridge's theme, he presents it in a manner associated with Mahler at his most solemn and expressive. Carter's first published work, *Tarantella* (1936) for male-voice chorus and piano four hands or orchestra, makes use of melodic material from a book of Neapolitan tarantellas. But apart from this, Carter avoided making stylistic allusions in his early neo-classical period. It was Stravinsky's objectivity and formal clarity that meant most to him. Messiaen, on the other hand, had no interest whatsoever in neo-classicism. His roots were in the French organ tradition founded in the late sixteenth century by Jehan Titelouze, a tradition which in its early stages made extensive use of plainsong. Messiaen's debt to Stravinsky lay in the rhythmic innovations of *The*

Rite of Spring, which he first made use of in his orchestral work *Les offrandes oubliées* (1930). Plainsong forms the basis of the melodic material, but the rhythm draws on Stravinsky's 'additive' principle, and the way he expands and contracts rhythmic cells.

Tippett was also drawn to Stravinsky's additive rhythm, as the last movement of his First String Quartet (1935) bears witness. In his oratorio *A Child of our Time* (1939–41) he followed Stravinsky's example in *Oedipus Rex* (1926–7) by turning to Handel's oratorios for a model. In Tippett's case, the model was *Messiah*. The incident on which *A Child of our Time* is based is the assassination of a German diplomat in Paris by a young Polish Jew, in protest against the treatment of 6000 Polish Jews stranded without possessions on the Polish border and prevented from crossing it. The event became the pretext for the Nazis to unleash a savage anti-Semitic pogrom, the first stage of which was the notorious Crystal Night destruction, beatings and arrests of 9 November 1938. As well as explicitly evoking items in *Messiah* to express the horror and the pity evoked by the situation, Tippett also drew on Bach's Passions, particularly the use of chorales. To make such communal, reflective moments more meaningful for modern audiences, he replaced the Lutheran chorales with black spirituals, ending the oratorio with soloists and chorus uniting in *Deep River*.

In essence, the musical situation after the Second World War was not dissimilar to that after the first. Established composers continued to pursue the style they had previously found for themselves, while those who were up and coming struck out on new paths. There was, however, a difference between the nature of the two wars. Although the slaughter was terrible in the first, it was confined mainly to the armed forces of the combatants. The second, on the other hand, was all-out war, with almost as many civilians killed as servicemen. The death toll amounted to 40 million, and when the war drew to a close the world also had to come to terms with the Nazi concentration camps and the atomic bomb. It was quite clear that young composers in the late forties would follow their forebears after the First World War and adopt an objective style. What was unexpected was the extreme nature of their response. Europeans took one direction, most American composers another, but for everybody the objectivity had to be absolute. Composers sought to suppress their personal identities by devising schemes that produced music automatically.

The means of achieving this in Europe came through the twelve-note method which Schoenberg had devised in the early twenties. His purpose was to ensure that the melodic and harmonic aspects in an atonal score had a common identity. The twelve notes of the chromatic scale were placed in an order that had to be retained throughout the work, and it was Schoenberg's belief that this ordering could be identified even when the notes were inverted or turned backwards, or when the twelve-note series was transposed. The method proved useful in creating unity, but it meant that freedom of choice was restricted. As far as pitch was concerned, composers could draw only on the twelve-note series. In all other respects, they were free to do what they wanted. To make a piece autonomous, however, this freedom had to be removed. All aspects of the score needed to be serialized. As far as possible choice had to be eliminated.

This is the procedure that lies behind Pierre Boulez's first book of *Structures* for two pianos (1951–2). Boulez admits that he took the elimination of personal invention to absurd lengths, but nevertheless it was probably his most fundamental experiment. Pitch, durations, dynamics and attack are all organized in sets of twelve, and Boulez allowed himself only a very limited amount of personal choice. The material comes from Messiaen's piano piece *Mode de valeurs et d'intensités* (1949), but apart from this Boulez's work bears little or no relation to any previous music. It marks a complete break with the past. The events, though logically consistent serially, appear to be utterly random aurally. Boulez was perfectly aware that this extreme form of automatism was self-defeating, and in later works such as *Le marteau sans maître* (1954) he allowed himself greater freedom. It then became apparent that this radical new style could open up worlds that had never been explored or even dreamed of before. *Le marteau sans maître* is a setting for mezzo-soprano and six instrumentalists of three poems by the Surrealist poet René Char, who once said that it is impossible to live without having the image of the unknown ever before one's eyes. What is striking about Boulez's score is the way his personal invention, his freedom to choose, to decide and to reject at any one moment, makes the apparently random world created by the serialization of the elements accessible to the listener – at least to a certain extent. It lifts one of the veils shrouding the mystery he always wants to create; it brings the unknown a little more into focus.

The creation of surreal worlds by the avant garde was greatly assisted by the advance in electronics after the war. In 1952 a studio for

17

Olivier Messiaen's class at the Paris Conservatoire. Karlheinz Stockhausen is seventh from the right. Yvonne Loriod, Messiaen's future wife, is second from the right.

electronic music was established in Cologne, and it was here that Karlheinz Stockhausen composed *Gesang der Jünglinge* (1955–6), an electronic piece in which the mysterious contains within it something familiar that the listener can latch onto and use as a point of reference. The strange sounds produced electronically in the studio can switch from a loudspeaker on the left to one on the right or in the centre, appear to be distant then near, and be radically transformed within seconds. But at every juncture can be heard the reasonable, familiar sound of a boy singing the well-known words of the Benedicite: 'O all ye works of the Lord, bless ye the Lord . . .' This sound is also transformed and shifted about; at one stage there appears to be not a single boy but a choir of boys singing in the distance. But the two sound worlds are not kept separate. The sound of the boy's voice may melt into the electronic sounds and vice versa. It means that the familiar and the unfamiliar, the known and the unknown, are always in contact with each other.

In all the pieces by Boulez, Stockhausen and their avant-garde colleagues, the initial material and the system that produces a structure out of it has to be devised by the composer. But for the American composer, John Cage, this was not radical enough. 'The composer', he said, 'must give up the desire to control sound, clear his mind of music, and set about discovering means to let sounds be themselves rather than vehicles for man-made theories or expressions of human sentiments.' His initial solution was to rely on chance operations. In his extended piano piece *Music of Changes* (1951), everything is determined by the tossing of coins and applying the results to the charts and hexagrams contained in the I Ching, the ancient Chinese book of oracles. In *Music for Piano* (1952–6), he obtained the pitches by tracing the imperfections on a piece of paper. His final step was to do absolutely nothing and to get people just to listen to the sounds going on around them in their everyday lives – the sound of birds perhaps, the hum of air-conditioning, distant traffic, the laughter of children.

Cage's philosophy was particularly influential in the fifties and sixties, and led directly to the minimalist movement which has been so prominent in America. No minimalist composer has ever gone to Cage's lengths to eliminate human volition; they have always used ideas that they themselves have invented. When Cage heard La Monte Young's *Composition 1960 no.7*, which consists of an open fifth to be held 'for a long time', he said that the attentive listener would be simultaneously struck by the simplicity of the action and by the complexity of the sound. Young then went on to compose *Arabic Numeral (any integer) for Henry Flynt* (1960). This is based on repetition, in this case the regular and uniform repetition of a heavy sound or cluster 'for a long time'. Ultimately repetition became the basis of minimalism. Like the music of the European avant garde in the early fifties, the purpose was to devise a formula that enabled the work to write itself, except that now the formula and the resultant music had to be simple rather than complex.

The period between 1947 and 1973 was one of unparalleled economic growth and expansion. At no other period in the twentieth century could a British politician have won a general election on the slogan 'You've never had it so good', as Harold Macmillan did in 1957. The confidence that this growth created was reflected in all the arts, not least in music. Summer schools, festivals and magazines arose specifically to perform and discuss new music, and even composers of the older generation were caught up in the excitement of the musical scene and incorporated some of the new ideas into their compositions. The only composers whose work lost its previous vitality were those who had come to maturity in the twenties, notably Walton, Prokofiev and Hindemith. Stravinsky, an older man, was much more adaptable. He took up the twelve-note method and enjoyed a late flowering, producing between 1952 and his death in 1971 some of his most inventive and cogent works.

Popular music also reflected the confidence of the post-war years. The dominant style in jazz was bebop, which had arisen in Harlem during the closing years of the war, and reflected the self-assertive brilliance of some of the virtuoso black musicians who were working there, in particular the trumpeter Dizzie Gillespie and the alto saxophonist Charlie Parker. In its first phase, bebop was 'hot', fast and exceptionally virtuoso; in its second 'cool', restrained, economic and

Richard Rogers' modernist design for Channel Four's headquarters in London.

relaxed. The style favoured small ensembles, placed greater emphasis on solo improvisation than had been the case in the swing era, experimented with much more complex harmonic, rhythmic and formal patterns than jazz had done in the past, and detached itself from dance music. As a result bebop eventually took jazz out of the realms of popular music and reduced it to a minority interest. This change was sealed when the alto saxophonist Ornette Coleman and seven of his colleagues recorded an album in 1960 called *Free Jazz*, inaugurating a style that makes no reference to any recognizable tune or chord sequence and in which everything is based on improvisation.

The music that replaced jazz and the songs of Tin Pan Alley in the popular esteem was rock – originally rock 'n' roll, a development of rhythm-and-blues cultivated by black musicians for black audiences between 1949 and 1969. The first rock 'n' roll record, *Rock Around the Clock*, appeared in 1955 and was performed by a white group, Bill Haley and the Comets. 25 million copies were sold, mainly to white teenagers. But even more significant for the early popularity of rock 'n' roll was Elvis Presley's recording the following year of *Hound Dog*, a raucous rhythm-and-blues number that came top of the rhythm-and-blues and the country-and-western charts, as well as the white pop charts. Inevitably there was considerable opposition to rock 'n' roll, not least from Tin Pan Alley and the recording industry that had grown up around it. Rock 'n' roll did not need top singing stars, arrangers and studio orchestras, only guitarists who could sing and a drum kit. For a time the market was flooded with watered-down versions issued by Tin Pan Alley. The only place where the original rock 'n' roll style could still be heard was Britain, and the American pop scene found a focus again only after the Beatles made their first appearance in the States in 1964. Tin Pan Alley then collapsed, and later the Rolling Stones and The Who rang its death knell. Despite the efforts of groups such as Pink Floyd and the Grateful Dead to bridge the gap between rock and 'serious' music, the differences between them are probably too great for reconciliation.

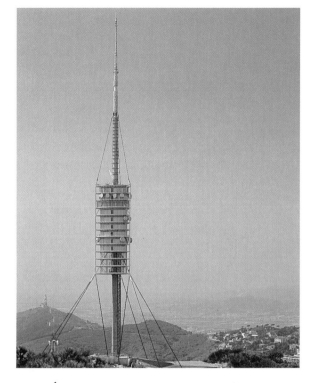

Communications tower, Barcelona, designed by Norman Foster.

Never before in the history of music has serious music been so estranged from popular culture, and never before has popular culture been so dominant.

Since 1973 the economic situation has been beset by recession and unemployment, and this has led to general uncertainty and lack of confidence. In recent years the situation has been exacerbated by the breakdown of communism in Eastern Europe and the instability of Russia in particular. Inevitably music has been influenced by this change of climate. In those periods of economic expansion, as before and immediately after the First World War and during the years 1947–1973, composers had the self-assurance to be experimental, introduce new ways of proceeding, and take things to extremes. In times of recession, they have been much more cautious, much more aware of the audience they are addressing. This was the case in the thirties and is also the case now. Nothing fundamentally new has emerged since 1973, either in serious music or in pop. Most composers want to be reconciled with tradition. All have had to recognize that most music lovers prefer to listen to Baroque, Classical and Romantic music rather than the music produced in the twentieth century. They therefore make use of music that is familiar and well loved. But this has happened throughout the century. In the twenties composer found their models in Baroque music, in the thirties in Classical music; now interest has shifted to Romanticism.

However, neo-romanticism is only one of many styles that co-exist at the present. Over the century the two world wars, economic fluctuations and social changes have resulted in frequent and sometimes abrupt changes in style, so that during the last quarter of the century it was inevitable that the musical culture would be pluralistic. A significant strand in this pluralism is the contribution women composers are making to the richness of the present musical scene. As yet women have not proved to be great innovators as composers, and this may be why they get scant mention in books about the history of music, where most attention is given to those who instigate trends or new ways of proceeding. But women have brought something to music which was encountered only rarely in earlier centuries. Nicola LeFanu, whose mother Elizabeth Maconchy was also a distinguished composer, puts it in this way:

Most people believe that music transcends gender, that you can't tell if a composition is by a man or a woman. I know, however, that my music is written out of the wholeness of myself, and I happen to be a woman. I'm not bothered by whether I compose better or worse than a man, because I take both possibilities for granted; but I am interested in what I can do that is different. In my thoughts and actions there is much that is similar to those of a man, and much more that is different. Can it really be otherwise in music? Could there be a music which did not reflect its maker? If we continue to have a musical culture which only draws on the creative talents of one sex, what kind of musical perspective shall we have?

The pluralism of our culture is due in great measure to the development of technology in the twentieth century. If you lived in a village or provincial town at the beginning of the century, you might have to wait months or even years before you could see an opera or go to a concert. You would be in regular contact with music only if you played an instrument or sang in a choir. But even then the range of music available to you would be limited. It is unlikely you would ever hear much contemporary music. The citizens of Birmingham who attended the first performance of *The Dream of Gerontius* ought to have considered themselves privileged. Nowadays the world's music is obtainable at the touch of a button. There are about ten first-class performances of the oratorio on CD, including the excerpts Elgar himself recorded in 1927. We take the pluralism of our composers and the wide range of music and performances available to us for granted. There is no turning back.

Chapter 2
Dancing on a Volcano

When a piece of music breaks with tradition, as has happened so often in the twentieth century, the gap between its first performance and its eventual acceptance by the music-loving public can often be quite long. It took fifty years for *The Rite of Spring* to enter the orchestral repertory and receive regular performances. It has taken Schoenberg's Five Orchestral Pieces and *Erwartung* even longer. Both were crucial to the evolution of music in this century, but performances of them are still comparatively rare. It may be that audiences still find their lack of a discernible harmonic framework disconcerting; or perhaps they are still baffled by Schoenberg's unusual concept of musical time. There are occasions, for instance, when he wants to stretch out a single moment so that it lasts half an hour or more; there are others when he wants to create the impression that time has been compressed, or that there is no past or future, only the present.

The tonal system, which Schoenberg abandoned before the First World War, is based on the idea that a piece of music should be like going on a journey, in which you know full well where you will end up – namely, back home – and, indeed, when you will arrive. It is a hierarchical system in which 'home' is the 'tonic' triad of the key that the composer has selected for the piece. Returning to the home key and ultimately finding rest on its tonic chord gives music written in the tonal system its sense of direction and purpose. As a result, all tonal music, whether a short song or a complex symphonic movement, is underpinned by a simple threefold structure, based on the principle that in order to confirm or stabilize something you have first to deny or undermine it. The first stage involves establishing the home key, the second journeying to another key and treating it as if it might be an alternative to the tonic, the third returning to the original key so that all doubts about where home is are dispelled. The third section must feel absolutely secure, and in a classical score, such as a sonata-form movement by Beethoven, it is usually dramatized so that the return home becomes the most decisive event in the structure.

Gustav Klimt, *Beethoven Frieze*, 1902: detail from 'The longing for happiness finds fulfilment in art'.

At the end of the nineteenth century, Europe was uneasily wriggling out of its old skin and was metamorphosing into something more complex, more dangerous. Just at the point where all the certainties and empires and the old social order were beginning to crumble, just at the point where Freud was beginning to show that unconscious order could be infinitely more powerful than the conscious, so music was leaving home, abandoning tonality, seemingly forever.

How firmly the home key needs to be established at the beginning of a movement depends on the character the composer has in mind for the piece. The tonic chords in the introduction to Beethoven's String Quartet in E♭, op. 127, are stated with great deliberation and nobility, because the overall character of the movement is 'maestoso'. But in the opening section of his next quartet, the elusive Quartet in A minor, op. 132, firm tonic chords are avoided. Here we have to sense the key from the way the other chords behave.

Tonality was as much a part of its social time as perspective was part of painting, as the hierarchical social order was of its political time.

Schoenberg's decision to abandon tonality was taken when he was composing his Second String Quartet in 1907–8. The first three movements are in F♯ minor, D minor and E♭ minor respectively, but, as in Beethoven's op. 132, the keys are not stated firmly – they have to be sensed. He also avoids giving them any dramatic emphasis when they return home. His main interest seems to be in the way his melodic material unfolds and develops. Throughout the work there is an increasing tendency for the melodies to float free of the harmony, and this desire for melodic freedom may explain why he quotes the last line of a popular Viennese song in the second movement and includes a soprano voice singing verses by the symbolist poet Stefan George in the third and fourth. The quotation comes from the old Viennese street ballad 'O du lieber Augustin', a perky little tune in D major. Some people have suggested that its last line 'alles ist hin' ('it's all up', or 'all is lost'), could be a reference to the crisis in Schoenberg's marriage occurring at the time. This certainly fits with the soprano's text in the third movement. It calls on God to end life's miseries and send the supplicant light: 'Take from me love, and give me your joy.' Schoenberg's setting is a theme with variations, but it is not until he comes to the words 'give me your joy' in the movement's coda that we get the sense that we are really in E♭ minor. The last movement, at least while the soprano is singing, abandons tonality altogether. The text begins with the line, 'I feel air from other planets,' and goes on to speak of floating up to higher spheres. In this atonal context, the soprano's line can indeed float. Without the gravity of a home key there is nothing to pull it down to earth.

From that moment onwards, Schoenberg organized all his music so that the governing factor was free-floating melody. In tonal music, melody springs from the harmony; in this new atonal style, the harmony springs from the melody. Schoenberg constructs his chords from the melodic intervals of the material they are accompanying.

26

But the absence of a tonal centre to provide a goal for the harmonic movement, and the seemingly illogical sequence in which one chord follows another have an equally strange effect on the way the music relates to the passing of time. Schoenberg was deeply conscious of this effect and drew attention to it when writing about the two short operas he composed between 1909 and 1913, *Erwartung* and *Die glückliche Hand*:

The common denominator of the two works,' he said, 'is something like this. In *Erwartung* the aim is to represent in *slow motion* everything that occurs during a single second of maximum spiritual excitement, stretching it out to half an hour, whereas in *Die glückliche Hand* a major drama is compressed into about twenty minutes, as if photographed with a time-exposure.

Everything in music, from the pitch of a single note to the colour of a great harmony, is the result of an operation in time – namely, the frequency of vibrations. Musical processes, the functions of melody, harmony and rhythm, are also, of course, operations in time. But these processes are primarily concerned with psychological rather than physical, measurable time. How we experience the passing of time is not subject to accurate measurement. It depends on our state of mind, mood or what we have to do in our everyday lives. Time can pass quickly or slowly. But in *Erwartung* and *Die glückliche Hand*, Schoenberg is dealing with time as experienced in altered states of consciousness or dreams. The events in *Erwartung* – a woman's search for her lover, her discovery of his dead body, her subsequent dementia and jealous outpourings about the other 'she' – could all be taking place inside her mind, the result of intense shock perhaps. The events in *Die glückliche Hand*, on the other hand, are too grotesque to be anything but a fantasy or dream about failure and inadequacy. It opens with the figure of a man lying face down on the ground with the teeth of a great cat-like beast fastened to his neck and ends with man and beast in the same posture. The symbolism seems to refer to the man's passion for a woman, and his inability either to satisfy her or to keep her close to him.

What is unfamiliar and disturbing about both operas is their lack of temporal direction. Without a tonic to pull the music forward into the future, the events seem to be taking place in a temporal vacuum. This is particularly apparent in *Erwartung*, where Schoenberg even

Peter Breugel's
The Triumph of Time
of 1557, a thesaurus of
emblems of time: the
may-pole, tides, clocks,
the sun and moon and,
trampled beneath the
procession, music.

eliminates all sense of the past. He takes free-floating melody to an extreme. Nothing is repeated. No sooner has a melodic phrase been introduced than it is abandoned, never to appear again. The surface of the music is in a constant state of activity, but deep down it is absolutely static. This strange dichotomy opened up new vistas for twentieth-century composers, and in retrospect Schoenberg's concept of musical time influenced Western music as decisively as the highly dynamic, goal-orientated concept of time that emerged during the Renaissance and was responsible for the tonal system.

In the Middle Ages, when music was underpinned by the old church modes, man defined himself in relation to a stable, cosmic order. Christian theology may have been apocalyptic, but most people associated time with the cyclic rotation of the seasons, the planets, the phases of the moon, the rise and fall of the sun. All things returned to themselves, and temporal beings achieved permanence through constant regeneration. But with the rise of Humanism during the Renaissance when people began to think of themselves as self-defining and dynamic, cyclic time was gradually replaced by linear time, the concept of time as a dimension directed towards a non-recurring future. It was this concept that gave rise to tonality. The tonic becomes the goal towards which everything moves. All the diversions, all the subsidiary cadences, keep this goal constantly in mind.

There are, of course, cadences in modal music, but they never exert

28

so strong a gravitational pull as those in the tonal system. In fact, the listener cannot be really sure which mode the music is in until the final note. The essence of the modal system is epitomized by the music of the Catholic church. Gregorian chant was devised so that each word of the biblical text could be dwelt on in an atmosphere of unhurried, unpressurized calm.

However, during the 300 years when the dynamic tonal system held sway, the old church modes never completely died out. Beethoven used one in the slow movement of the A minor Quartet. The movement, written as a 'thanksgiving to God by one recovering from illness', alternates between a slow, hymn-like section and a lively dance. The *A* sections of the movement's *ABABA* structure are cast in the Lydian mode (the mode with a final on F). The *B* sections, on the other hand, are a dance in the key of D major, expressing 'the feeling of renewed strength'. In other words, the contemplative state of mind needed for prayer is contrasted with the dynamic state of mind suitable for activity. In fact the sections are not repeated verbatim: Beethoven decorates them on their return. The *B* section becomes livelier and more impulsive, the *A* section more deeply contemplative. On its final appearance the *A* section is not very far removed from what Schoenberg was to achieve nearly a century later: the surface of the music has movement, but deep down it is still, almost timeless.

Arnold Schoenberg's painting, *Hand*, 1910.

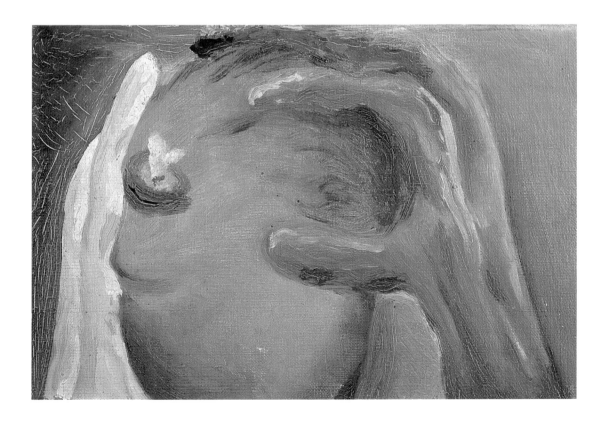

At the very heart of Beethoven's music is the idea of transformation. Usually the transformation is one of mood or state of mind, but in the Diabelli Variations it involves a change of character. The 'vulgar little waltz' which Diabelli gave him is ultimately transformed into an elegant minuet; base metal is turned into gold. Behind all these transformations lie the optimism, the outgoing spirit of the Enlightenment. This is why most classical works end in joy and affirmation. The deeply contemplative mood of the A minor Quartet's slow movement has to be followed by a vigorous march and a finale ending in ebullient high spirits. The Cavatina in the next quartet, the Bb major, op. 130, has to be followed by the 'Grosse Fuge'. This is hardly joyous, but is nevertheless regarded as being the most powerful affirmation of the will ever written. There is nothing in music quite so dynamic and goal-orientated. It might be said that from then on tonality was bound to go into decline. None of the composers who followed Beethoven could equal his will-power or faith in the future.

This is already apparent in Schubert. He may have stayed firmly within the classical tradition in most of his instrumental works, but at least half of his songs reflect the sentiments of the German Romantics, many of whom had a decidedly pessimistic turn of mind. They sought death rather than life. In death the soul leaves this vale of sorrows and finds a 'milder land'. Many of Schubert's songs ignore the principle that a tonal piece should begin and end in the same key. In his setting of Goethe's 'Ganymed', where the young Ganymede is taken up to Olympus to be the cup-bearer of the gods, Schubert portrays his journey upwards through the sky in two ways: not only does the piano accompaniment at the close of the song rise higher and higher, but, more important, the piece begins in Ab major and ends in the sharper key of F major. The traditional notion that the tonality should eventually return home has been replaced by the Romantic desire to transcend the mundane.

This desire found its highest expression in Wagner's *Tristan and Isolde*, the work that is always cited as being the greatest influence on the breakdown of tonality. The inspiration behind it was Schopenhauer's *The World as Will and Idea*, a deeply pessimistic philosophical treatise dating from 1818. Schopenhauer maintained that we experience the world from outside as idea and from inside as will. The will – will-power – is not an attribute of the individual, it is the unseen

dynamic force which generates all phenomena, animate or inanimate, and the source of all striving, craving, egoism, malice, sin, suffering and conflict. It is not enough to die to be released from its bondage because in Schopenhauer's opinion death is not the end: in all likelihood we shall all be born again. To be released one needs to reach the state Buddhists call Nirvana.

What must particularly have attracted Wagner was the status Schopenhauer accorded to music. Schopenhauer believed that music is the direct and immediate manifestation of the will itself, and that therefore it gives us an insight into our deepest state of being. Equally important is the fact that when we listen to music all our striving and craving become dormant. We find a measure of inner peace. In *Tristan and Isolde*, Wagner's subject is the will as it manifests itself in sexual yearning. Not only is his music highly sensuous, it expresses a longing that can never be appeased because the lovers never have the chance to satisfy their sexual yearning for each other. As a result his harmony never resolves except at the end of an act; it never achieves a sense of arrival. His main focus is on the colour and expressive quality of the discords he introduces to express the sense of yearning.

Wagner establishes his musical procedures for the opera in the Prelude to Act 1. All the music is taken from the scene near the end of the act when Tristan and Isolde take the love potion given to them, look long and deeply into each other's eyes and then pour out their hearts to each other. At this point, however, the climax is interrupted by a change of harmony, indicating that the lovers are always going to be sexually frustrated. The structure is based on the standard threefold formula discussed earlier, except that here the return occurs at the height of the climax and there is no sense of tonal stability before or after. The chord that Wagner places at the peak of the climax is the famous 'Tristan chord', a highly chromatic discord which first appeared at the opening of the Prelude. There it was preceded by a long, swelling note on the cellos, and suggested the couple's stabbing pain for each other. It is a chord that can behave in a variety of ways, depending on its context. At the opening it sounds as if it belongs to

Wagner, Prelude to *Tristan and Isolde*: the 'Tristan' chord.

A minor, but at the climax, although the notes are exactly the same, it sounds as if it belongs to E♭ major, and at the very end of the opera, when the couple's love is eventually transfigured in death, Wagner resolves it, again without transposition, into B major. The ambiguous nature of the chord sums up the ambiguity of Wagner's harmony as a whole, but he repeats it so often that after a while it becomes an entity in its own right. We begin to enjoy its colour and expressive quality for their own sake. We begin to accept that it is the pleasure of longing itself and not necessarily the fulfilment that matters. And as soon as we accept that, the temporal perspective shifts away from the future, from what is going to happen next, and focuses on the present, on what is enjoyable in the moment.

This use of a harmonic entity as a constant point of reference, and the shift in temporal perspective resulting from it, are probably the most significant aspects of *Tristan*, at least as far as twentieth-century opinion is concerned. Nineteenth-century musicians were more interested in Wagner's chromatic harmony in general. When Schoenberg had his string sextet *Verklärte Nacht* ('Transfigured night') submitted to a committee of the Tonkünstlerverein in Vienna for possible inclusion in one of the society's concerts in 1900 or 1901, one member said that he thought it would sound 'as if someone had smeared the score of *Tristan* while the ink was still wet'. It is true that several of the chords are unorthodox, but none of them functions as the Tristan chord does, and from a tonal point of view the work is actually far from radical. The first part is cast in D minor and, after the usual diversions to other tonal areas, the opening key returns quite properly as D major.

What is radical about *Verklärte Nacht* is not its harmony but Schoenberg's method of developing and transforming his melodic material. In this respect it looks forward to the melody-based styles of his atonal and twelve-note music. Undoubtedly the reason he chose to base the work on Richard Dehmel's poem was because transformation is its very essence. Dehmel's poetry is primarily concerned with social compassion and the spiritualization of sex. In *Verklärte Nacht*, a man and a woman are walking together on a cold, moonlit night in winter; the woman confesses that she is pregnant as the result of a brief affair with another man at a time when she felt her life was empty and meaningless and she desperately wanted a child. Now that she is in love with the man by her side, she bitterly regrets what she

Richard Wagner in 1871, photographed by Franz Hanfstaengl.

Gustav Klimt, *Fulfilment*, 1905/09.

has done and is consumed with guilt. The man tells her she should not feel oppressed. In the moonlight, the world around them is radiant. The woman has brought brightness into his life, and the child will be his as well as hers. It will be transfigured by the love and warmth of their relationship.

The woman's confession constitutes the first subject, transition, second subject and development sections of an expanded sonata form; the man's response the recapitulation. But instead of bringing back the exposition more or less verbatim, as is usually the case, Schoenberg transforms it so that material which was once anguished and guilt-ridden becomes as 'radiant' as the night.

Everything in the score has its origins in a low, soft, descending scale, first heard on viola and cello at the beginning of the work. This scale is clearly meant to convey the couple's muted and pensive mood, and perhaps even their footsteps. During the introduction, Schoenberg develops its shape and character so that it becomes a figure designed to express the woman's increasing agitation. Thereafter no descending scale of significance occurs until the climax of the woman's confession. Here, however, instead of a minor scale, a chromatic one is pounded out as loudly as possible by the whole ensemble playing in octaves. For the man's reply, Schoenberg goes through the same process again. But in this instance, the minor scale is transformed little by little into a phrase which lyrically and warmly elaborates the notes of a descending major scale. At this stage it becomes clear that Schoenberg has been reserving these scales for the moments of greatest importance. All that remains now is for him to transform the major version of the scale into music descriptive of the transfigured night. And for this magical moment all he needs is the first three notes.

Wagner said that the art of composition was the art of writing good transitions, and no one was better at getting smoothly from one idea to another than Schoenberg. But, as several major twentieth-century composers have proved, good transitions are not always necessary. Stravinsky, Varèse, Messiaen, Tippett and Birtwistle, among others, have shown that music can be equally effective if blocks of apparently unrelated material are placed side by side and listeners have to make the connections themselves. These juxtapositions may be ambiguous, but ambiguity is the essence of poetry. Mahler was particularly adept at exploiting the ambiguities created by juxtapositions and cross-cuttings. But because he was so masterly in the art of writing transitions, the juxtapositions and disjunctions he includes in his scores are unexpected and can be extremely disquieting. They throw the smooth and logical into disarray.

Mahler belonged to the same generation as Elgar and, like Elgar's, his music can overflow with self-confidence one moment and express a deep sense of loss the next. It is as if both men were conscious that the world they loved would soon crumble away. Elgar's sense of loss is conveyed by recalling earlier material nostalgically – as in the Violin and Cello concertos, for instance – while Mahler's comes from the nature of the material itself. He was what Schiller would have called a 'sentimental' artist in that he looks back at childhood as being a lost paradise. This is particularly evident in his early music. The song that ends the Fourth Symphony, for example, is a child's vision of heaven, and the whole symphony evokes the world of the very young. Mahler himself called the opening theme in the first movement 'childlike, simple and entirely unselfconscious'. During the development section this innocent world becomes increasingly threatened. At the climax a low trumpet plays an ominous fanfare. But nothing comes of it: the recapitulation occurs as if nothing had happened. The effect is strikingly apt, for children live in the fullness of the moment – they are entirely focused on the here and now. Once a threat is removed, it is immediately forgotten.

Mahler completed the Fourth Symphony in 1901, roughly four years after he had moved to Vienna to take up his appointment as principal conductor of the Imperial Court Opera. The position involved producing as well as conducting the bulk of the operas, and in his ten years there he raised standards to legendary heights. The Viennese worshipped him as a conductor, but found his music difficult to stomach. Viennese society in the years before the First World War prided itself on being a bulwark of stability. Everything had its appointed place. So a composer whose musical language undermined the stability of the established order was bound to meet with disapproval, especially if he was a Jew. And yet, as Stefan Zweig pointed out in his autobiography *The World of Yesterday* (1942), it was the Jews of Vienna (Mahler, Karl Kraus, Hugo von Hofmannsthal, Arthur Schnitzler, Peter Altenberg) who gave to what was Austrian, and Viennese, 'its most intensive expression'.

Nowhere is this more evident than in Mahler's Seventh Symphony of 1904–5. All its material can be directly related to the Austrian

Hans Lindloff's caricature of Gustav Mahler.

Mahler in 1907.

Mahler once said, 'When the end of the world comes I shall go back to Vienna, because everything arrives there twenty years too late.'

musical vernacular, even by those who have never been to the country. And although the marches, dances and songs are torn apart, parodied, and even mocked at times, Mahler always gives the impression that he loves and respects his models. He described the symphony as being 'predominantly of a cheerful character'. There are no references to childhood or the fullness of the moment. In fact, the opposite is the case. Each of its five movements seems to be the embodiment of adult self-consciousness. The central movement is a shadowy scherzo, alluding to the Viennese waltz and to tunes that could have come out of Viennese operettas. On either side of it are two movements Mahler entitled 'Night Music'. The first, with its march-like rhythm, alpine horns and cow-bells, suggests a night-time walk in the mountains, the second a serenade. The outer two movements are dominated by military music, their irony and humour deriving mainly from the context in which Mahler places the marches, fanfares, voluntaries and calls to order. The first movement opens with the rhythm of a funeral march, suitably muted and hushed, but the melody, when it enters, is (as Mahler put it), 'a roar of nature', a full-throated affair, bellowed out by a tenor horn. In the last movement, where the marches are more ceremonial, Mahler places them cheek by jowl with a mock minuet and a mock Turkish march – Turkish military music having been the butt of Austrian musical humour ever since the eighteenth century.

If these outer movements belong to the public world, the central movement, the scherzo, belongs the private world of inner thoughts. Its formal design is the *ABA* of the standard scherzo and trio, but inside this traditional framework Mahler unfolds a sequence of events suggesting the antics of some ghoulish dance. The sequence consists of a scurrying figure, a sentimental or plaintive tune and a waltz. But every time Mahler goes through it something bizarre and quite unexpected is thrown up. There are probably more cross-cuttings and dislocations in this movement than anywhere else in his output. Nothing is ever allowed to 'be'. The music flickers from point to point, just as the mind flickers from point to point when day-dreaming.

William James in his *Principles of Psychology* (1890) talks about the 'stream of consciousness' being in a constant state of change. 'No state once gone can recur and be identical with what it was before.' The portrayal of the 'stream of consciousness' later became a standard literary device, two of the most celebrated examples being the opening of Virginia Woolf's novel *Mrs Dalloway* and the closing pages of James Joyce's *Ulysses*. In Vienna, Arthur Schnitzler made use of it as early as 1900 in his story *Leutnant Gustl*. The lieutenant, believing that he has lost his honour when he is insulted at a concert, spends the night walking and sitting about in the Prater, going over and over in his mind what he thinks the consequences will be. The author's main purpose was to expose the lieutenant's hypocrisy, and by implication the hypocrisy of the Viennese in general. But as well as being a writer, Schnitzler was also a doctor with special interests in psychology, and it was his skilful exploitation of the lieutenant's shapeless inner musings that made the greatest impact at the time. Mahler's scherzo could also be considered an example of the stream of consciousness, and it may well have had an influence on Schoenberg's *Erwartung*.

But for many Viennese, the stream of consciousness was merely the tip of an iceberg. With Sigmund Freud in their midst how could it be otherwise? He had shown them that the workings of the mind were not as rational as everybody had believed. His first publications dealt with hysteria, which he attributed to sexual repression and, in the case of one of his patients, to father-fixation. When Hugo von Hofmannsthal wrote his play *Elektra* in 1903, it is thought that he was already familiar with what Freud had to say about Hamlet's father-fixation in *The Interpretation of Dreams* (1900). Although the play is a study in hysteria, Hofmannsthal's decision to write *Elektra* arose from a crisis in his own life totally unrelated either to hysteria or to father-fixation. This was the realization that he could no longer continue to write the precious poetry he had been producing since he was a child – poetry entirely devoted to a celebration of the past. It had cut him off from the present, and as a result he felt

Vienna at the close of the nineteenth century and, as ever, decay smells sweet. Looking back on it now, we can see it's the end of an era. We can see an old world crumbling.

Schoenberg's painting
The Red Gaze, 1907.

Elektra is a gigantic teenage tantrum. It seemed at the time the most outrageously barbaric, nihilistic, destructive piece of music that had ever been written.

estranged from the real world. _Elektra_ was his attempt to face the crisis head on, and his text later became the libretto of Richard Strauss's opera.

The action takes place in Argos just before and after the return of Electra's brother, Orestes, to avenge the murder of their father Agamemnon by their mother Clytemnestra and her lover Aegisthus. Hofmannsthal modelled his play on Sophocles, but unlike Sophocles his concern is entirely focused on the psychology of the three women living in the claustrophobic atmosphere of the palace in Mycenae: Electra, Clytemnestra and Electra's sister Chrysothemis. Hofmannsthal reveals that for different reasons all three have lost the sense of a real present. They live either in the past or in the future. Electra has focused all her attention on her father's death and the

Felicity Palmer (_centre_) as Klytemnestra and Janet Hardy (_left_) in the title role of Welsh National Opera's production of _Elektra_ by Richard Strauss.

prospect of her brother's revenge; Clytemnestra wants to obliterate from her memory the past and all thoughts of her husband's murder, but lives in dread of Orestes' return and the vengeance that will follow; Chrysothemis can think only of the time when she will have a husband and children. All three are paralysed, quite unable to act – none more so than Electra; afflicted with the classic symptoms of hysteria, she cannot even hand Orestes the axe to commit the longed-for act of revenge, and then can hardly find the strength to dance her dance of triumph on the deaths of Clytemnestra and Aegisthus.

Richard Strauss completed his score in 1908, shortly after Schoenberg had finished the Second String Quartet. It is undoubtedly Strauss's most radical and dissonant work, and, as in Schoenberg's quartet, there are passages that are virtually atonal. The most extreme occur in the scene between Electra and Clytemnestra, notably when Clytemnestra tells her daughter about the monsters that haunt her dreams. The episode concludes with a tonal cadence (as does the last movement of the quartet), but before this the discords are as harsh and the harmony as rootless as the images Clytemnestra conjures up. For both characters Strauss wrote music that is basically bitonal: one key is superimposed on another. For Clytemnestra he selected B minor and F minor, for Electra E major and D♭ major. When the tonic triads of Clytemnestra's keys are played simultaneously the sound is particularly dissonant because both are minor triads and they have no note in common; the B clashes against the C, the F against the F♭. When Electra's triads sound together the effect is less grating, but no listener can fail to detect that, like her mother, she has no centre to her being.

Strauss in his study in the 1940s.

Strauss was one of the first to make use of bitonality, but he was too committed to Romanticism to make any further contribution to the development of the ideas unfolding during the radical years before the First World War. The next opera he and Hofmannsthal produced, *Der Rosenkavalier*, turned away from the problems raised in *Elektra* and found refuge again in the past.

Only Schoenberg had the vision to realize that what was needed at the time was a style that could be more 'present-centred' than anything the tonal or even the modal system was able to produce – a style to capture, or at least strongly evoke, the fullness of the moment. He achieved it in the last of the Five Orchestral Pieces, which he composed between May and August 1909, immediately before *Erwartung*. When they were published, Schoenberg supplied the pieces with titles. He was rather reluctant to do so at first, but they prove helpful in providing the listener with clues as to the purpose behind the music's temporal perspectives. This is to move stage by stage from a state of 'becoming' to a state of 'being'. Schoenberg had attempted to accomplish this transition in *Verklärte Nacht*, but there he could only hint at the sense of 'being' the lovers have achieved when they move off into the night.

Arnold Schoenberg in 1911.

Schoenberg called the first piece 'Premonitions'. Here the state of 'becoming' is represented by the development of a motif and its accompaniment through four sections, each longer than the one before. At the end of the first it becomes clear that the goal of each section is a rapidly repeated note, pitched low on a brass instrument. It is towards this that the music pounds. In the last two sections the note is turned into a chord, played very loudly by low

Self Portrait (1907) by
Richard Gerstl.

trombones, and the repetitions are flutter-tongued. To some ears these may sound like 'raspberries' – in which case the goal is at least distinctive and memorable!

The next piece, much slower and calmer, is also developmental. Schoenberg calls it 'Vergangenes', which could be translated as 'Yesteryears'. The title suggests that his intention was to go back in time and base the music on the methods he would have used in the past. As far as the motivic development, harmony and form are concerned, this is exactly what he does. The form could be considered a variant of sonata form, and at critical points – the opening section, the return of the opening after the development, and the end of the piece – the harmony strongly implies D minor. The music is therefore directional. But what rivets the ear and distracts the listener's attention away from the music's destination and what might happen next is the emphasis Schoenberg places on spatial depth. At any one time there can be six lines of counterpoint accompanying the leading voice in the foreground. They are all recessed, some appearing to be more distant than others. Schoenberg achieves this simply by applying the principle that objects in the distance or middle distance are less clear than those in the foreground, and will often appear distorted, fuzzy or incomplete. To draw the listener's attention to these distant objects, Schoenberg distorts and fragments the leading voice, making it difficult to follow as a line. This means that, instead of tracing the linear progress of the music, the listener is drawn deep inside the sounds as they appear in the moment.

In the third piece, called 'Colours', the spatial dimension becomes even more important, for here there are no themes or motifs, only changing colours heard as if coming from indefinable places in the middle- and background. At one time Schoenberg thought of calling it 'Summer Morning by a Lake', but this would have located the sound too specifically. The piece simply consists of a five-note chord, which alters very slowly, one note at a time. The colours are created by the constantly changing orchestration, and the feeling that they come from somewhere in the vague distance is suggested by occasional flashes of sound played by piccolos, flutes, harp and celesta, which appear to be very close at hand in the registers Schoenberg selects for them. The overall effect is one of great stillness and peace, but the lack of melodic material also creates the impression of emptiness. To capture the fullness of the moment, Schoenberg needed to preserve the present-centredness of this pivotal piece and combine it with melodic richness.

'Peripeteia', the title of the fourth piece, was the word Aristotle used to describe the sudden reversal that results in the ending of a tragedy being wholly different from what the audience has been led to expect. Like the first movement, it is very fast, and appears to be rushing headlong towards a goal. The exposition of its material certainly gives the impression of pursuing a state of 'becoming'. But the energy is soon dispelled and there is no development. The same material returns at exactly the same pitch, different only in that it is juggled around, accelerated or reordered.

The next and final step in Schoenberg's progression from 'becoming' to 'being' has to be the removal of all repetitions. And this is achieved in 'The Obbligato Recitative' – a strange title because the

Wassily Kandinsky's *The Blue Rider* (1903), later the title of an exhibition at which Schoenberg presented his *Visions* and *Gazes*.

piece has nothing remotely like an obbligato or recitative in it. But 'obbligato' literally means 'that which must be done' and recitatives are those sections in operas where prose text is set to music. Given this, Schoenberg must have meant that it was a piece he had to write, and which he had to cast in a form resembling prose. The nearest traditional equivalent to such music is Gregorian chant, where each phrase has to be new because nothing in the prose of the biblical text is repeated verbatim. But the two differ in that Schoenberg's music is atonal, nothing is pulling it forward, and its texture is a complex network of lines with spatial depth. Like *Erwartung*, 'The Obbligato Recitative' contains no motivic development. The correspondences that do occur from time to time appear like veiled memories, lying in the back of the mind. Everything is focused on the uniqueness of the moment.

It was while he was composing the Five Orchestral Pieces and *Erwartung* that Schoenberg was at his most active as a painter. In 1907 he met and became friendly with Oskar Kokoschka and Richard Gerstl, two members of the group known as the Vienna Secession who at that time were turning away from art nouveau and embracing Expressionism – the movement in which artists sought to give free rein to their inner feelings. They not only encouraged Schoenberg, they also gave him advice and occasional lessons. Kokoschka was a writer as well as a painter, and in 1907 he produced three significant literary works: a stream of consciousness poem about the dreams that pass through the mind of an adolescent during puberty, and two of the earliest expressionist plays. Schoenberg probably saw the two plays when they were given in an open-air theatre in 1908. One of them, *Mörder Hoffnung der Frauen*, which Hindemith was later to set, had a deep influence on Schoenberg's text for *Die glückliche Hand*. Gerstl was even closer to Schoenberg. He was a frequent visitor to the Schoenberg household, and Schoenberg's wife, Mathilde, left him to live with Gerstl for a while. Shortly after she had been persuaded to return home, Gerstl committed suicide. Mathilde suffered a severe psychological breakdown and retreated into herself. One visitor to Schoenberg's apartment described her as being 'a frail, sick-looking woman, who sat silently in the corner of the couch, always wrapped in a shawl'.

Most of the paintings Schoenberg produced after this incident are of disembodied faces, which look in many ways like masks, except for their terrifying eyes: Schoenberg called them *Visions* and *Gazes*. Others are less disturbing, and three of these were shown in the *Blaue Reiter* exhibition of December 1911, organized by Wassily Kandinsky and Franz Marc in Munich. Early in 1912 Schoenberg was commissioned to write a melodrama for the Viennese actress Albertine Zehme. The outcome was *Pierrot Lunaire*, the work which seems to have purged him of his obsession with masks.

The text consists of German translations of twenty-one poems by the Belgian poet Albert Giraud, who modelled his Pierrot on the great nineteenth-century French mime Baptiste Debureaux. It was Debureaux's portrayal of Pierrot which Jean-Louis Barrault made famous in Marcel Carné's film *Les enfants du Paradis*. In Schoenberg's 'twenty-one melodramas' Pierrot is portrayed as the very epitome of the split personality. The actress half sings and half speaks, so that like Electra and Clytemnestra she appears to have no centre to her being. Furthermore she plays the part of a man and is dressed entirely in white, her face covered in chalk or white powder so that it resembles a mask. Accompanying her, but hidden from view by screens, are a group of five instrumentalists. Schoenberg arranged the poems in three groups of seven and the contents reveal an inner world that is utterly bizarre. Pierrot always refers to himself in the third person, and the images he conjures up are those of one who can make contact only with the macabre. To contain these often violent fantasies, the poet cast the thirteen-line poem in a formal mould, the first and second lines recurring as the seventh and eighth, the first returning again to round the poem off. Schoenberg's music is likewise very formal at times. One number is a passacaglia, several contain elaborate contrapuntal procedures such as canons, others are parodies of familiar genre pieces such as the Viennese waltz; there is also a 'Waltz à la Chopin'.

Pierrot is deservedly Schoenberg's most frequently performed work, but its formal features are not in line with what he had achieved in the last of the Five Orchestral Pieces or *Erwartung*. It also raises questions about his commitment to atonality, for in the last number, when Pierrot's mood becomes less fanciful and he makes the decision to return to his home in the *commedia dell'arte*, Schoenberg stabilizes the music in E major. In fact, even though *Pierrot* is always thought of as being basically atonal, E major lies in the background throughout the work: the opening few measures of the first number, for instance,

Schoenberg said that the true artist has no need of beauty, all he really needs is truthfulness.

Jean-Louis Barrault (right) as the mime in Marcel Carné's *Les Enfants du Paradis*.

could easily be interpreted as an elaborate version of its dominant seventh. This is why, when E major comes to the surface at the end, its appearance seems inevitable.

The twelve-note system, which Schoenberg formulated in the early twenties, was simply the rationalization of the melody-based style he had been using ever since the last movement of his Second String Quartet. The rationale was that everything in a piece should be based on a twelve-note melody derived from the twelve pitches of the chromatic scale. The melody would preserve its identity, he believed, even when it was reversed, turned upside down, or transposed. It would also form the substance of all the chords the composer required. But at no time should any one note be allowed to predominate. Tonal implications should be avoided at all costs. Schoenberg thought the system would ensure the supremacy of German music for a thousand years. However, it was not taken up extensively until after the Second World War, but the new generation of composers had scant regard for Schoenberg's twelve-note works, seeing them as merely a regurgitation of Brahms; the only works of his that they respected came from the period which produced the Five Orchestral Pieces and *Erwartung*.

Gidon Kremer playing Berg's Violin Concerto.

During the twenties and thirties, the twelve-note system was used by hardly anyone but Schoenberg and his pupils, Berg and Webern. Berg is at his best in large-scale works. Listening to him may be compared to reading a rich, complex novel, full of subtle cross-references but containing nevertheless a vivid story line. He was a Romantic by inclination and always attempted to place the twelve-note system within a tonal context. Webern, on the other hand, was somewhat austere in his approach to music and preferred always to write short pieces. He pared everything down to its essentials, and this was one reason why the iconoclastic generation of post-war composers looked on him as one of their godfathers.

Berg held on to tonality because he frequently needed to have recourse to its emotive power. One of his most moving uses of it comes near the end of his atonal opera *Wozzeck*, where, after Wozzeck's suicide, the music plunges into D minor, more or less forcing the audience to empathize with the soldier's tragic fate. A similar incidence occurs at the end of his Violin Concerto, which he completed just before his death in 1935. He had felt a premonition of his death, and originally the concerto was intended to be a requiem for himself; but in the event it was dedicated to the memory of Alma Mahler's daughter, Manon Gropius, who, at the age of eighteen, had died of infant paralysis. The twelve-note row on which the concerto is based outlines the triads of G minor, D major, A minor and E major, and concludes with the first four notes of a Lutheran chorale, *Es ist genug*. Eventually, towards the end of the work, the chorale is played in full in Bach's harmonization: 'It is enough; Lord, if it pleases you, set me free. My Jesus comes: now, oh world, good-night. I leave all my sorrows behind.'

As often as not Berg underpins his music with strict, traditional forms, as if he needed to restrain or discipline his extraordinarily fertile imagination. But he always disguises their presence. The last of his *Altenberg Songs* of 1912, for instance, is a passacaglia, but the repetitions of the theme on which it is based are so varied that it is difficult to tell where they begin. What is noticeable – and is noticeable in all Berg's music – is the *ABA* form in which the song is couched. Berg's practice was to cast the first *A* section as the exposition, the *B* section

The young Manon Gropius, with Franz Werfel and Alma Mahler in Venice, 1920.

Berg was not only writing a requiem for a young girl that he loved dearly, but also a requiem for the culture around him that was disappearing.

Berg's note row for the Violin Concerto.

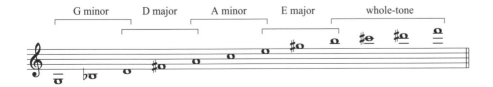

as a huge development, and the second *A* section as a transformed recapitulation of the first. The song is called 'Hier ist Friede', and the words 'Here is peace' occur at the beginning of the first and last lines of the four-line poem. The passacaglia theme consists of three phrases, which overlap with each other and are played on different instruments in different tessituras. The announcement of the complete theme constitutes the exposition, the varied repetitions of it the development, and the transformed recapitulation the coda. The coda occurs after the soprano has repeated her opening words. At this point the passacaglia's three phrases appear in reverse order, the song ending with the notes of the first of them played backwards.

Reversals are an essential feature of Berg's way of thinking and have a direct bearing on his very Nietzschean concept of 'eternal recurrence', the idea that Nietzsche expounds several times in *Thus Spake Zarathustra*. Time may appear to be a linear process, but it is actually cyclic. The same events will keep on returning over and over again. In the first scene of Wozzeck, this is the thought that obsesses and terrifies the Captain while Wozzeck is shaving him. The Captain, a restless, fidgety man, who jumps from one idea to another, constantly asks Wozzeck 'to take his time'. He likens time to a mill-wheel and cannot bear the thought that it will go on turning for ever. 'What will you do with the great expanse of time before you?' he asks Wozzeck. Berg casts the scene in the form of a Baroque suite, which he overlays with his customary tripartite structure. The Prelude constitutes the exposition, the Pavane, Cadenza, Gigue, Gavotte and Air the development, and the Postlude, in which the notes of the Prelude are played backwards, the transformed recapitulation. The juxtaposition of these different types of piece illustrates the way the Captain flits from one topic to another like a butterfly. All are themselves in *ABA* form, except for the Air, which provides the music for Wozzeck's response to the Captain and is through-composed. This is simply because Wozzeck's reply leads logically to a conclusion. He knows that he and his kind can never escape being poor and that, being poor, he can never be virtuous. The best he can hope for is that when he goes to heaven he will become one of the thunder-makers!

It is, however, the mill-wheel image that prevails, for Berg constructs the opera to represent one great turn back to its starting point. The last bar of each of the first two acts could lead immediately into the first bar of the next, and the last bar of the third act could lead

In February 1933, four weeks after Hitler became Chancellor of Germany, Berg had gone to Munich to judge a music competition. It was carnival time, and he wrote to his wife, 'The whole town and all its inhabitants are quite drowned in carnival din, masks and confetti, and on top of that the news of the Reichstag fire. Dancing on a volcano.'

straight back to the beginning. This means that the very last scene of the work, in which the dead Wozzeck's little boy is playing in the street, could be followed without a break by Wozzeck's scene with the Captain. And if this were to happen we should witness history repeating itself, for the child is treated in the same callous, insensitive way by his companions as Wozzeck has been treated throughout his life. 'You,' they shout out to him when the body of the woman Wozzeck has murdered has been found, 'Your mother's dead.'

It has now been established that, like Richard Strauss, Berg needed either a programme or a text to set his imagination in motion. The programmes he chose, however, were all of a kind, and had relevance only to himself. They all sprang from an event which happened in 1902, shortly after the production of Arthur Schnitzler's play *Reigen* ('Round dance'). Later, in the fifties, a watered-down version of the play was made into a film by Max Ophuls and called *La ronde*. Berg probably never saw the play but

Max Ophuls' film *La Ronde*, based on Schnitzler's *Reigen*.

he certainly read the text in the summer of 1904. Its subject is the sexual merry-go-round. A prostitute couples with a soldier, the soldier with a chamber-maid, the chamber-maid with a gentleman, and so on, until the cycle is completed when an aristocrat couples with the prostitute who appeared in the first scene. Each scene has the same cyclic structure. It begins with the couple greeting each other and preparing to make love; then, after a blackout, the process is reversed – they adjust their clothing and say farewell. For Berg, the important thing was that Schnitzler fashioned the events to resemble the medieval dance of death. Everyone takes part in it – young, old, rich and poor. Throughout his life Berg regarded all extramarital love affairs, including his own, as being part of the sexual merry-go-round. And his music suggests that behind them all stands the figure of death.

In 1902 Berg had a brief affair with one of the maids in his parents' summer house in Carinthia. The result was the birth of a daughter and his attempted suicide. This is the incident that lies behind the programme of the Three Orchestral Pieces of 1914–15 and, more remotely, that of the Violin Concerto, where he introduces a Carinthian folk tune. But Berg did not want the event exposed to public view, so he makes the references virtually impenetrable. Who would know that the words of the folksong express pleasure at waking up in 'Mizzi's' bed? On the surface the Three Orchestral Pieces are his tribute to Mahler. Behind the first (Prelude) stands the first movement of Mahler's Ninth Symphony, which Berg considered to be a premonition of death, and behind the third (March) stands the last movement of Mahler's Sixth – it even includes Mahler's three great hammer blows of fate. The central movement, however, is entitled 'Round Dance', and at its centre Berg even provides the blackout – a long pause in which the orchestra is silent. The title apparently refers to a waltz, where the couple goes round and round in close contact, for it is a waltz that leads up to the pause and is resumed when the music begins again, though now it is played backwards.

Another illicit love affair provided Berg with the programme for his *Lyric Suite*, a work in six movements for string quartet, dating from 1925–6. In the fourth movement, marked 'Adagio appassionato', he quotes a passage from Alexander von Zemlinsky's *Lyric Symphony* (1923) – 'You are my own, my own' – while in the last, a bleak Largo desolato, he quotes the Tristan chord and makes oblique reference to Baudelaire's poem 'De profundis clamavi': 'From the depths of the dark gulf into which my heart has fallen, I implore your pity, you, the only one I love.' The lady in question was Hanna Fuchs-Robettin, the wife of a wealthy industrialist, whom Berg met in 1925. In the copy of the score that Berg gave to her as a present he explained the cryptic symbolism he had devised. As well as using their initials (AB and HF – the German note names for the pitches A–B♭–B♮–F), he decided that she could be represented by the number 10 and he by the number 23. Multiples of these numbers can be found everywhere in the score. The movement in which the music goes in reverse is the

Hauptmann (Udo Holdorf) and the Doktor (Michael Devlin) in Netherlands Opera production of Berg's *Wozzeck*.

third, a scherzo with a trio marked 'estatico'; the trio represents either their love-making or perhaps simply the moment when they confessed their love. But, as the later movements make clear, their love was doomed. Berg was not prepared to leave his wife, nor Hanna her husband. The quotation of the Tristan chord suggests that, like Tristan and Isolde, they could be united only in death.

The reversals in several of Berg's works take the strict form of a palindrome. In his Chamber Concerto for violin, piano and thirteen wind instruments, which he completed in 1925 to celebrate Schoenberg's fiftieth birthday, a palindrome occurs at the central point of the Adagio, the second movement. But the literal retrograde version lasts only a few bars: thereafter the reversal no longer affects the details, merely the larger gestures. The movement was intended to be a character study of Schoenberg's wife, Mathilde, who was dying of cancer when the work was begun. She had still not recovered from Gerstl's death and was still withdrawn. The piano is silent except at the point where the music turns round, when it plays a low C♯. The solo instrument is the muted violin, which enters very quietly on a high note just before the first movement ends; its presence is noticeable only when the other instruments, representing Schoenberg and his noisy pupils, suddenly become silent. Berg spells out Mathilde's name on a muted trumpet, using the musical letters German speakers have at their disposal, and above it he has the oboe play a phrase associated with Mélisande in Schoenberg's tone poem *Pelleas und Melisande*; the implication is that if Mathilde is Mélisande then Richard Gerstl must have been Pelléas and Schoenberg Golaud, the jealous husband who is responsible for his rival's death and his wife's withdrawal. It is no wonder that Berg disguised the quotation from *Pelleas und Melisande* and tried to make his programmes as obscure as possible. The true interpretation of the *Lyric Suite* came to light only when his sketches for the work were examined in the eighties.

Unless they are short, palindromes and reversals can have only a symbolic function in music. Aurally, they are not easy to detect. This may be why in *Lulu*, his second opera, Berg placed the palindrome symbolizing the reversal of Lulu's circumstances in a three-minute film sequence. It occurs as an interlude between the two scenes of the central act and shows, in accelerated action, her imprisonment for the murder of her husband, Dr Schön, and then her escape. In the ascendant phase of her life, leading up to her imprisonment, Lulu is

Louise Brooks as Lulu in the 1929 film of Wedekind's *Pandora's Box*.

the *femme fatale* who brings disaster to the men in her life. In the descendant phase, culminating in her death at the hands of Jack the Ripper, she brings disaster on herself. The roles of Dr Schön and Jack the Ripper have to be played by the same singer to underline the fact, as in *Wozzeck*, that the victim can become the predator, the predator the victim.

Berg based his libretto on two plays by Frank Wedekind, in which the extent of the havoc wrought in modern life by the exercise of the will (in Schopenhauer's sense) is revealed. What dominate our lives are sex and the desire for power and prestige. And, as in Schnitzler's *Reigen*, these drives result in a perpetual merry-go-round, a perpetual dance of death. If Lulu had found love she might have been able to jump off the merry-go-round. But, as Berg's music makes clear, her love is stifled, never allowed to blossom. In the last movement of his *Lulu Suite*, containing items from the opera, he includes a moving passage in D♭ major associated with Lulu's capacity to love. Emotionally it is extraordinarily powerful, and since the last movement of the suite takes music from the opera's last scene, those who have not seen the opera would assume that this is how it ends. But they would be wrong. In the event, Berg resisted the temptation to engage the audience's compassion, as he had done at this point in *Wozzeck*. The

D♭ major passage is absent. Lulu's love has truly been stifled.

Webern also made use of palindromes, notably in the first movement of his Piano Variations, op. 27, of 1935–6; but in his case they have a purely musical function and do not relate to any extra-musical circumstances. Like so many works by the composers of the so-called Second Viennese School (Schoenberg, Berg and Webern), one form is here superimposed on another. The ten variations are overlaid with a three-movement sonatina form: the first three variations make up the first movement, the fourth the second movement, and the remaining six the third. Palindromes are the most symmetrical structures imaginable, and if short can sound very contrived. Webern starts with a movement consisting of nothing else but short palindromes, some sounding particularly stilted. But this is only because he wants to end with a movement in which there are no apparent symmetries at all, where everything sounds utterly spontaneous. In this respect, the structure as a whole is not unlike that of Schoenberg's Five Orchestral Pieces.

Webern has the reputation of being one of the century's most radical composers. Most music lovers still find his work a stumbling block, which is why it so rarely appears in concert programmes. But he thought of himself as being steeped in tradition. As a young man he studied musicology in Vienna and edited several volumes of music by the great Renaissance composer Heinrich Isaac. As a conductor, he found Schubert and Mahler closest to his heart, and when talking about his own music he always insisted that Bach, Beethoven and Brahms stood behind him. In the Piano Variations, it is Bach who is prominent. Like the Goldberg Variations, Webern's work is an exercise in the art of crossing hands. He himself confessed that he had in mind the Badinerie from the B minor Suite for flute and strings when composing the lively second movement. And the fact that virtually the whole piece consists of a single unaccompanied line suggests that he must also have been thinking of Bach's unaccompanied violin partitas and sonatas. The few, sparse chords that do occur are mostly confined to the last movement. There they encapsulate the ambiguity and mystery towards which the music has been moving ever since the formal palindrome that opens the work. A single unaccompanied line, however, is the last thing a listener would expect from a work written for the piano, the harmony instrument *par excellence*. But like Bach, Webern had the skill to make a melodic line yield a rich

Anton Webern in 1933.

contrapuntal harvest. By having it leap from register to register he creates the impression that there is not one line but several moving along simultaneously. Part of his skill in this respect lies in the way he characterizes each note, particularly in variation 5, the lyrical focal point of the work. He groups the notes into pairs, each pair having its own distinctive articulation (legato, staccato or tenuto, for example), so that the two notes can always be linked up wherever they might appear. The resulting texture sounds as rich as if one were listening to a network of counterpoint. This is undoubtedly why the work has been considered the apotheosis of the melodically based twelve-note technique, and why the avant-garde composers who emerged after the Second World War regarded it as a model to be emulated.

Stravinsky said that Webern was important because he discovered a new distance between the musical object and ourselves, and in so doing discovered a new measure of musical time. By this Stravinsky was presumably drawing attention to the fact that when we listen to a piece of music in which related events are separated by a long period of time, we have to stand back from the music to grasp the connections. But if we apply the same listening technique to Webern's work, particularly some of his very short pieces, the music is almost bound to sound trivial. To get the most out of it we have to move in close and listen not just to the sound but to the quality of the sound, the nuances that lie within each fleeting whisper. The exercise is not unlike listening to the second of Schoenberg's Five Pieces, where the spatial depth diverts the attention away from the flow of the music through time and focuses it on what is happening in the moment. But ideally this kind of listening has to be prepared for. We need time to become adjusted to present-centred listening. This is almost certainly why Webern reserves those mysterious chords in his Piano Variations until the last movement. To penetrate the mystery we have to move close and get into them, we cannot stand back. Webern therefore begins the work with palindromes that demand to be listened to from a distance. He then has us gradually shift our position *vis-à-vis* the music, so that by the time we reach the lyricism of variation 5 we should be fully prepared for the chords. From there we are only a few seconds away from variation 7 where they begin.

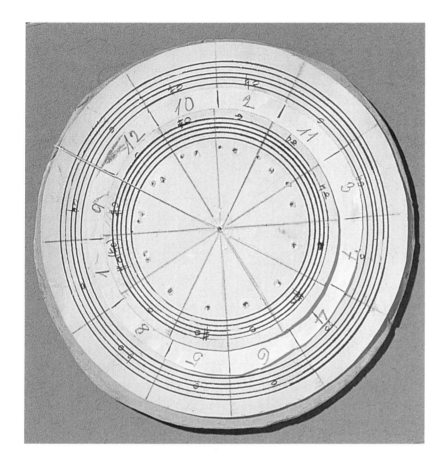

The device Schoenberg made to work out note-row formations in his Brass Quintet, op. 12. There are such devices for several of Schoenberg's twelve-note pieces.

Schoenberg, speaking about Webern's aphoristic Six Bagatelles for string quartet (1911–13), said: 'You can stretch out a glance into a poem, a sigh into a novel; but to express a novel in a single gesture, a joy in a breath, such concentration can only be present in proportion to the absence of self-pity.' The absence of self-pity is what distinguishes Webern from Berg, for self-pity can be experienced only by those who are self-conscious, and Webern is one of those rare composers who are fundamentally naïve in their outlook and consequently have little or no sense of the tragic. He had no sense of the division between man and nature, and, with the sole exception of his Six Pieces for large orchestra, op. 6, which he composed in 1909 after the funeral of his mother, all his works are a celebration of the unity of things. What excited him about the twelve-note system was that it ensured unity.

Nevertheless, in the Piano Variations Webern was not above flouting Schoenberg's 'rules' forbidding the use of privileged notes. All the notes in variation 4 (the second movement, based on Bach's Badinerie) are symmetrically arranged around the A above middle C, while all the notes in variation 5 gravitate towards the final E♭. The whole work, in fact, oscillates between these two notes. The climax of the third movement consists of notes cascading down from three iterations of a high A, while the mysterious chords ultimately find their destiny in a low E♭. In modal and tonal music A–E♭, the interval of a diminished fifth, is a discord which needs resolving. The standard resolution would be to have the A move to B♭ and the E♭ move to D, or (if the E♭ is read as D♯) to have them move in the opposite direction, to G♯ and E. But Webern resolves the tension in a highly unorthodox

The poet Hildegard Jone's sketches of Webern conducting.

way. He does so by supplying in the bass the note towards which the coda has been moving – a low B. It may be unorthodox, yet it feels right (perhaps because his basic note row ends on B).

The procedure is a prime example of a harmonic technique that became very prevalent after Webern's death in 1945. It involves setting up harmonic tension of some kind, but never revealing how it will be resolved until the end of the piece. However, this procedure is not new: as we saw earlier it is one of the features of the old modal system. As will become apparent in the following chapters, the use of modes has been every bit as important to the organization of pitch in the twentieth century as the twelve-note system, perhaps even more so. Being a Renaissance scholar, Webern may have been instinctively aware that modal thinking would come into its own again.

Chapter 3
Rhythm

An excess of order produces sterility and boredom, an excess of disorder chaos, so that in music, as in life, the two must be held more or less in balance. The relationship between order and disorder can probably be heard most clearly in the music of a jazz pianist such as Art Tatum. Order is represented by the regular pulse in his left hand, disorder – or at least relative disorder – by the rubato, syncopations and cross-beats in his right. There are passages in his celebrated 1933 recording of Duke Ellington's *Sophisticated Lady* where Tatum suspends the regular beat completely and moves into an entirely different rhythm: he allows caprice to take over – but not for long. In fact, Tatum is never out of control. He always keeps the basic pulse going, even though it cannot be heard. He therefore has no difficulty in restoring order after his flights of fancy.

The same principle holds good in the music of Bach, Beethoven and Brahms, except that there the pulse is less obtrusive and the cross-rhythms never so flamboyant. Greater emphasis is given to the harmonic rhythm underpinning of the music's flow. This long-established relationship between regular pulse and the melodic and harmonic events that save it from monotony was shattered in 1913 by Stravinsky's *The Rite of Spring*, first performed by Diaghilev's Russian Ballet in Paris. In those days no ballet dancer had ever encountered any music that did not have a regular beat. But *The Rite of Spring* contains some dances where the time signature changes constantly – in one section of the 'Games of the Rival Clans' successive bars run: $\frac{3}{2} - \frac{4}{4} - \frac{3}{2} - \frac{4}{4} - \frac{5}{4} - \frac{4}{4}$. Diaghilev had asked Nijinsky to be the choreographer, and Stravinsky remembered him standing on a chair in the wings at the first performance, beating out the rhythm with his fist and shouting numbers to the dancers 'like a coxswain'.

Diaghilev founded the Russian Ballet in 1909 and during the twenty years of its existence sixty-eight ballets were produced, most of them specially

If rhythm before had been measured by the heartbeat, by the pulse, with all its strange, cranky, individual humanity, in the twentieth century rhythm would be measured in a much more exact way.

Jean Nouvel's responsive building, the Arab Institute in Paris, with electronically adjustable apertures for windows.

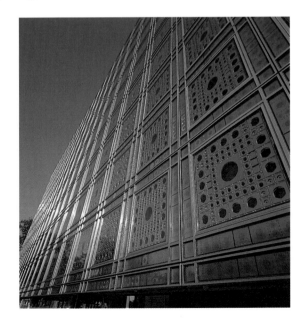

Stravinsky in 1934, at the time of composing the Concerto for two pianos.

Stravinsky talked about trying to recapture the violence, the sense of the earth cracking that he witnessed each spring in Russia. But at a deeper level *The Rite of Spring* is a metaphor for the cracking of an exhausted era.

commissioned by Diaghilev. Among these were major scores by Ravel, Debussy, Strauss, Satie, Falla, Prokofiev, Poulenc and Milhaud, as well as Stravinsky. The company never performed in Russia itself. Diaghilev's purpose was to dazzle western European audiences with the brilliance of the Russian dancers, choreographers, designers and composers he had assembled, and to give the West a taste of Russian exoticism. Stravinsky's first ballet, *The Firebird*, was based on a fantastic Russian fairy-tale; *Petrushka*, his second, on a bizarre and tragic event in a Russian puppet theatre. He said that the idea for *The Rite of Spring* came to him quite spontaneously: 'I saw in imagination a solemn pagan rite; wise elders, seated in a circle, watching a young girl dance herself to death.' To help him construct a scenario, Stravinsky sought the advice of the stage designer Nikolai Roerich, who had written about and painted pictures of the pagan rites of the ancient Slavs, some of whose customs still survived in Russia. They divided the action into two parts: the first part culminates in the 'Dance of the Earth' after one of the elders kisses the earth in a moment of 'mystic terror'; the second in the 'Sacrificial Dance', in which a young girl dances herself to death and the elders dedicate her body to the sun god.

Stravinsky's score is as important to modern music as Picasso's painting *Les demoiselles d'Avignon* is to modern art. Picasso broke away from the classical norm for the human figure and the

Art Tatum, jazz pianist of genius.

spatial illusion of one-point perspective, Stravinsky from the pre-eminence of melody and harmony. But whereas Picasso had examples of African masks and Oceanic statues in front of him when painting *Les demoiselles*, for Stravinsky there was a complete lack of any suitable models. There was no ancient Slavic music to draw on, so he had to invent the past. This meant stripping away those qualities considered essential for civilized modern life – the willingness to compromise, to make allowances and to see the other person's point of view. Stravinsky's score is consequently characterized by its obsessiveness, its determination never to yield. When the elder leaves the village to plant his ritualistic kiss on the earth, the music accompanying him is a phrase played over and over again by four tubas with practically no deviation; they cut across everything going on around them, and persist with an iron determination that becomes terrifying.

Stravinsky said that the Prelude to the ballet was meant to represent the awakening of nature, 'the scratching, gnawing, wiggling of birds and beasts'. The action proper starts with the 'Auguries of Spring', a dance in two parts, the first half for men, the second for young girls. An obsessive four-note quaver figure (Db–Bb–Eb–Bb) is played throughout, mainly by the cor anglais; about half way through the second part, the pitch falls a semitone, and this constitutes perhaps the only significant change in harmony in the entire movement. Everything, therefore, depends on rhythm. The scene starts with a stomping dance for the men, the strings pounding out insistently and relentlessly a powerful discord. The notes come from the superimposition of two chords lying a semitone apart – Fb major and a dominant seventh on Eb. Normally, in tonal music, one chord would eventually have to give way to the other – there would be some kind of resolution. But not here. And to increase the tension Stravinsky adds irregular accents to the pounding quavers, so that the men are forced to move convulsively. On top of this relentless rhythm are snippets of melodic material: a menacing trumpet fanfare, echoed by oboes and pizzicato violins; a short, four-note diatonic tune, tossed in the air by flutes; the same four notes turned into a rustic dance for bassoons.

In 'The Dance of the Young Girls' it becomes apparent that the melodic material is all derived from Russian folk music. The only

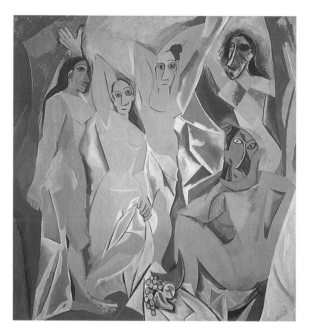

Picasso, *Les demoiselles d'Avignon* of 1906–7.

genuine folksong is the one given to the bassoon at the very opening of the work, but Stravinsky said that throughout *The Rite* he was able 'to tap some unconscious "folk" memory'. When the girls enter, the first horn, sounding as if from the distance, plays a simple modal tune built from five notes. This is immediately followed by a decorated version on the first flute. A little later the same tune appears on the alto flute, a minor third higher. Then more characters enter, among them a group of elders, who are represented by a stately melody for trumpets. Meanwhile the girls continue to dance, their music being the horn's tune and its decorated version, split into short units and shuffled around so that the order can never be predicted. The dance ends with ostinatos and unpredictable patterns piled on top of one another to represent the bustle of the various groups on stage.

The rhythmic complexities of 'Auguries of Spring' are as nothing, however, compared to those of the 'Sacrificial Dance' which brings the ballet to its conclusion. This is the only dance for a solo performer, and it is evident from the music that the chosen victim dies not from exhaustion but from the violence of her convulsions. Stravinsky cast the dance in rondo form – *ABACA*. Apart from snippets of melodic material in sections *B* and *C*, rhythm is pre-eminent, melody and harmony are reduced to subsidiary functions. There is a pulse, but it is very irregular, particularly in the *A* sections. In the 1921 version of the score, the dance gets under way after a preparatory bar of $\frac{3}{16}$, and a pause. Then follow two four-bar units, the second being a repeat of the first. The time signatures are: $\frac{2}{16} - \frac{3}{16} - \frac{3}{16} - \frac{2}{8}$. The main accent falls on the first beat of the second unit, and the motion leading up to it might be described as controlled rubato; the note values in the $\frac{3}{16}$ bars hold back the momentum, those in the $\frac{2}{8}$ bar push it forward. Most of the chords articulating the rhythm are placed on the off-beats. The difficulties this creates for the players make the sound edgy and tense. Furthermore, Stravinsky never repeats the pattern note for note: he either varies it or permutates its units, as he had done in the 'Dance of the Young

Girls'. Yet, although heavy accents fall at the beginning of many of the bars, they never feel like down-beats. The whole dance feels as if there were nothing but up-beats, and the suspense this creates gives the impression that the girl is actually willing herself to die.

At the first performance, even though the house was in tumult and the music could hardly be heard above the noise, Marie Piltz, the dancer, and Pierre Monteux, the conductor, carried on to the end. There has never been such an uproar at a first performance in the whole history of music. The audience felt that all its civilized standards had been affronted. And so, in a way, did Stravinsky. He was a man who led a very ordered existence, and the violence and chaos that characterize *The Rite* took even him by surprise. It was as if he had allowed something he wanted to repress to come to the surface. Perhaps this was why he felt that the work had willed itself into existence: 'I heard and I wrote what I heard,' he said. ' I am the vessel through which *Le Sacre* passed.' In later works, notably those composed in the neo-classical style, he kept disorder in check. Even so, most of the scenarios he selected for his ballets and dramatic works hinge on an irrational act – the power of a 'joker' to cause disruption, the power of the sphinx, the devil or a covetous fairy to wreak havoc.

Stravinsky's first neo-classical score was a ballet based on music by the eighteenth-century Neapolitan composer Pergolesi which Diaghilev had found in various libraries. The scenario concerns the disruptive exploits of Pulcinella, the favourite 'joker' of the Neapolitan *commedia dell'arte*. Diaghilev asked Stravinsky only to orchestrate the pieces, but, as in *The Rite of Spring*, Stravinsky turned out a score that 'invented the past'. He creates the impression that his is the music of the Neapolitan *commedia dell'arte*, and Pergolesi's just a refinement of the abrasive original. The abrasive elements are found in the harmony, the orchestration, the texture, and the unexpected syncopations and off-beat accents; on the whole, the pulse itself is fairly regular. But this

Stravinsky (*left*), with Mrs Kovchinsky, Diaghilev and the designer Leon Bakst, 1915, in Lausanne.

The scene of the slave auction, from D. W. Griffiths' film *Intolerance*, 1916.

does not mean that Stravinsky had abandoned the rhythmic innovations of *The Rite*, for he followed *Pulcinella* with the *Symphonies of Wind Instruments*, where he returned to his earlier Russian style.

Symphonies was composed in 1920 as a tribute to Debussy, who had died two years earlier. Stravinsky called it 'an austere ritual which is unfolded in terms of short litanies between different groups of homogeneous instruments'. There are essentially three kinds of material: a slow chorale, which eventually comes into its own at the very end of the work; fast, bell-like music, summoning people to the commemoration; and folk-like material in a tempo midway between the chorale and the bell-like music. The way in which Stravinsky cuts from one to another recalls the technique of the film director D.W. Griffith. In his film *Intolerance* (1916), four stories, set in Judea, Babylon, medieval France and modern times, are woven together to treat the theme of bigotry through the ages. Stravinsky's cross-cutting is as bold as Griffith's: if all the bell-like passages were placed in a sequence, they too would make a coherent 'story', as would all the chorales and all the folk-like passages. Cross-cutting is a constant feature of Stravinsky's style. The most cogent example occurs in the last scene of his ballet *Orpheus*, where a fugue for two horns is twice interrupted to make room for a two-bar harp solo; Stravinsky admitted that all he had done was to cut the fugue off 'with a pair of scissors'.

As well as providing a bold example of cross-cutting, the *Symphonies of Wind Instruments* also clearly illustrates Stravinsky's need to create 'ametric' rhythms, especially in his Russian works. This rests on the fact that the pace at which music proceeds is governed not only by tempo but also by the rate of harmonic change. Although the frequency of harmonic change depends on the nature of the work, in almost all circumstances it accelerates at the approach to a cadence; the increase in movement helps to give the cadence weight and importance. Stravinsky adopts the conventional procedure, but he reserves it for cadences that have special significance. Generally in the Russian works the harmony tends to be extremely slow-moving, even static, and this means that the increase in pace has to be effected by durations (that is, note values). Stravinsky's usual procedure is to divide the durations into two contrasting units and to alternate them. *Symphonies* begins with seven bars of the bell-like music, containing no harmonic change at all. The first unit (let us call it *a*) functions as an up-beat; the second (*b*) as a down-beat, and Stravinsky's pattern is *ababab*. Both units get successively shorter, except for the last *b*, which has to be lengthened because it functions as the cadential point of rest. The chorale that follows is also harmonically static, at least to begin with, for it starts with the fivefold repetition of a single chord. In this instance the first unit is a sustained chord, the second a staccato one. The durations of both units decrease by a quaver on each appearance: the durations of the sustained chord are thus $5 : 4 : 3$, and the staccato chord $3 : 2$. When these alternate with each other the result is $5 : 3 : 4 : 2 : 3$, a pattern which, although logical, escapes the tedium of being too predictable.

Traditionally, rhythm has proved to be one of the most difficult aspects of music to notate. The problem exercised medieval composers for well over 300 years. The first published edition of Stravinsky's score of *Symphonies*, a piano reduction dating from 1926, indicates that the notation of these five chords caused Stravinsky considerable difficulty. The staccato notes fall within a triplet grouping, and even Koussevitzky, who conducted the first performance, may have found them tricky to place. But the fact that the revised version of 1947 makes the placing of them only marginally easier suggests that Stravinsky always intended the pattern to be rather wayward. Here all the chords are notated on off-beats, the metric pattern being $\frac{3}{4} - \frac{2}{8} - \frac{3}{8} - \frac{3}{4} - \frac{3}{4}$. To get them to sound precisely together the players must be extremely attentive. And this is exactly why Stravinsky chose to notate the chords as he did. He never wanted them to sound relaxed. He always wanted them to sound slightly edgy, and this quality cannot be achieved unless the players are slightly tense.

Although *Symphonies* uses all the rhythmic procedures found in *The Rite*, it has none of its violence and obsessiveness. These have been tamed. The French composer Edgard Varèse

Debussy (*left*) with Stravinsky in 1912, the year of the première of Debussy's *Prélude à l'après-midi d'un faune*.

Edgard Varèse in 1958, at the time of his *Poème électronique*.

(1883–1965), studied and worked in Paris and Berlin before being invalided out of the French army in the early months of the First World War and settling in the United States. In the mid-twenties he produced a piece called *Intégrales* (1924–5), in which barbarity and the taming of barbarity can be witnessed in one and the same work. Varèse's music, like Stravinsky's, is fairly static harmonically, and he too relied on rhythm to propel it forward. But his rhythms seem to be far more spontaneous than Stravinsky's. It therefore seems strange that when he talked about his music he presented it in the language of higher mathematics or science.

'Intégrales' means the sum of a large number of infinitesimally small quantities, or, as Varèse put it more technically, 'the value of the function of a variable whose differential coefficient is known'. How this definition could possibly apply to the music he had written is difficult to imagine. When giving advice to his listeners on how to approach the music, Varèse said that they should 'visualize the changing projection of a geometrical figure on a plane, with both plane and figure moving in space, but each with its own arbitrary and varying speeds of translation and rotation'. The problem with talking in these terms is that, although they may be perfectly valid from a purely structural point of view, they give absolutely no idea of the musical imagery or the kind of transformation that takes place in the piece. Like Stravinsky when talking about *The Rite of Spring*, it is as if Varèse wanted to distance himself from the barbarity of his music.

Varèse also resembled Stravinsky in thinking of himself as the inventor of worlds – not only ancient worlds, but worlds that have been lost or may not yet have come into existence. The first piece he composed in the United States, a big orchestral work called *Amériques* (completed in 1921), is not about America as it is today but about 'new worlds on earth, in the sky or in the minds of men'. *Arcana*, an equally impressive orchestral work from 1925–7, carries on its title-page a quotation from the *Hermetic Astronomy* of Paracelsus: 'One star exists higher than all the rest. This is the apocalyptic star. The second star is that of the ascendant. The third is that of the elements, and of these there are four, so that six stars are established. Besides these there is

The impact of New York turned Varèse into music's skyscraper mystic. 'Today is an age of speed, synthesis and dynamics. Consequently, we expect contemporary forms to reflect those qualities. I tell people I am not a musician; I work with rhythms, frequencies and intensities. Tunes are the gossips in music.'

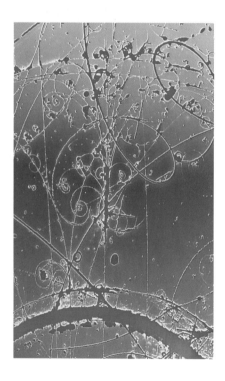

A picture of the atomic age: particle tracks in a bubble chamber.

still another star, imagination, which begets a new star and a new heaven.'

In *Intégrales* Varèse imagines a world that is probably much more ancient than that of *The Rite of Spring*. The work opens with the simplest music of all, a sequence of calls and responses. There is only one harmony and nothing resembling a melody, so the whole substance of the music relies on rhythm and timbre. A sopranino clarinet opens with a call on a single note, articulated by an accelerating rhythm; this has none of the neat, interlocking procedures found in *Symphonies of Wind Instruments* – it is much too impetuous and raw. Altogether there are eleven calls on the same note and all are rhythmically different. The response consists of two three-note chords, one on high woodwind, the other on low trombones. The percussion instruments supply the pulse, but it becomes regular only once, when a marching rhythm momentarily occurs on a snare drum. In the next section the pitch drops a minor third, and the calls come from a low horn. The effect is like some prehistoric Hagen, calling for his men on a great cow-horn.

In the second part, the calls and responses are of a completely different nature. All the calls come from an oboe, playing a sensuous, very pliant melodic line. While it plays, the other instruments remain silent, as if listening. The responses now are the calls heard in the first part, but gradually they become shorter and less aggressive until eventually the four instruments that have asserted themselves most strongly – sopranino clarinet, horn, trumpet and trombone – play a repeated chord in rhythmic unison with the oboe. In this moment, it could be said, civilization is born.

Five years after writing *Intégrales*, Varèse produced the first piece composed exclusively for percussion instruments – *Ionisation* (1929–31). This time the title comes from physics. Nicolas Slonimsky, who conducted the first performance, said that Varèse was referring to the process in which an atom liberates an electron and assumes a positive electric charge. 'The free electron travels until it is captured by another atom, which then assumes a negative charge.' By a huge stretch of the imagination it might be possible to see how this matches what happens musically, but Varèse would have made his intentions clearer had he simply

Ionisation: a false-colour image of the response of particles to chemical reaction.

explained the work in terms of its sound. The musical material derives entirely from the contrast between two kinds of sonority: the deep, resonant sonority of the tamtam and the dry sonority of the military drum. When a tamtam is struck midway between its rim and its centre there is an initial attack but the vibrations only slowly reach their peak; they then die away gradually. Varèse uses other sustaining percussion instruments, including gongs, cymbals, two sirens, a lion's roar and rolled snare drums, to emulate and enhance these characteristics in their own ways. The military drum's sonority, on the other hand, has little more to it than a dry attack; its companion instruments are claves, bongos, woodblocks, maracas, slapstick and various types of snare drum.

The work is in two parts, both ending with a chorus. The first is an exultant ensemble for the 'dry' instruments. Until this point, most of the material for these instruments has been associated with the military drum's marching rhythms, but when they join forces for the chorus, they swing into a triplet rhythm, the sudden change of gear resembling the rhythmic juxtapositions found in Balinese music. The second chorus, which ends the work, is for the sustaining instruments, with piano, bells and glockenspiel added to lend weight to the resonances. Remnants of the military drum's marching rhythms can still be heard on the tarole (a high snare drum), but they gradually fade away to nothing. As in *Intégrales*, war-like sounds are eventually pacified by warmer, darker, more mysterious ones.

Perhaps the most arresting sound in *Ionisation* is the eerie scream of the two sirens. The images they conjure up – distant police cars or fire-engines, cats wailing in the night, the weird calls and cries of the primeval forest – seem like echoes from some surreal dream world. The Surrealist movement arose in France after the First World War and attracted mainly writers and painters living in France and the Hispanic countries; it hardly touched music until the advent of electronic techniques in the fifties. The purpose of Surrealism was to draw upon the subconscious and shake off the control of reason. It is not known whether Varèse was sympathetic to its ideas, but the Latin-American poems he selected for *Offrandes*, his two songs for soprano and chamber orchestra (1921), are surrealist, and the music evokes landscapes that could only be imagined by a mind searching for worlds 'beyond reality'.

The rhythmical innovations in the works of Stravinsky and Varèse have long been acclaimed, but those of Charles Ives (1874–1954), who was experimenting with rhythm as far back as 1898, have been dismissed as the work of an amateur. Perhaps because he was a full-time businessman and had no need to make a living from music, Ives has been consistently underrated. In fact, the idea that his experiments were of no more than personal interest can easily be disputed, as we shall see in Chapter 6. Some of his most ambitious rhythmic procedures can be found in his orchestral music, where he places groups of players at different locations on the platform and gives them quite independent roles. Music in one rhythm and tempo is superimposed on music in another rhythm and tempo. *The Unanswered Question* (1908) makes use of three such locations. Throughout the piece, a muted string orchestra, sitting in the background, ideally out of sight, plays very slow, very quiet, hymn-like music. (This too could be thought of as being 'beyond reality'.) In the foreground a solo trumpet reiterates, as if it were a question that urgently needs to be answered, a short chromatic figure in a different tempo. The answer comes from four flutes, placed further back than the trumpet, or on the opposite side of the platform. But the humdrum answer does not satisfy the trumpet, nor do their longer, faster, more discordant and more frenzied subsequent answers. Eventually the flutes give up the struggle, and when the trumpet repeats its question for the last time it is greeted by silence. The listener is left to conclude that the answer really lies in the quiet music being played in the background.

In a piece called *Calcium Light Night*, which he composed while he was still a student at Yale in 1898, Ives recalls a night of student celebrations, when he stood listening to snatches of college songs being sung in different parts of the campus and watching a parade go by. Instead of using the Doppler effect to create the illusion that the parade is approaching and then moving

Charles Ives' handwritten score of part of the Fourth Symphony. Ives suffered at this time from a palsy that rendered most of his scores nearly illegible.

When you look at a Charles Ives score you can see immediately that it is not ordered in any way – it's messy. It's music written by a truly original ear, an innocent ear of enormous intelligence.

away, Ives managed to notate a controlled accelerando and ritardando. As the parade gets closer the tempo of the marching rhythm gets faster, and as the parade moves off it gets slower. The snatches of songs, however, are played in real tempo. The result is accelerating and decelerating time at one level and strict time at the other.

Ives's extraordinarily bold use of rhythm and tempo reaches its zenith in his Fourth Symphony, written between 1908 and 1916. The first movement, scored for chorus as well as orchestra, is basically a triadic setting of the hymn *Watchman, tell us of the night*. The middleground contains snatches of *In the sweet bye and bye*, *Something for Thee*, the Westminster chimes and Arthur Sullivan's hymn tune *Proprior Deo*. In the background, a distant choir of two violins and harp plays without stopping, and throughout the movement, a line from the hymn tune *Bethany* (*Nearer my God to Thee*).

Ives said that the second movement, an Allegretto,

is not a scherzo in the accepted sense of the word, but rather a comedy – in which an exciting, easy and worldly progress through life is contrasted with the trials of the Pilgrims in their journey through the swamps and rough country. The occasional slow episodes – Pilgrims' hymns – are constantly crowded out and overwhelmed by the former. The dream, or fantasy, ends with an interruption of reality – the Fourth of July in Concord – brass bands, drum corps, etc.

The movement is rhythmically so complex that two conductors are needed. At one stage there are ten independent rhythms running against one another. At these moments, the world seems to be plunged into chaos. Only when the tumult momentarily stops can a choir of strings be heard playing something quiet in the background.

Order is restored in the third movement, a double fugue on the hymns *From Greenland's icy mountains* and *All hail the power of Jesus' name*. But it is not order that Ives is after, it is the realization of a spiritual aspiration. And this comes in the finale. Far away in the distance four or five percussionists quietly play rhythmic patterns, quite unconnected with everything else that is heard. Nearer at hand a choir of five violins and two harps plays snatches of *Bethany*, as in the first movement. In the foreground the main body of the orchestra interweaves snatches of other hymns. Near the end of the movement the choir re-enters to sing wordlessly the second half of *Bethany*. The very last sound, however, comes from the distant percussion, finally fading away into silence.

The Fourth Symphony was not performed in its entirety until 1965, nine years after Ives's death. The person who was mainly responsible for bringing it to the attention of Leopold Stokowski and the Philadelphia Orchestra was Elliott Carter (born 1908) who had got to know Ives when he was sixteen. Ives wrote a recommendation for the lad to attend Harvard, where Carter read English, philosophy, mathematics and classics. Like several other composers of his generation, he later went to Paris to study under Nadia Boulanger. However the neo-classical style she encouraged him to adopt eventually gave way to the

Part of Elliott Carter's Double Concerto showing his extraordinary rhythmic devices, sevens changing into threes, threes into twos, giving the effect, as he says, of 'projecting time onto a curved screen'.

ideas to which Ives had introduced him as a teenager. *The Unanswered Question*, *Calcium Light Night* and the Allegretto of the Fourth Symphony were the works Carter cited in an article he wrote for *The Score* magazine in 1955 called 'The Rhythmic Basis of American Music'. He summarizes Ives's innovative procedures as: (1) the superimposition of different speeds that can be expressed in notation with a common unit; (2) the presence of strict time at one level and notated rubatos at another; and (3) the presentation of two or more unrelated levels heard simultaneously. Carter himself has the reputation of being highly inventive in the field of rhythm, but it must be said that the basis of his innovations resides in the three procedures of Ives that he summarized in 1955.

Carter's rhythmic concerns first became evident in his Cello Sonata

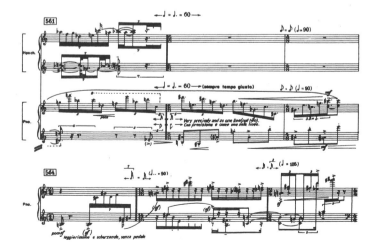

(1948). He decided that the work should not try to disguise the differences between the two instruments but should play on them. The sonata opens with the piano presenting a rhythm as precise and inexpressive as the ticking of a clock. When this is established the cello comes in with a long, warm melody in free style, its articulations falling just before or just after the piano's pulse and sounding quite independent of it. In other words, the relationship between piano and cello is very like the relationship between Art Tatum's left hand and right hand: one marks the pulse, the other plays rubato. In fact the influence of jazz becomes even more apparent in the second and fourth movements. But the truly innovative features of the work are Carter's use of metric and tempo modulations, the way he makes the transition from one metre to another and from one tempo to another, smoothly and without any noticeable 'gear change'. The trick is to use the same basic unit in both metres or both tempos. At first the piano's ticking rhythm is heard as four regular ticks in a bar of $\frac{4}{4}$, then as five ticks in a bar of $\frac{5}{4}$, then as a group of five ticks in a slower bar of $\frac{4}{4}$. Thereupon the process is reversed and Carter returns by the same steps to the original $\frac{4}{4}$ tempo. He uses the same method when he wants to modulate permanently to a slower or faster tempo, as for instance in the last movement, when he modulates from crotchet = 140 to crotchet = 112 (the tempo of the first movement).

A precedent for the procedure of tempo modulation occurs in the first two movements of Sibelius's Fifth Symphony, where the music moves from *molto moderato*, $\frac{12}{8}$, to *presto*, $\frac{3}{4}$, and then at the very end of the second movement *più presto*. Sibelius's 'gear changes' are not as smooth as Carter's, and he has to rely on the conductor to make the accelerando from *largamente* to *allegro moderato* and from *allegro moderato* to *presto*. Carter never has to resort to this. All his accelerandos and ritardandos are notated. He manages to modulate between tempos as effortlessly as Wagner was able to modulate between keys.

Carter says that the piano's ticking and the cello's rubato represent the contrast between chronometric time and psychological time. When the two are combined the result is musical or 'virtual' time. Chronometric time is linear, but psychological time could well be circular. This is why Carter links the four movements of the Cello Sonata: in terms of psychological time they form an unbroken continuity, and he ends the work by returning to the beginning, except that now it is the cellist who marks the ticking pulse and the pianist who plays rubato. Carter might have likened the overall circular shape to Berg's *Wozzeck*, but instead he referred to *Finnegans Wake* – possibly because Joyce's novel is a dream sequence.

The relevance of this becomes apparent when we turn to Carter's First String Quartet of 1951, a work that makes use of all three of Ives's rhythmical procedures. Carter says that the general plan for the four movements was suggested by Jean Cocteau's film *Le sang d'un poète* (1930), where:

the entire dream-like action is framed by an interrupted slow-motion shot of a tall brick chimney in an empty lot being dynamited. Just as the chimney begins to fall apart, the shot is broken off and the entire movie follows, after which the shot of the chimney is resumed at the point it left off, showing its disintegration in mid-air, and closing the film with its collapse on the ground.

To parallel this, the quartet begins with a cadenza for the cello and ends with the violin taking it up where the cello left off; but instead of collapsing downwards, the music for the violin rises higher and higher! 'On one level,' Carter added, 'I interpret Cocteau's idea (and my own) as establishing the difference between external time measured by the falling chimney (or the cadenza) and internal dream time (the main body of the work) – the dream time lasting but a moment of external time but from the dreamer's point of view, a long stretch.'

On two occasions, the dream is interrupted. The quartet does indeed have four movements – a fantasia (Maestoso), a scherzo (Allegro scorrevole), an Adagio and a set of variations. But the fantasia runs into the scherzo and the adagio into the variations. The breaks that normally occur between one movement and another are displaced, and instead of the normal three there are two, falling half way through the scherzo and some time after the variations have got under way. This means that as far as the players and audience are concerned, there are only three move-ments. There is no reason why the players cannot tune their instruments and wipe their brows during the breaks. When they start playing again, they take up where they left off. Clock time goes on but musical time stops.

Carter's main preoccupation is with the relationship between simultaneous events moving at different velocities. As Einstein indicated in his paper of 1905 on relativity, our sense of time comes from our capacity to co-ordinate these simultaneities. Herein lies the rationale for the rhythmic complexity of Carter's quartet. When the Fantasia gets under way after the cello's cadenza, although all four instruments have $\frac{4}{4}$ as their time signature, only the cello plays in this metre. The first violin plays in $\frac{10}{12}$, the second in $\frac{5}{16}$ and the viola in $\frac{6}{4}$. The viola's rhythm becomes the means of making the smooth modulation to a new tempo ten bars later. At this point, everyone's time signature becomes $\frac{3}{2}$, but only the second violin maintains it: the first violin plays in $\frac{15}{8}$, and the viola begins in $\frac{3}{2}$ but changes to $\frac{6}{4}$, while the cello plays freely but always just before or just after the beat. The temporal events proceed at different velocities, but we know where we are in the temporal flow because from time to time they coincide.

It would be a mistake to conclude from these descriptions that Carter's music is dry and intellectual. His main purpose is to produce textures of great richness, and to show how different types of material can complement one another. Nevertheless, his music is far from easy to perform. It could only have been produced by someone brought up in a jazz culture, whose approach to rhythm is essentially 'laid back'. In any case, not all of the quartet is as complex as the opening of the Fantasia. The Adagio, for instance, is comparatively straightforward, at least for the listener. Here the two lower strings are dramatically pitted against the two upper ones. This is also the most Ivesian section of the work, for against an impassioned, rugged recitative for the viola and cello, the two muted violins play softly and contemplatively in a high register a two-part or sometimes three-part texture, which sounds as if it were coming from somewhere in the distance. Eventually the two lower strings abandon their rhetoric, put on their mutes

Nancarrow's music has the cranky, hand-made quality of one of Tinguely's friendly machines.

Jean Tinguely's
L'Avant-Garde of 1988.

and join the violins. As in Ives, the calm, distant voice is the one that prevails.

Carter acknowledged his debt to Ives by quoting the opening theme of his First Violin Sonata in the first movement of the Cello Sonata. In the last, he quotes a passage from Conlon Nancarrow's Rhythmic Study no. 1 for player piano, which had been published in ordinary musical notation by the *New Music Quarterly* in 1951. Conlon Nancarrow's music is rarely heard in the concert hall, but most if not all of his player piano studies are available on disc. He was born in Arkansas in 1912, studied composition with Walter Piston and Roger Sessions, and played trumpet in various jazz bands. In 1937 he enlisted in the Abraham Lincoln Brigade and fought in the Spanish Civil War against Franco. When he returned to the United States, the government, uncertain about its policy concerning Spain, considered him undesirable and revoked his passport. He consequently settled in Mexico, where, deprived of contact with fellow composers in the States, he wrote his rhythmically complex music for player piano (or 'pianola', as it is sometimes known), punching the holes in the piano rolls himself.

The Rhythmic Study no. 1 is indebted to jazz and sounds as if several Art Tatums were improvising at breakneck speed simultaneously. In one section there are five metric pulses running along at the same time, respectively in $\frac{7}{16}$, $\frac{9}{32}$, $\frac{4}{4}$, $\frac{7}{8}$, and $\frac{15}{32}$ – which alone makes the study more complex than anything Carter has written. Yet, because the principal feature of the piece is a regular ostinato, built from a pattern of diatonic chords in the middle register, we get the equivalent of the jazz man's necessary beat. Several of Nancarrow's later studies are devoted to rhythmic canons, each voice moving in its own tempo. In these, a regular beat is noticeably absent. No. 15 has two voices moving at a ratio of 3 : 4, no. 19 three voices in ratios of 12 : 15 : 20, no. 36 four voices at ratios of 17 : 18 : 19 : 20. No. 27, a study in acceleration and

A page of Nancarrow's transcription of his Study no. 37 for player piano. A canon played at twelve different speeds giving rise to polyrhythms such as 21:20, 25:24 and 15:14.

It's not just that two human hands could not get round this music, but you would need two or more human brains controlling them.

Conlon Nancarrow with the machine for punching out his piano rolls.

deceleration controlled by an ostinato figure in the middle voice, which Nancarrow calls 'the ticking of an ontological clock', may suggest affinities with Carter's Cello Sonata. But Nancarrow's accelerations and decelerations are considerably more variable and precise than anything that could be obtained by human instrumentalists.

Nancarrow's music was designed for two special Ampico player pianos, one with wooden hammers and the other with steel hammers covered in leather. The composer Charles Amirkhanian has said that 'no recorded image of his compositions will ever reproduce the overwhelming sensation of the raw power and excitement generated when sitting in Nancarrow's soundproof studio in Mexico City and listening to his rolls in the flesh'. Not many people have had that privilege, so composers who have wanted to emulate Nancarrow's achievements have had to get to know his music through listening to discs. One such is Harrison Birtwistle (born 1934) who for his opera *The Mask of Orpheus* composed six taped inserts which are even faster than Nancarrow at his most breathtaking. Birtwistle created this music at the Institut de Recherche et de Coordination Acoustique / Musique (IRCAM) in Paris, the most sophisticated electronic studio in the world. The inserts are self-contained pieces, lasting about three minutes each. The material stems from notes and chords played by a harp, then analysed and synthesized by a computer to produce what Birtwistle calls 'a mad, mechanical percussion instrument'. Altogether, there are some 400 individual sounds ranging from what appears to be a bass drum at one end of the spectrum to an impossibly high piano at the other. In between are what could be marimbas, bongos, vibraphones and guitars. Birtwistle left the 'voicing' of the pieces to his assistant, Barry Anderson, while he himself focused on 'the important things' – the rhythms. Birtwistle became fascinated by the ability of a computer to divide a second into, say, thirteen or seven with absolute precision. None of the rhythms are written down and they are far too fast to be analysed by ear, but apparently they all sprang from the nature of the material as it slowly evolved in the studio.

The Mask of Orpheus looks at the Orpheus myth from every conceivable angle, and the taped inserts are cut into the action to tell the stories that Orpheus told to the rocks and trees as he sat on the mountain after failing to rescue Euridice from Hades. They accompany a group of actors who mime the stories at a speed comparable to accelerated motion in the cinema. When the actors come on stage, everyone – conductor, orchestra and singers – must freeze, even if they are in the middle of a phrase or taking a breath. They may move again only when the episode is over, at which juncture they take up where they left off. Birtwistle says that his purpose was to make what follows seem as if it were taking place in slow motion. 'Music is the one medium where time can transcend itself,' he says. 'With poetry you are always up against language and meaning – in theatre too – while in painting you're up against the frame, which limits size and scale. Time scale in music is something which has nothing to do with the length of a piece – and new concepts of time are my main compositional preoccupation.'

Birtwistle likens what he does to looking at an object from different perspectives. In *The Mask of Orpheus* we see Orpheus as a man (a masked singer), as hero (a masked mime) and as myth (a huge puppet whose voice comes from an amplified singer off stage). Because it is re-enacted at several points, we also witness his death from different perspectives. Birtwistle has adopted this approach ever since he came across Satie's *Trois gymnopédies* (1888) as a student. Unlike other sets of piano pieces, where the tempos and moods of the items usually contrast, these are virtually identical in tempo and mood. If you have a visual imagination, as Birtwistle does, listening to them is like looking at three facets of a crystal. They are simply themselves, unhurried and devoid of rhetoric.

'To be interested in Satie,' said John Cage, 'one must first be disinterested to begin with, accept that a sound is a sound and a man is a man, give up illusions about ideas of order, expressions of sentiment, and all the rest of our inherited claptrap.' For Birtwistle, Satie was the first composer he had come across whose music was not linear and goal-orientated. For Cage, Satie was important because he took no heed of established conventions and his music referred to nothing but itself. For the minimalists

The Mask of Orpheus, by
Harrison Birtwistle.

who followed in Cage's wake, Satie's music was the epitome of simplicity. The *Trois gymnopédies*, written at the same time as Strauss composed *Don Juan* and *Macbeth*, Tchaikovsky his Fifth Symphony and Mahler his First, established the precedent for those who wanted to challenge the complexity of music in their own time. Terry Riley, who, with La Monte Young (they were both born in 1935), was one of the founding fathers of minimalism, has explained why the movement came into being. Minimalism emerged not because there was an intellectual desire to strip music down to its essential factors, but because it was in accord with the spirit of its time, with the spirit of hope. According to Riley:

The musics of Webern and Schoenberg were created during a time of great distress on the planet – World War One, the discovery of psychotherapy and the dark sides of the mind. The influence of that very gnarled, anguished music continued on through most of the first half of the century in some form or another. Some composers were outside it, but most were touched by it – even Aaron Copland and people like that who were essentially bright-sounding composers. After World War Two there was a change in the climate, just before the 1960s – in my view the high point of the twentieth century in terms of really wanting to be free, to tear off the bonds of society which said you had to live a certain way or do certain things to be a valid individual – and that was when minimalism happened.

The climate was one of hope, or deepening spirituality, as was the whole of the 1960s. That changes in the 1970s. As far as I was concerned, by the time the public caught up with minimalism, the real heart of the movement had gone.

Riley's *In C*, the work that brought the movement to international attention in 1964, has an insistent pulse on a high C played throughout by a piano. The piece can go on for as long as the energy of the players (and there is no limitation to the number) lasts out. The elements cutting across or fitting in with the insistent pulse are fifty-three short fragments of various lengths taken from standard patterns found in music of the eighteenth century. All are 'in C' and can be played by any melodic instruments at speeds of the players' choosing. The players may go on repeating the fragments for as long as they like, but each player must go through all fifty-three in the order Riley stipulates. In effect, the fragments create a varied but very simple rhythmic counterpoint to the insistent pulse.

Steve Reich (born 1936) managed to go two steps further in the quest for simplicity. The first involved a technique known as 'phase shifting', the other 'pattern accumulation'. Phase shifting occurs when two tape recorders, playing the same recording synchronically, begin to run at different speeds so that the tapes no longer synchronize with each other. In *Come Out* (1966), Reich used a recording of a nineteen-year-old youth saying: 'I had to, like, open up the bruise and let some of the bruise blood come out to show them.' After the third repetition of this sentence, Reich accelerates the speed of the second tape recorder so that the words become jumbled up. With more acceleration the two tapes get back into synchronization and comprehensibility is restored. The following year, Reich applied the principle to *Piano Phase* for two pianos. The first piano repeatedly plays two six-note patterns; once the repetitions have become established the second piano follows suit, but then begins to accelerate, so that it gets a quaver ahead of the first piano. Piano 2 then reverts to the basic tempo for a while, before accelerating again to creep ahead by

Terry Riley.

Steve Reich.

Reich has taken the most extreme example of clock time and turned it into music.

another quaver. This sequence of events continues until the two instruments eventually return to unison. The technique is the same as the one Ives explored in *Calcium Light Night*, Carter in his Cello Sonata, and Nancarrow in his Rhythmic Study no. 27, except that here it is stripped down to its essentials. Reich says that the importance of the phase-shifting process lies in its impersonality. Once the process has been set up, it works itself out inexorably.

When the two patterns get out of synchronization completely, however, even phase shifting can sound complex. So, to create a still simpler music, Reich devised a system of pattern accumulation. *Music for Pieces of Wood* (1973), for example, is scored for five tuned claves, the highest playing (as in Riley's *In C*) an insistent pulse throughout. When the pulse has become established, the second clave enters with its complete pattern and goes on repeating it. The other claves come in one by one, but they build up their patterns slowly. When all the patterns have been worked through, the process starts again with shorter patterns, and after these it is repeated with even shorter ones.

The minimalism of *Music for Pieces of Wood* is not as extreme as some of La Monte Young's early pieces (*Composition 1960 no. 7*, for instance, consists only of an open fifth, with the instruction 'to be held for a long time'). This is undoubtedly why minimalism has become so popular, even though, in Terry Riley's opinion, the heart had gone out of the movement by the early seventies. Composers who wish to engage the attention and the imagination of their listeners have spurned the minimalists' excessive use of repetition. Most twentieth-century composers have wanted to avoid repetition and only a few have wanted to maintain an absolutely regular pulse throughout a movement. This applies even to composers like Michael Tippett (born 1905), who have their roots deep in tradition. Tippett considers his 'mentors' to have been Beethoven and English composers of the late sixteenth and early seventeenth centuries. But as far as rhythm is concerned he also acknowledges a debt to Stravinsky and certain jazz musicians. One of his favourite recordings is Bessie Smith's and Louis Armstrong's version of the *St Louis Blues*; more recently the trumpet and flugelhorn playing of Miles Davis has meant most to him. The first work he published, the

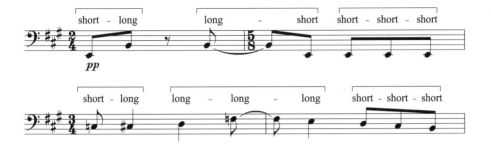

First String Quartet (completed 1935), ends with a fugue, the subject of which has close rhythmic affinities with the chorale near the beginning of Stravinsky's *Symphonies of Wind Instruments*. The fugue theme should start with a $\frac{9}{8}$ bar: short–long, long–short, short–short–short. But to give it vitality Tippett writes it as two bars: $\frac{2}{4} : \frac{5}{8}$. This means that the long of the second group falls across the bar line and creates a syncopation. The next two bars have a similar pattern except that the second group is expanded to long–long–long, making a pattern of short–long, long–long–long, short–short–short. This is written in two bars of $\frac{3}{4}$, and here the second long of the second group falls across the bar line. Because these syncopations thrust the music forward, Tippett calls the technique 'sprung rhythm'.

The term 'sprung rhythm' had previously been used only by the nineteenth-century Jesuit poet Gerard Manley Hopkins, who wanted to escape from the running 'sing-song' patterns that had crept into English poetry since the seventeenth century and return to an older tradition, based on the irregular patterns characteristic of the spoken language. In addition to this, Tippett was also thinking of the buoyant, lilting rhythms found in Elizabethan and Jacobean madrigals.

What is so impressive about Tippett's handling of rhythm, especially in his early period, is that he can draw on disparate procedures (regular pulse, jazz rhythms, and the additive rhythms of Stravinsky) and yet produce music that is perfectly unified. The Second String Quartet, which he composed during the war (1941–2) and clearly wanted to sound as English as possible, draws on madrigal technique in the first movement, the dragging rhythms often found in English consort music in the second,

The opening of the third movement of the First String Quartet, showing Tippett's 'sprung rhythm'.

79

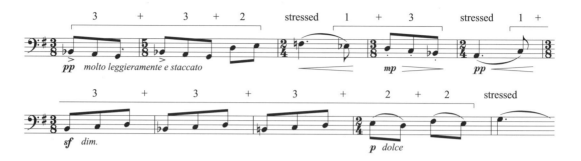

'Additive rhythm': cells of
unevenly grouped quavers,
leading always to the same
down-beat.

sprightly additive rhythms reminiscent of the light-hearted can-
zonettas of Morley in the third, and sprung rhythms in the fourth
– here set against a pounding beat reminiscent of jazz.

'Additive rhythm' is a term coined in 1959 by the musicologist
Carl Sachs to define the difference between the standard rhythms
of Western music and those found in certain non-Western cultures. Traditionally Western rhythms have been constructed by
multiplying or dividing units: an eight-unit rhythm is invariably
constructed on the basis 2 x 2 x 2; a nine-unit rhythm on the basis
3 x 3. In certain non-Western cultures, on the other hand,
rhythms are put together by adding or subtracting units: an
eight-unit rhythm could be 3 + 3 + 2 or 3 + 2 + 3 ; a nine-unit one
2 + 3 + 2 + 2. Tippett uses additive rhythms in the scherzo of the
Second String Quartet because its textures are thin – often just a
single line or two lines – and he wants to keep the movement lilting and buoyant. He employs only three durations – quaver (one
unit), crotchet (two units) and dotted crotchet (three units) – and,
as Stravinsky had done in *The Rite of Spring* and *Symphonies of
Wind Instruments*, he uses additive groupings for dynamic purposes to drive towards a cadence or a note that needs to be
stressed. He starts with a sprightly tune in three phrases, played
in octaves by the second violin and cello. Each phrase consists of
quavers leading to a dotted crotchet, the note that needs to be
stressed. In the first phrase the quavers are grouped 3 + 3 + 2; in
the second 1 + 3, and in the third 1 + 3 + 3 + 3 + 2 + 2. As a result
the three dotted crotchets vary in the rhythmical stress they
receive: the last gets the greatest because it has the longest preparation. However, Tippett contrives to disguise the stress by
adding unexpected accents to certain other notes. Like all good
composers, at the beginning of the movement he creates the feel-

ing that all is not yet settled: it must run for some time before the stress pattern will be stabilized.

For both Stravinsky and Tippett – and indeed for all the composers discussed so far in this chapter – rhythms, whether they are additive or multiplicative, are related to bodily activity – stamping, walking, dancing. Even the complex metres Carter and Nancarrow have devised fall into this category. But because additive rhythms do not produce regular metres they can only be used for group activity on certain occasions. The additive rhythms in the 'Sacrificial Dance' of *The Rite of Spring* were intended for an individual dancer. So too are the dance-like additive rhythms of Tippett's scherzo. This is a dance for someone who wants to feel free and trip it 'on the light fantastic toe'.

Additive rhythms are also used, paradoxically perhaps, by composers who want their music to escape from earthbound activity and float free. One such was Olivier Messiaen (1908–1992), who in 1931 became organist of the church of La Sainte Trinité in Paris, a position he held for more than sixty years out of devotion to the Catholic liturgy and, above all, Catholic theology. Initially it was the music of the liturgy, particularly plainsong, which most strongly influenced his work as a composer. For Messiaen plainsong is 'truly religious because it is detached from all exterior effect and from all intention'. The rhythm of plainsong was never notated: medieval monks must have learned by example the conventions for singing the rhythmically free prose of the Latin biblical texts. During the seventeenth and eighteenth centuries, it became the practice to sing plainsong in a slow, heavy style, each note accompanied by a separate chord on the organ. When the Abbey of Solesmes near Le Mans was established in 1833, the monks swept this dullness aside. Their detailed research suggested that plainsong should be sung freely at a faster pace and without accompaniment. When written out in modern notation their rhythms look very like the additive rhythms of Tippett's scherzo though without the bar lines. In performance, however, the quavers would be treated very freely; the pace would be calm and devotional, the sound mellifluous.

Messiaen with his pupil and sometime critic, Pierre Boulez, at the Odéon, Paris, in 1966.

Several of Messiaen's melodies are based on specific pieces of plainsong. The first movement of *Les corps glorieux* (1939) for organ uses the Marian antiphon *Salve Regina* as its model; the opening of the tenth movement of *Vingt regards sur l'enfant Jésus* for piano (1944) is based on the gradual *Haec dies* for Easter Sunday. But whether or not a plainsong melody is actually present, the additive rhythms of plainsong are never far from Messiaen's mind when the atmosphere is devotional and he wants the music to float: one has only to listen to the opening melody of *Les offrandes oubliées*, the orchestral piece he composed in 1930, to realize as much. The melody is given to the strings playing in octaves and proceeds in even quavers. Crotchets are introduced to mark the ends of phrases, or to lengthen a note that needs to be lingered over. There are three aspects of the music, however, which differ from the plainsong norm: the very slow speed (quaver = 44), the inclusion of two full, heartfelt outbursts for the strings; and the mode.

French composers had been using modes ever since the 1860s. Fauré and later Satie, Debussy and Ravel often had recourse to them. Mostly the modes in question were the old church modes, but Debussy also made use of the whole-tone scale. Messiaen found that the church modes lacked the symmetry he was always looking for, so he too used other scales, and even invented his own. His favourite mode was the octatonic scale, which Stravinsky had inherited from his teacher Rimsky-Korsakov and used throughout *The Rite of Spring*. Messiaen chooses this mode for the opening of *Les offrandes oubliées*. It consists of alternating semitones and tones – in this case B–C–D–E♭–F–F♯–G♯–A–(B). Messiaen had just got to know *The Rite of Spring* when he wrote *Les offrandes oubliées*, and he constantly referred to it when teaching composition. None of the three detailed analyses he made has been published, but his pupil Pierre Boulez (born 1925) drew on them in his essay 'Stravinsky Remains' (in *Notes from an Apprenticeship*). It is evident that Messiaen was fascinated by the symmetries of Stravinsky's music, as well as his additive rhythms. He noted that there are passages, particularly in the 'Dance of the Earth', where the rhythms are mirror images of each other. Messiaen calls these 'non-retrogradable' rhythms because they are the same back-

Is there still a place in the twentieth century for rhythm to be emotional – the kind of visceral force that made people jump and dance over the centuries? The answer is a resounding 'yes!'

wards as they are forwards. They represent perfect balance and can be found, he says, 'in all the decorative arts, in the veins of the leaves of trees, in butterfly wings, in the human face and body, and even in ancient magic formulae'. The opening of the sixth movement of *Quatuor pour la fin du temps*, which he composed in 1940 when he was a prisoner of war in Germany, has a non-retrogradable rhythm in each bar. The unit is the semiquaver, and the first bar runs $3 + 5 + 8 + 5 + 3$, the second $4 + 3 + 7 + 3 + 4$, the third $2 + 2 + 3 + 5 + 3 + 2 + 2$, and so on.

Messiaen was also fascinated by the way certain rhythmic figures in the 'Dance of the Earth' get progressively longer, while at the same time others get progressively shorter, after which the situation is reversed. Messiaen saw this as the antagonism between two rhythmic forces, and although Stravinsky never allows the patterns to become too predictable, they furnished Messiaen with ideas which were eventually to bear fruit in the fifth movement of his *Turangalîla Symphony* of 1946–8.

The word 'Turangalîla' comes from two Sanskrit words. 'Turanga' means 'time', 'rhythm', 'movement' – 'time that runs like a galloping horse,' said Messiaen, 'that flows like sand in an hourglass'. 'Lîla' is variously used to describe the play of divine action on the cosmos, and the physical and spiritual union found in love. Messiaen first came across the word 'turangalîla' in 1935, when, in a French encyclopedia, he found it in a list of 120 Indian rhythms compiled in the thirteenth century by an Indian scholar called Sharngadeva. Most of the rhythms are ametric, some are non-retrogradable, others contain units that expand or contract. The *turangalîla* rhythm is a contracting one: two dotted semiquavers are followed by two semiquavers – $3 : 3 : 2 : 2$. The list was of importance to Messiaen for two reasons: first because it placed at his disposal an invaluable reservoir of additive rhythms, a fact that immediately became apparent in his nine meditations for organ, *La nativité du Seigneur* (1935), and the nine *Poèmes pour Mi* for soprano and piano or orchestra (1936–7); and second because all 120 rhythms have Sanskrit names, and some of the titles had cosmic overtones which were of significance to him.

The *Turangalîla Symphony* is a vast, ten-movement work for piano, ondes martenot (an electronic keyboard instrument capable of sustaining notes and producing glissandos) and orchestra.

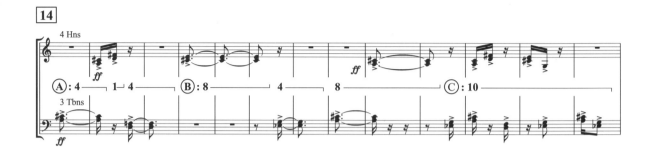

Messiaen marks the *personnages rhythmiques* in the score of the *Turangalîla Symphony*, counting out the groups in numbers of semiquaver beats.

Messiaen called it a love song, a hymn to joy – 'love that is fatal, irresistible, transcending everything, suppressing everything outside itself; joy that is superhuman, overflowing, blinding, unlimited'. The 'love' music is nearly always cast in floating additive rhythms and played by the highly mellifluous ondes martenot, the 'joy' music in corporeal rhythms with, as often as not, a strong, swinging beat. The exultant fifth movement that ends the first half, 'Joie du sang des étoiles' ('Joy of the blood of the stars'), was always cited by Messiaen as the best illustration of the 'vast counterpoint of rhythms' pervading the work.

In fact 'Joie du sang des étoiles' is not the most complex section in the symphony, but it contains what Messiaen calls 'personnages rythmiques'. The whole movement is based on a theme 'in weighty thirds and nearly always played on the trombones fortissimo', which is first heard at the very beginning of the symphony. Messiaen calls it the 'statue theme' because it evokes the 'oppressive, terrifying brutality of Mexican monuments'. The *personnages rythmiques* occur in two passages in the central section of the movement, and Messiaen describes them in this way:

Imagine a theatrical scene. There are three characters on stage: the first is active, has the leading role in the scene; the second is passive, acted upon by the first; the third witnesses the conflict without intervening, being only an observer and not stirring. In the same way three rhythmic groups are in action: the first augments (this is the attacking character); the second diminishes (this is the character attacked); the third never changes (this is the character who stands aside).

Messiaen's purpose in 'Joie du sang des étoiles' was not to create something explicitly dramatic, but to attain a symmetry which would symbolize the physical union of the two lovers,

one balancing the other in perfect harmony. What is interesting is that the third rhythmic character, far from being the one who stands aside and never changes, is in a state of constant transformation. It is this character who is the real actor, and who eventually brings about the perfect symmetry.

In the first episode shaped by the *personnages rythmiques* the augmenting rhythm of the 'attacking character' is produced by the addition of a semiquaver to each of its durations at successive occurrences (4:1:4, 5:2:5, 6:3:6, 7:4:7), the diminishing rhythm of the 'character attacked' by the successive subtraction of a semiquaver (8:4:8, 7:3:7, 6:2:6, 5:1:5). The 'observer' begins with the set of durations 1:2:2:2:1:2, but thereafter the pattern is varied, sometimes beyond recognition. In the second episode, which happens about thirty seconds after the first is completed, all three rhythmic characters appear, with mirror images of themselves running alongside them. This means that even the haphazard patterns of the 'observer' have become symmetric. Since the 'observer' initiates the addition of the retrogrades, and not the 'attacking character', who took the lead in the first episode, the 'observer' must get all the credit for the overall symmetry and balance.

Shortly before the first performance of the *Turangalîla Symphony* in 1949, Messiaen composed a short piece for piano called *Mode de valeurs et d'intensités*. It had a profound influence on the thinking of the young up-and-coming composers of the day, for it appeared to defy the whole of tradition and open up the possibility of making a completely fresh start in music. The piece had no melody, harmony, pulse or discernible rhythm. It appeared to be nothing but a series of random single notes. Stockhausen likened it to looking at stars twinkling haphazardly in the sky at night, Boulez to a carillon of bells set in motion by the wind. As far as Messiaen was concerned it was probably an exercise in the art of making music out of material that was absolutely fixed. It was the kind of exercise composition teachers give their students to test their imagination and ingenuity. He took thirty-six pitches, twenty-four durations, twelve types of attack (staccato, tenuto, various kinds of accent, etc.) and seven dynamic markings (ranging from *ppp* to *fff*) and arranged them into three descending scales that overlap with one another. A glance at the score reveals that he applied his musical skills with all the imagination and ingenuity he would have expected from the best of his students: each scale makes as convincing a line as is possible in the circumstances, and the three lines work together to produce good counterpoint. However, the ear cannot pick up what the eye can see. For those who heard the work at Darmstadt, the annual summer school devoted to discussing and playing the advanced music of the day, its appeal was due to the impression it gave of being wholly untouched by human volition. Their response can be summarized by the phrase Messiaen once used to describe plainsong – namely that it sounds as if it were utterly 'detached from all exterior effect and from all intention'.

The young composers felt that the secret lay in Messiaen's adoption of fixed material. To create music that sounds as if no human will has shaped it, one must set up processes that, once established, will generate the music almost automatically. And this indeed is what composers did in the early fifties. In his first book of *Structures* for two pianos, which he and Messiaen performed for the first time in 1952, Boulez took the highest of the three scales in *Mode de valeurs et d'intensités* and set out to discover:

how far automatism in musical relationships would go, with individual invention appearing only in some really very simple forms of disposition – in the matter of densities, for example . . . it was an experiment in what one might call Cartesian doubt: to bring everything into question again, make a clean sweep of one's heritage and start all over again from scratch, to see how it might be possible to reconstitute a way of writing that begins with something which eliminates personal invention.

86

No one has ever taken automatism so far since, but it proved a very useful procedure and many composers have relied on it, and still do, to a certain degree: it releases them from unnecessary drudgery, produces unexpected results and enables them to escape from clichés. But the rhythmic pointillism which became fashionable after *Mode de valeurs et d'intensités* soon became tedious. Composers realized that they could not do without lines. By the time Boulez came to write his *Second Improvisation on Mallarmé* in 1958 he had already discovered other ways of making them appear to float. This is probably why he chose for the text 'Une dentelle s'abolit', for the poem is about a lace curtain wafting aimlessly in a half-open window. He later rescored the piece as part of *Pli selon pli* (1957–62), his five-movement 'portrait' of Mallarmé for soprano and orchestra, but the first version is for relatively small forces: soprano, harp and nine percussionists. The poem is one of Mallarmé's most obscure: its images are the lace curtain billowing against the pale glass of the window, a mandore and a bed – or rather the absence of a bed. Described as 'an allegory of birth, of aborted creation, of the dominating passion of an absent work', the overall impression is that it concerns Mallarmé's difficulties in giving birth to a poem, and that the lace curtain symbolizes his uncertainties: at one moment it suggests fullness, the next emptiness.

To mirror these states of being, Boulez alternates between two vocal styles, one melismatic, the other syllabic. The melismatic sections are based on additive rhythms: each note is preceded and often terminated by grace notes, which are unmeasured and therefore rhythmically quite free. The material comes from a succession of beautifully spaced chords, each note being fixed in its octave so that, as the singer leaps from one to another, she conveys not only the fullness of the curtain in certain moments but also the variety of shapes it can assume. In the syllabic sections, all the grace notes are removed. The rhythm consists of a succession of semibreves, each with a pause marked over it. The first two phrases contain eight semibreves each and the singer is requested to sing each phrase in one breath. Because singers vary in their capacity to sustain a long phrase, there can be no specific tempo marking: they will float from note to note in their own time. The only point at which the vocal line becomes metric and has neither grace notes nor pauses, is when Boulez comes to the words 'Tristement dort une mandore' ('sadly sleeps a mandore'). A mandore is a small plucked instrument with a rounded body, and Mallarmé makes great play with the resemblance of its shape to that of a pregnant woman. The mandore's belly, however, is empty. One reason why Boulez selected harp, tubular bells, vibraphone, piano and celesta to accompany the soprano may have been that their combined sonorities could be taken to represent the sound of the mandore, magnified to sound larger than life. But the principal reason must have been that once struck their sounds fade away. They die at birth.

The use of floating rhythms might be said to have reached its zenith in *Atmosphères* (1961) by the Hungarian composer György Ligeti (born 1923). 'Music should not be normal, well-bred, with its tie all neat,' he said.

First in Cologne in 1957 and later during my long stay in Vienna in the '60s, I gradually evolved a musical style in which I abandoned structures conceived in terms of bars, melodic lines and conventional forms. In this respect my first two orchestral works, *Apparitions* and *Atmosphères*, are the most radical. *Atmosphères*, although polyphonic, is just floating, fluctuating sound.

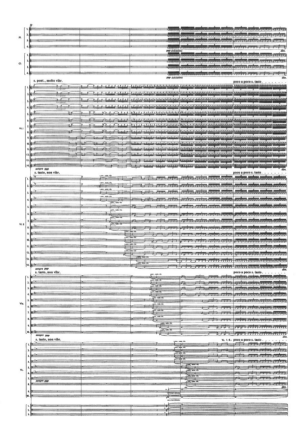

Atmosphères by György Ligeti. Even the pattern on the page gives the impression of a mass of coagulating lines.

The title was aptly chosen because all one hears is atmosphere, and Ligeti achieves the shimmering effects by means of the polyphony he mentioned. The piece is scored for full symphony orchestra with individual parts for twenty-eight violins, ten violas, ten cellos and eight double basses, which play a dense network of canons. You can see these by a close examination of the score, but you cannot hear them. What you hear, says Ligeti, is an impenetrable texture, 'something very like a very densely woven cobweb'.

Ligeti left his native country, where he had been severely restricted in the kind of music he could write, during the Hungarian uprising of 1956. *Atmosphères* dates from 1961, and although it brought him into the international limelight and was widely imitated, it was really the end of a line. Within a very short time he was working with rhythm again, 'not rhythm in its former sense, but a kind of exaggerated rhythm, with completely automated rhythmic processes'. His very next piece was *Poème symphonique* for 100 metronomes (1962)! Later, in a piece called *Self-Portrait with Reich and Riley (and Chopin is also there)* (1976), he developed his own form of minimalism.

This does not mean that the era of floating rhythms is at an end. They will continue to be employed, at least for as long as there are composers like Boulez and Stockhausen for whom regular rhythms have sinister connotations. Near the end of the war the Nazis had military marches pumped out through loudspeakers on nearly every street corner in Germany to bolster morale. Stockhausen said that he never wanted to hear a march, or indeed any other music with a pulsating beat, again. It was therefore to everyone's surprise that in 1974 Boulez should produce *Rituel in memoriam Bruno Maderna*, a piece in which regular pulse is not simply a feature but a feature of such importance that it seems to defy everything he had done before. However, the regular rhythm denotes not a military march but a funeral march of the deepest solemnity. Boulez called the work a 'litany for an imaginary ceremonial; a ceremonial of remembrance – whence these recurrent patterns, changing in profile and perspective; a ceremonial of death – ritual of the ephemeral and eternal: thus the musical memory – present / absent, in uncertainty'. The Italian composer and conductor Bruno Maderna was one of Boulez's closest colleagues and friends, and these gnomic words prefacing the score were clearly intended to prepare the listener to approach the music in the right spirit.

The piece is scored for an ensemble of eight groups, each one larger than the last: oboe, two clarinets, three flutes, four violins, a wind quintet, a string sextet, a woodwind septet, and a group of fourteen brass instruments; each group also contains a percussionist, except the brass group, which has two. The percussionists

Von Spreckelsen's Grande Arche at La Defense in Paris.

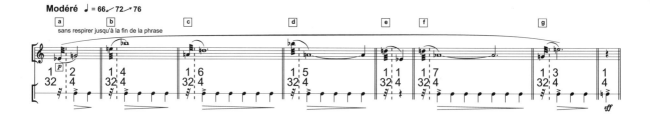

The first verse of Boulez's *Rituel*. An oboe and a tabla define the pattern of fast up-beat with sustained, pulsing down-beat.

in the brass group are distinguished from the others because they play the seven gongs and seven tamtams which are mainly responsible for establishing and maintaining the ritualistic and hierarchic atmosphere of the music. Boulez divides the work into fifteen sections, each, in the main, longer than the one before The odd-numbered sections (1, 3, 5, 7, 9, 11, 13, 15) are in a slow tempo, function as refrains or responses, and always contain the brass group with its gongs and tamtams; the even-numbered ones are in a faster tempo, function as verses, and never include the brass, gongs and tamtams.

The work opens with three slow gong strokes and a long seven-note chord played by the brass. This chord is the basis of the whole work. It will be transposed and its notes will be redistributed, but its basic sonority will remain constant. In the following odd-numbered sections the gong strokes and the sonority of the opening chord are expanded; other groups join in, maintaining sound characteristics and tempos of their own. As in 'Une dentelle s'abolit' the chords begin and end with grace notes, but here, because they are written for an ensemble, they have to be timed. A pattern is therefore established of fast notes followed by a long note, and then more fast notes. As lovers of Donizetti, Bellini and Verdi will recognize, this gives the rhythm a suitably Italianate character: in a typical Italian operatic aria of the nineteenth century, the fast notes are used to articulate the words, the long notes to sustain the ringing tone of the singer.

The Italianate character of the rhythm becomes even more overt in the even-numbered sections. The first one, for the oboe, is a long melody derived from the notes of the basic chord. Each note is a different length and each is preceded by a single demisemiquaver. In later sections, this single note is expanded into a group of up to seven demisemiquavers. The percussionist measures the length of the long notes in regular crotchets, but is silent in the bars where the short notes occur. The rhythmic pattern of the first verse is therefore: $\frac{1}{32} - \frac{2}{4}, \frac{1}{32} - \frac{4}{4}, \frac{1}{32} - \frac{6}{4}, \frac{1}{32} - \frac{5}{4}, \frac{1}{32} - \frac{1}{4}, \frac{1}{32} - \frac{7}{4}, \frac{1}{32} - \frac{3}{4}, \frac{1}{4}$. This means that the percussionist, playing in this instance a tabla, has a regular pulse with an occasional limp in it, because the last crotchet in each of the long bars appears to have an extra demisemiquaver added to its length. In later sections, when other groups join in, their tempos need not co-ordinate with one another, and the effect of this is to make the even-numbered sections sound like improvisations.

The texture is at its fullest at the beginning of the last section, when all the melody instruments help to sustain the brass choir's chords, the tamtams become increasingly to the fore, and the crotchet pulses are also present. But the process that has built up this texture is now reversed: one by one the groups fall out until, at the end, only the seventh and eighth are left to play a unison B♭ – the highest note in the work's opening chord. The gongs, which from the beginning have played long, irregular notes, now join the other percussionists' long-term pattern of regularly pulsating crotchets. Pulse has been tested and not found wanting.

Chapter 4
Colour

If you were to ask a Frenchman to name the work that marks the beginning of twentieth-century music, he would probably overlook *Erwartung* and *The Rite of Spring* and nominate Debussy's *Prélude à l'après-midi d'un faune*, a piece composed six years before the century began. This is certainly Pierre Boulez's nomination:

The flute of the *Faune* brought new breath to the art of music. What was overthrown was not so much the art of development as the very concept of form itself, here freed from the impersonal constraints of the schema, giving wings to a supple, mobile expressiveness, demanding a technique of perfect instantaneous adequacy. Its use of timbres seemed essentially new, of exceptional delicacy and assurance in touch; the use of certain instruments – flute, horn and harp – showed the characteristic principles of the manner in which Debussy would employ them in later works. The writing for woodwinds and brasses, incomparably light-handed, performed a miracle of proportion, balance, and transparency. The potential of youth possessed by that score defies exhaustion and decrepitude; and just as modern poetry surely took root in certain of Baudelaire's poems, so one is justified in saying that modern music was awakened by *L'Après-midi d'un faune*.

Edouard Manet's portrait of Mallarmé, painted in 1876.

Stéphane Mallarmé believed his poem to be eminently suitable for music, but Debussy's purely orchestral version seeks to capture only its essence – it does not go beyond establishing a suitable mood. The poem concerns the musings of a lascivious faun attempting to recapture the world of an erotic dream. It is based on one of the amorous adventures of Pan, the god who preferred to live in Arcadia, tend sheep and spend his afternoons dozing and dreaming in the sun. In one episode he pursues the chaste nymph Syrinx and her sisters to the River Ladon, where the goddess Diana turns them into reeds so that

Pan cannot distinguish them from all the others in the river. To compensate for his loss, Pan fashions some of the reeds into a panpipe so that every time he blows into it he can imagine the erotic pleasures he might have enjoyed with the nymphs had he caught them. Mallarmé's poem opens with the faun awaking from a dream in which he has been making love to two nymphs. He tries to reconstruct the contents of the dream, but finally reluctantly recalls that, just as he was reaching his sexual climax, the nymphs escaped from his grasp and started to make love to each other. The poem ends with the faun saying farewell to the shadowy creatures and falling asleep again. Its subject, therefore, is the tantalizing, the elusive, the something that is always just beyond one's reach.

Mallarmé places in italics and inverted commas the three short episodes where the faun tries to construct a narrative of what happened in his dream; the rest of the poem is devoted to the faun's hopes, comments and final understanding. The structure of Debussy's *Prélude*, however, is determined by musical considerations rather than literary ones. There are two melodic ideas, which are distinct though related, and the subtleties of instrumental timbre and harmony are crucial to the form. The opening melody, played by a solo flute, is sensuous and chromatic, and appears to be unable to find its way to a satisfactory conclusion, a consummation. It is the heart of the piece, and must have been written for the great French player Paul Taffanel who, in 1894, was the principal flautist in the orchestra of the Société des Concerts du Conservatoire. Taffanel's relaxed technique and warm, expressive tone had completely revolutionized flute playing.

The long note, a C♯, which opens the work and returns over and over again, is probably the most flexible note for tone quality on the modern instrument. The colour of the flute's opening solo, however, does not come solely from the instrument's timbre: equally decisive is the colour of Debussy's harmony – the contrast between a languid chromatic scale (the word 'chromatic' means 'coloured'), dropping from C♯ to G♮, in the first two bars, and the much more sprightly diatonic harmony in the following two. Debussy's key signature of four sharps indicates C♯ minor, but C♯ feels too unstable to be a tonic. A much more likely candidate for the key note is G♯ (the dominant), but

Vaclav Nijinsky as the faun in the scandalous performance of Debussy's ballet at the Théâtre du Chatelet in 1912.

although this appears to be the goal the flute is aiming for, it too lacks stability. C♯ and G♯ are stabilized only in the central section of the *Prélude*, when the strings play in octaves a sensuous but whole diatonic melody in D♭ major (the tonic and dominant notes of which, D♭ and A♭, are the enharmonic equivalents of C♯ and G♯). This melody has several significant characteristics: the solo flute is here replaced by massed strings playing with mutes, in a key which denies them the use of sympathetically vibrating open strings to give their sound brightness; moreover, it reaches its climax on a phrase which is already falling to a cadence, and thus to the feeling of closure that was lacking before. All of this suggests that the faun's attempts to reproduce the 'dark', sensuous moments of his love-making have come to fruition. Yet once the strings have completed their theme they never surface again. The flute's melody returns, with its varied harmonic colourations and its vain attempts to find a satisfactory continuation. On two occasions, Debussy scores it for the plaintive oboe, and just before the end we hear a fragment of it on a distant horn. The last two notes, C♯ and G♯, are given to the flute, but they now belong to the other key containing four sharps – E major. Although the C♯ is not sounding at the very end, its resonance lingers on in the memory, like a pale shadow of its full colour.

The orchestra came into existence specifically to provide music with a wide range of timbres. In a Florentine *intermedi* (a kind of masque) dating from 1539, each of three sirens was accompanied by a lute hidden in a shell, and three sea monsters by three transverse flutes situated so as to give their sound the brittle, brassy timbres of trumpets marine. In Monteverdi's *Orfeo* of 1607, strings, recorders, organs, harpsichords and plucked continuo instruments are used for the pastoral scenes in Thrace, while cornetts, trombones and the reedy sound of the portative regal organ are reserved for the scenes in Hades. In some passages Monteverdi leaves the instrumental colouring to the discretion of whoever is in charge of proceedings, but when the action becomes dramatically significant he is specific in his

Debussy in 1910.

Whereas in Wagner chords are all about development, tension, release – what they're becoming – in Debussy they are there for the glory of their inherent properties, for their sound.

95

The model of a classical symphony orchestra, the CBSO.

requirements. In Act 2, for instance, the organ is heard for the first time at the moment when the Messenger arrives to announce Euridice's death, rather than – as one might expect – during the wedding festivities. Instrumental colour is also used to create spatial depth. The audience knows that the dimensions of Hades are vast not only because of the echo effects Monteverdi makes use of in Orfeo's 'Possente spirto', but also because the timbres of the groups of solo instruments, which play, in turn, the ritornello – violins, cornetts and double harp – are successively more resonant in tone quality.

Spatial depth became a major consideration as the modern symphony orchestra developed from the middle of the eighteenth century. Most of Haydn's and Mozart's early symphonies are scored for two oboes, two horns and strings – timbres that can either blend or contrast, but can also be used to define a musical space. The oboe can be piercing when played loudly, and thus sound closer than it really is. The horn always has its bell facing away from the audience so that the sound they hear is always reflected from the back and side walls and the ceiling of the hall, making it seem more distant than it really is. As orchestras grew larger during the nineteenth century they offered not only a greater range of timbres and a more powerful sound, but also spatial characteristics that were more than just an illusion.

In the modern symphony orchestra players may be sitting twenty or thirty yards from each other. This has allowed composers to make musical use of spatial layout, and in pursuit of particular effects they have often specified how they want the orchestra to be seated.

Debussy did not go this far; he accepted the standard seating arrangement of the time because he was making use of the illusion of space rather than the physical deployment of the players to produce the effects he wanted. As soon as the flute brings its first two phrases to a half-close at the beginning of the *Prélude à l'après-midi d'un faune*, for example, there is a brilliant, reverberating glissando on the harp, heralding an echo of the flute first on one horn, in the middle distance, then on another, sounding still further away. It is as if a curtain has been lifted and we can see a landscape receding to the horizon, an imaginary landscape, one that we could never enter, always there but always out of reach. At the end of the *Prélude*, it is the horns, this time muted, that carry the flute's chromatic phrase out of earshot, their fading sound enhanced by the very delicate reverberations of two antique cymbals.

The references to distance and landscape here are not merely poetic. As Karlheinz Stockhausen pointed out in an article called 'Music in Space' (published in the journal *Die Reihe* in 1961), the criterion we use for judging distance by means of sound is not

Debussy in 1916, with his daughter, Claude-Emma, affectionately known as 'Chouchou'.

loudness. 'If the source of the sound,' he said, 'is right next to us, and the sound level changes from weak to strong, we by no means have the impression – not even with closed eyes – of far and near, but rather of unaltering distance and mere change of sound.' The criterion we use is the degree of noise in a sound, the amount of 'deformation' it contains. 'A sound occurring in Nature is always less distinct, more "faded", in the distance than the same sound from nearby.' In an enclosed space such as a concert hall, distance is judged by the amount of noise that gets mixed into the sound as it is reflected by the various surfaces. 'The

Schoenberg (*right*) and his
pupil Webern in Vienna.

**The idea that colour could be a
form in itself must have seemed at
the very least slightly sinful and at
the worst desperately revolutionary.**

nearer one sits to the source of sound in an enclosed space, the more direct sound one gets, and one judges the distance mainly according to the degree of deformation of the sound.' This is why Debussy's antique cymbals appear to be receding into the distance. The player will almost certainly be sitting at the back of the orchestra, and although the notes are crystal clear when struck, the ensuing reverberations become increasingly deformed as the sound fades away.

One of the most vivid examples of the dramatic use of distance in a piece dating from early in the century can be found in the Funeral March of Webern's Six Pieces for large orchestra, op. 6, a piece the composer associated with the funeral of his mother. 'Even today,' he said to Schoenberg just before the first performance in 1913, 'I do not understand my feelings as I walked behind the coffin to the cemetery. I only know that I walked the entire way with my head held high, as if to banish everything lowly all around.' His manipulation of distance, however, creates the impression that the experience was a nightmare for him. He scored the piece for percussion and wind without oboes or strings, and in the first of the three sections he establishes the space he wants his listeners to imagine – the huge, empty, desolate space of a Viennese cemetery. The work opens with the distant rumble of a bass drum and the equally indistinct sounds of a tamtam and two low bells of unspecified pitch, played extremely quietly. These create the background; chords passed between groups of upper woodwind, muted horns, muted trumpets, lower woodwind and muted trombones lay out the fairly distant middleground; then to locate the foreground Webern brings in a melodic line very high and clear on a piccolo. In the second section this line is taken up successively by clarinet, muted horn and muted trumpet, so that the sound recedes into the middle distance. Set against it in the background, but gradually moving forward, is a slow, uneven march rhythm played by the bass drum, with a low chord for muted trombones and tuba falling just before each of its hollow strokes. Because the chord is particularly low and discordant the individual notes cannot be distinguished so it sounds almost as blurred as the drum. The overall effect is not unlike those moments in nightmares when the fearful object creeps steadily nearer and nearer, and the dreamer can do nothing to stop its progress. The feeling of terror reaches its climax in the final section, when the instruments join forces to fill the whole space with a great crescendo, which Webern leaves the percussion to complete.

Webern composed the Six Pieces in 1909 at about the same time as Schoenberg was writing his Five Pieces, op. 16, the central movement of which is 'Farben' ('Colours'). Two years later, at the end of the great tome he wrote about harmony (the *Harmonielehre*), Schoenberg put into words what he had been trying to do in 'Farben' – though he presents it as if it were an idea for the future. He believed that the distinction between pitch and tone colour (that is, timbre) could not be sustained. His contention was that a sound becomes perceptible only by virtue of its tone colour, of which pitch is only one dimension. If it is possible to make a melody out of pitch then it should be equally possible to make a melody out of tone colour. It may seem a fantastic idea, which could be realized only in the future, but in his opinion such melodies would heighten 'the sensory, intellectual and spiritual pleasures offered by art'. They would bring us closer to the illusory stuff of our dreams. 'Tone-colour melodies! How acute the senses that would be able to perceive them! How high the development of spirit that could find pleasure in such subtle things! In such a domain, who dares ask for theory?'

The term 'tone-colour melodies' (*Klangfarbenmelodien*) has usually been interpreted as meaning melodies in which pitch is still the most important element but where the notes are passed from instrument to instrument so that a sequence of different colours emerges. But Schoenberg was referring to a situation where colour was the primary element as in 'Farben'. Unfortunately, he never developed the idea any further in music, but it has proved to be prophetic, as several electronic works dating from the 1980s and 1990s have shown. However, colour does play a crucial role in his stage directions for *Die glückliche Hand* which he finished in 1913. One scene takes place in a grotto workshop where the man miraculously makes a brilliant diadem by splitting an anvil with a hammer. He then bends down to pick up the sword he dropped in order to wield the hammer.

As his left hand touches the sword, darkness falls on the grotto. Dark drapes blot out all trace of the workshop. With the darkness, there

Schoenberg, in writing 'Farben', was giving us a practical impossibility. Instruments simply cannot dissolve into each other in the way that colours can. I'm sure that he would have leaped on the possibilities of electronic changes, distortions, the ability of a whole new type of instrument to make these colours. As he said, maybe his ideas were a fantasy for the future, and maybe the possibilities of the future are here now.

Schoenberg's sketch for his music drama *Die glückliche Hand*, 1913.

arises a wind, first blowing faintly, then swelling menacingly. With the crescendo of wind, there goes a crescendo of illumination, beginning with faint reddish light from above. The Man has to enact this crescendo of light and storm as if emanating from himself. In the reddish light, he looks at his hand, which then falls slowly and wearily to his side. There follows brown turning to dirty-green light – his eyes become excited. Next, dark blue-grey, succeeded by mauve – his excitement grows. This gives rise to an intense dark-red, becoming brighter and louder – his limbs stiffen convulsively. When blood-red is reached, he stretches out trembling arms, stares from bulging eyes, and drops his jaw in terror. Into the blood-red is blended some orange, and then some bright yellow, until at last the glaring yellow light alone remains . . .

Schoenberg's interest in colour undoubtedly stems from his activity as a painter. But these stage directions indicate clearly that colour had symbolic and possibly spiritual significance for him. The symbolism of colour plays a key role in the theosophy of Swedenborg, which Schoenberg had encountered in Balzac's novel *Seraphita*, and he made extensive use of it in his oratorio *Jacob's Ladder* (the first version of which he completed in 1922). It could be said that all twentieth-century composers who have made colour paramount in their music have been drawn to it for its mystic symbolism. This is true too of certain painters, such as Schoenberg's friend Wassily Kandinsky, who was also immersed in theosophy. In his *Concerning the Spiritual in Art* (1912), Kandinsky says that Schoenberg's music 'leads us into a new realm where musical experiences are not acoustic but purely spiritual'. As far as colour is concerned, he believed that for those who are spiritually sensitive each colour will create a 'corresponding vibration in the human soul', ranging from 'the total restfulness of heavenly blue' to the 'harsh trumpet blast of earthly yellow'.

As a Russian, Kandinsky was caught up in the almost apocalyptic atmosphere that pervaded his homeland during the years preceding the First World War. Rimsky-Korsakov's choral opera *The Legend of the Invisible City of Kitezh and the Maiden Fevronia*, which was produced in the Maryinsky Theatre in St Petersburg in 1907, was one of several musical works that reflected the religious mysticism of the period. But perhaps no composer caught this spirit more fervently than Alexander Scriabin (1872–1915), whose mystical way of thinking was deeply influenced by the theosophy of Helena Blavatsky. Rimsky-Korsakov and Scriabin both believed that the relationship between music and colour was so precise that each key was associated with a particular colour. They came to this realization separately, and their views about which colour matched which key differed. In his symphonic poem *Prometheus: The Poem of Fire* (1908–10) Scriabin called for an organ, 'a giant reflecting machine', whose keyboard, instead of producing sound when a chord was played, would illuminate the hall with a particular colour. When the chord changed, the colour changed. The music constantly makes use of a 'mystic' chord which Scriabin had invented, and the purpose of the piece is

The Deposition, an icon from the Novgorod school of the fifteenth century. One of the icons that was revealed in its true colours by the Russian restorers of the late nineteenth century.

Wassily Kandinsky, *Impression III (Concert)*, 1911, painted after Kandinsky had been to a concert of Schoenberg's music.

to reveal how the mystery of human enlightenment came into being with the gift of fire given to man by Prometheus. The changing colours are meant to represent not only the flickering fire but the spiritual implications for man of Prometheus's gift. Unfortunately the reflecting machine never functioned correctly when the work was performed in Scriabin's lifetime, and nowadays the colour effects have to come from the music itself.

Around the turn of the century a new preoccupation with colour made itself felt in Russian art, coinciding with the rediscovery of a great national art form. Shortly before, a programme had been launched in Russia to restore old religious icons, which had long been neglected; the dirt and varnish of centuries were removed and the full glory of the original luminous colours was revealed. They stood out clearly; there was no blending, no smoothing of edges. Painters and composers in those radical years before the First World War came to realize how highly medieval Russians had valued colour, and it made a deep impression. The first exhibition of Russian medieval art did not take place until 1913, but most Russians who had an interest in the arts had seen specimens of the restored icons long before then. When Diaghilev founded the Russian Ballet, mostly with performers from the Maryinsky Theatre, colour played a crucial role in their performances: stage designs, costumes, make-up and the music itself, were all intended to contribute to a gorgeous spectacle. Diaghilev had been so impressed with Stravinsky's brilliant use of orchestral colour in *Fireworks*, when it was first performed in 1909, that he commissioned a new ballet score, *The Firebird*. In the event, Diaghilev's choice was amply justified: Stravinsky demonstrated what an orchestra could sound like when the timbre of each instrument was kept pure and unsullied. He swept away the classical notion of orchestration as a blending of tone colours, and applied the instrumental colours distinctly and separately, just as they did in the medieval icons.

Stravinsky establishes his intentions straight away. Throughout the introduction, every tone colour can be heard distinctly, even at the very opening where the violas, cellos and double basses are joined by the sombre weight of the trombones. Some way into the movement Stravinsky devises a sound colour that was completely

Mikhail Fokine and Tamara Karsavina in Stravinsky's *The Firebird* in 1910. Fokine was the choreographer of the ballet, which featured costumes by Leon Bakst.

new to the orchestral palette, a magical glissando played as string harmonics. In passages involving flutes, clarinets, bassoons, horns, trumpets, trombones and strings, the timbres are still clearly distinguished, and despite the number of instruments playing, none is ever allowed to obscure another. The same clarity is preserved even in the full textures of sections of the 'Infernal Dance of King Kashchei', where, to maintain the independent voices within the big tutti, each instrument or instrumental group has its own figuration and can be heard as a separate strand. Stravinsky always preferred the hard-edged sounds of wind instruments to those of the more flexible string department, and it is this preference that helps to make the orchestration of *The Firebird* so lucid.

In the first few years of his company's existence, Diaghilev commissioned ballet scores from composers who were brilliant orchestrators. These were not only Russians: the ballet had its greatest successes in France, and French composers were equally preoccupied with the possibilities of orchestral colour. The scores of Nikolay Tcherepine and Reynaldo Hahn have since fallen by the wayside, while Ravel's *Daphnis et Chloé* (1909–12) has become an orchestral favourite, and Debussy's *Jeux*, though performed less often than *Daphnis*, is now considered a pivotal work in twentieth-century music.

Ravel had proved his ability as an orchestrator with *Rapsodie espagnole* (1907–8), but in *Daphnis* he turned away from the colour of Spain to the much more austere atmosphere of classical Greece. He said that the picture he had in his mind when composing *Daphnis* was 'fairly closely related to the Greece imagined and depicted by French painters at the end of the eighteenth century'. The painter he particularly dwelt upon was Jacques Louis David (1748–1825), whose work was the most neo-classical of all the Revolutionary artists. Yet the orchestration of *Daphnis* is far from being restrained or chaste. The score is one of the most opulent Ravel ever produced, and it even includes a wordless chorus. For the French it has become the epitome of *la belle époque*.

Jeux (1912–13), on the other hand, was intended to epitomize an era that had left behind *la belle époque*, one that was thoroughly modern. Vaclav Nijinsky, the dancer and choreographer who devised it, intended it to be 'the plastic apologia for the man

'The Infernal Dance of King Kashchei' is here because it is full of colour, but my God, what carniverous colours these are! It's not a matter of pale washes or of light diffusing; this is rapacious, dangerous music.

The CBSO, with three conductors, performing Stockhausen's *Gruppen* in Birmingham: the modern world's answer to Scriabin's dream of an instrument that would flood the hall with coloured light.

of 1913'. He told Debussy that he wanted it to be based on the spirit of youth, some athletic event in modern life: 'les jeux de sport, les jeux de l'amour'. The action takes place outside a tennis court in a park just as an evening game is finishing. It is getting dark, and under a huge electric candelabra, which casts a fantastic light around them, a young man and two girls run on stage looking for a lost ball. We never discover whether all three have been playing a game on the same court, but when they see one another, the search is forgotten and they begin to flirt. First one girl becomes the object of the man's attention and then the other. All three play hide-and-seek, chase one another, lose one another, squabble, and sulk for no reason, and, when the man cannot make up his mind about whom to run after next, the girls begin a flirtation between themselves. He then decides that somehow or other he must chase them both simultaneously. But from somewhere a tennis ball lands near them, 'thrown', said Nijinsky, 'by a malicious hand'. Casting scared glances at one another, the trio run off into the darkness.

Before he embarked on the score, Debussy knew that Nijinsky wanted to base the choreography on a series of small athletic gestures, so that the fleeting emotions and half completed actions of the characters could be expressed in angular yet light, unforced types of movement. Except at the beginning, when the eerie, mysterious atmosphere of the park has to be established, and near the end, when the mystery is deepened by the appearance of the tennis ball, Debussy's *poème dansé* establishes just this kind of movement. The bulk of the music is a scherzo in triple time, which, when slowed down slightly, becomes a waltz. Most of the musical gestures are short, up-beat phrases. The old idea of beginning with a theme and then developing it has been scrapped in favour of a structure that consists of the search for a theme, which, if it is found at all, does not appear until the culmination or even the end of the work. There is an impression in *Jeux* that the music is leading to a climax –

Debussy calls this passage of preparation 'joyous' – but the climax evaporates into thin air. A theme that begins to emerge more strongly at the end likewise disappears. The only point at which the ballet itself gives us a sense of completion is when the trio glance at one another and run away. But the music that accompanies them is not an ending or a completion, it is simply meant to represent the tennis ball bouncing into a flowerbed or the undergrowth.

At the opening of the ballet, Debussy establishes the atmosphere of the twilight park, and then uses the orchestra to depict clearly a game of tennis, which is happening off stage and ends when the ball first bounces into sight, followed by the dancers. This 'game of tennis' consists of five two-bar phrases – versions of a short up-beat phrase (*a*), and a variable complementary phrase (*b*). The two types alternate to make the pattern *a1–b1–a1–b2–a2*. Debussy splits each phrase into short units which he tosses across the orchestra: *a1* – violas to cellos and first bassoon; *b1* – tambourine to suspended cymbal; *a1* – violas to cellos and first bassoon again; *b2* – pizzicato violas to pizzicato violins to a chord on flutes, oboes and clarinets; *a2* – first horn and xylophone to third horn, with violins in counterpoint rushing up a scale to suggest something flying into the air. In effect, the scoring is like a *Klangfarbenmelodie*, the melodic line passing from one instrumental colour to another. There is, however, evidence that Debussy was using timbre not only for descriptive purposes but also to signpost important structural junctures. The two-bar motif that accompanies the first entrance of the young man, returns whenever a new 'game of love' is initiated. It always appears on a woodwind instrument: a clarinet on the first few occasions, then the cor anglais, and when the music begins to move towards the last climax, an oboe. Admittedly the timbre changes, but the phrase lies in the clarinet's so-called 'throat' register in the middle of its range, and this would be unsuitable for the occasions when the sound needs to be more penetrating and assertive.

A much more cogent example of the structural potential of timbre can be found in Webern's

Leon Bakst's painting of Diaghilev in 1906, at the beginning of his career as a ballet impresario.

Nijinsky, with Karsavina and Scholler, in Debussy's *Jeux* in 1912.

Nijinsky with Maurice Ravel, playing the latter's *Daphnis et Chloé*.

Variations for Orchestra (1940), scored for flute, oboe, clarinet, bass clarinet, horn, trumpet, trombone, tuba, timpani, celesta, harp and strings. The binary-form introduction consists of two lines of counterpoint built from four-note units, each unit having its own tone colour. The principal line in the first part contains eight four-note units, the eight tone colours being those of the double basses, oboe, trombone, first violins, bass clarinet, solo violin, cellos, and finally flute, oboe and clarinet playing in unison. The second part is shorter and to construct it Webern brings back five of these units, four of them in their retrograde versions, his choice being determined by the harmonic movement they create. As in the Variations for Piano discussed at the end of Chapter 2, the harmonic poles of attraction are A and E♭. The movement is therefore from A to E♭ and then back to A. Webern moves from one polarity to another in minor thirds lying within the octave below and above middle C (A–C–E♭–G♭(F♯)–A). The first part starts on the lower A, establishes the harmonic orientation, and ends on the E♭. The colours of the five four-note units are those of the double basses (A–C), oboe (E♭–G♭), first violins (A–F♯), bass clarinet (E♭–C), flute, oboe and clarinet (G♭–E♭). The four units carrying the movement which return the harmony to A have the colourings of the tuba (C–A), bass clarinet (C–E♭), oboe (E♭–G♭), solo violin (F♯–A). The inconsistencies in Webern's use of timbre all stem from the position of the units in the structure as a whole. To be consistent with the other occasions when G♭ and E♭ are linked together, for example, these two notes at the end of the first part should be played on the oboe alone, not doubled by flute and clarinet. But the unit is preceded by two loud notes on the trombone and therefore the oboe needs to be reinforced.

Despite the care that Webern takes to make timbre fulfil a more structural role than usual, no one could possibly say, as Messiaen did about his *Couleurs de la cité céleste*, that 'the form of the piece depends entirely on colours'. For Webern, timbre, though important, was ancillary to pitch and rhythm. But

Messiaen was one of those rare composers who suffer from (or are blessed with) a condition known as 'coloured-hearing synaesthesia', others being Rimsky-Korsakov, Scriabin and Arthur Bliss. The condition is completely involuntary. Whenever he heard music Messiaen saw colours, and not just primary colours: he said that one particular chord caused him to see 'a yellowish orange with a reddish tinge'. The score of *Couleurs de la cité céleste* (1963) specifies the names of the colours he visualized on every page. His purpose, he said, was to inform the conductor about the colours he had in his mind so that his visions could be conveyed to the players. 'It is essential', he said, 'that the brass "play red", that the woodwind "play blue".'

The problem for those without coloured-hearing synaesthesia is that those who have the condition are never in agreement. The relationship between chord and colour is entirely personal. Rimsky-Korsakov saw C major as white and F♯ major as greyish-green, Scriabin saw them as red and bright blue. Messiaen may say that the form of *Couleurs de la cité céleste* depends entirely on colours, but this is not something the listener can detect, especially since the timbres he uses are limited to the mainly percussive and brassy sounds of solo piano, three clarinets, ten brass instruments, three xylophones (xylophone,

Messiaen said that God's greatest gift to the world was to have given people things to listen to.

Messiaen transcribing birdsong.

Max Oppenheimer's portrait of
Webern, 1908–10.

xylorimba, marimba) and percussion. What listeners hear from piano, clarinets and xylophones is birdsong and from the brass four plainsong Alleluias, transformed according to St John's description of the celestial city in his Revelation:

And there was a rainbow round the throne . . . And the seven angels had seven trumpets . . . And to the star was given the key to the bottomless pit . . . And the light of the Holy City was like a jasper stone, clear as crystal . . . And the foundations of the wall of the city were garnished with all manner of precious stones: jasper, sapphire, chalcedony, emerald, sardonyx, sardius, chrysolyte, beryl, topaz, chrysoprasus, jacinth, amethyst.

Listeners will have no trouble with the seven trumpets or the music representing the bottomless pit; they may even recognize the plainsong Alleluias which form the basis of most of the melodic material, but it is doubtful whether they will be able to relate the colours of St John's precious gems to Messiaen's *couleurs*. He was convinced that the listeners would be able to detect the difference between one harmonic colour and another. They undoubtedly can, but this does not mean that they can also see visions. In the end the piece relies for its coherence not on a shared perception of harmonic colours but on its melodies, harmonies, rhythms and textures.

On the other hand, there are pieces by Messiaen, particularly some of those in *Catalogue d'oiseaux* (1956–8) for piano, where the colours themselves can be easily detected by listeners. One of the pieces in the first volume deals with the golden oriole (*le loriot*), a relation of the starling; the male has brilliant yellow plumage trimmed with black, and an unmistakable short song in the alto register which Messiaen describes as being 'flowing and golden'. His intention is to equate the bird's colouring and song with the midday sun, and the chord he uses to symbolize the sun is E major – a symbol that has its roots in the eighteenth century. But he does not have to rely on anything as specious as eighteenth-century colour symbolism to make the equation clear, because his transcription of the golden oriole's song is centred on E, as are the background chords that represent the bird's early morning environment. When the chord of E major eventually appears at the climax of the piece, after a long build-up, we know that it can represent nothing else but the sun at its zenith. Messiaen directs it to be played quietly and as if a choir of brass instruments has suddenly come to the aid of the pianist. Immediately afterwards we get the golden oriole's full song and a quotation from Messiaen's choral piece *Cinq rechants*, which clearly relates the piece to that other *loriot* – Yvonne Loriod, his wife. In the pianist's left hand are the chords from *Cinq rechants*, in the right hand the song of the golden oriole slowed down to an eighth of its original speed. Only someone familiar with Messiaen's music will know that he is quoting an intimate love song, but even the uninitiated will recognize that the harmonic colouring and relaxed style of the passage refer to some 'golden' memory as well as the bird.

Given the interest of most twentieth-century composers in exploring new ways of handling timbre and harmonic colour, it is surprising that this has not been reflected in the invention of new instruments. The orchestra Messiaen specified for *Chronochromie* (literally 'The colour of time', 1960), the work he composed immediately after *Catalogue d'oiseaux*, contains more or less the same instruments that Debussy might have used in 1900, the only difference being that Debussy would have employed fewer percussion instruments and might not have heard of the marimba. The only significant additions to the orchestra in the second half of the century have been percussion instruments originating in Africa, Asia and Latin America. Even oriental composers such as Toru Takemitsu (1930–1996) are prepared to accept the tonal palette of the standard orchestra. In *Dream / Window*, a fairly recent piece dating from 1985, the only unusual instrument (at least as far as the symphony orchestra is concerned) is an amplified guitar, which he uses as a substitute for the Japanese koto. Where Takemitsu differs from earlier twentieth-century composers, such as Debussy, is in stipulating how the orchestra should be laid out. The strings are to be divided into two orchestras sitting as far apart from each other as possible to the left and right of the conductor. In between are various chamber groups: flute, clarinet and string quartet at the front; two

Three masters of musical colour: (*from left*) George Benjamin, Olivier Messiaen and Pierre Boulez.

harps, celeste and guitar in the middle distance; woodwind and brass still further back; and furthest away the percussion.

A dream, says Takemitsu, provides you with a glimpse of what lies deep inside you; a window allows you to get a glimpse of the outside world – the natural environment perhaps. But the Japanese words for 'dream' and 'window' also form the name of a sixteenth-century Zen monk, famous for the gardens he created in and around Kyoto. A Japanese garden is meant to be a miniaturized version of a natural environment. Colour is used sparingly, because great splashes of it are so rarely seen in nature. The most distinguished garden in Kyoto, the garden of Ryoanji, consists of five groups of rocks laid upon a rectangle of raked sand to suggest a wild beach or a seascape with rocky islands. Takemitsu said that the serenity, clarity and formal beauty of gardens such as this were the structural and aesthetic model he always had in mind when writing music. *Dream / Window* is slow enough for the audience to hear how the colouration of one group of instruments gently filters through another, how perspectives change, and how the entire sound takes on new colours when, for instance, the double basses come in with a low D or the upper strings begin playing glassy harmonics.

Takemitsu was also influenced by his work in the electronic studios of Japanese Radio in the late fifties. On the one hand, the dense clusters of string harmonics and filtration techniques are typical of the way noise can be gradually transformed into sound colours in an electronic studio; on the other, his spatial distribution of the sound resembles the stereophonic effects obtainable with multiple loudspeakers in the late fifties. There is no doubt that electronic music has made the greatest contribution to timbre, harmonic colour and space in twentieth-century music.

The tape recorder, which made electronic music possible, was invented in 1935 and used by German Radio to record some of Furtwängler's concerts with the Berlin Philharmonic during the Second World War, but did not become widely available until the early fifties. Pierre Schaeffer (1910–1996), a sound technician for French Radio, had access to one in 1948 and used it to produce early examples of *musique concrète* – music consisting of the electronic manipulation of sounds recorded on location or in a studio, such as railway trains, the human voice, musical instruments, bells and so forth. Four years later, Herbert Eimert established an electronic studio at the West German Radio Station in Cologne, where purely electronic music could be produced without the aid of recorded sounds. As well as the variable-speed tape recorders, filters and echo chambers which Schaeffer had been using, the studio contained oscillators and noise generators. The first outstanding piece of electronic music produced in Cologne, Stockhausen's *Gesang der Jünglinge*, makes use of electronically generated sound and a recording of a boy singing the *Benedicite* – the song of the three boys in the burning fiery furnace: 'O all ye works of the Lord, bless ye the Lord . . .' Two years after its first performance in 1956, Varèse's *Poème électronique*, which had been composed in a studio at Eindhoven, was played over 350 loudspeakers in the pavilion designed by Le Corbusier for the 1958 world exhibition in Brussels. It too combined pure electronic music with *musique concrète*, in this instance an imprecation sung by a female soprano. Other than short studies, the first piece composed entirely from electronically generated material, without recourse to *musique concrète*, was Stockhausen's *Kontakte* (1958–60).

These pieces reveal what appears to be a fundamental dichotomy in electronic music. On the one hand, it draws the listener's attention away from the meaning of discourse and focuses it on sound *per se*; on the other, it opens up hitherto unexplored worlds which need to have meaning imposed on them. Although, when listening to *Gesang der Jünglinge*, our attention may be entirely focused on the transformation of one sound into another, we nevertheless have to find an explanation for the inclusion of the *Benedicite*. The transformation of sounds is one of the essential features of electronic music, even in early pieces of *musique concrète* such as the *Symphonie pour un homme seul* (1950) by Schaeffer and Pierre Henry. Nothing like this had been done since Schoenberg composed 'Farben' forty years earlier, using conventional instruments. To organize the transitions in *Gesang der Jünglinge*, Stockhausen devised two sets of scales, one for the purely electronic sounds, the other for the voice of

The sound paths for Varèse's *Poème électronique* at the Philips Pavilion at the Brussels World's Fair in 1958. The 'hyperbolic paraboloid' shape of the pavilion was invented by the composer Iannis Xenakis, then working as an architect in Le Corbusier's studio.

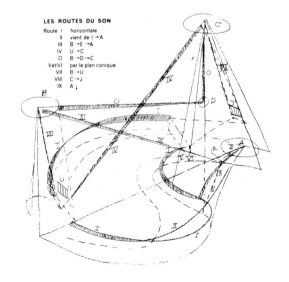

the boy. Those for the electronic sounds range between dark and
bright timbres, pure pitch and random noise bands, the darkest
noise and the brightest noise; those for the voice between dark
and light vowels, vowels and consonants, and the range of consonants produced by the voice. But the electronic and vocal
sounds are not kept separate. There are moments when what initially seems to be a vocal sound turns out to be an electronic one,
and *vice versa*. In other words, there is a constant effort to find
points of contact between the vocal and electronic sound
worlds, between what is familiar and what is strange.

Most German speakers will know the German text of the
Benedicite and will be able to supply its meaning even when the
words and syllables are split up and rearranged. What will surprise them is the emergence of new words formed by the dislocations – words that are not in the dictionary but that nevertheless
have meaning as poetic communication: 'Schneewind', 'Eisglut',
'Feuerreif' ('snow-wind', 'ice-heat', 'fire-ripe'). The feeling that
we have entered a surreal world when listening to this piece is

enhanced by Stockhausen's manipulation of illusory and physical space. At one moment the boy's voice appears to be close at hand, the next it has become an ethereal choir singing far away in the distance. This, of course, is simply an acoustic illusion, created by mixing noise into the sound, the superimposition of several recordings and the application of reverberation. The manipulation of physical space comes from relaying the stereo recording through five loudspeakers, four on the walls of the hall, the fifth in front: the sound can come from one side or the other, from all sides, or move clockwise or anticlockwise from one side to the other.

The gardens at Ryoanji, Kyoto.

For *Kontakte*, Stockhausen used a four-track tape and discovered a method of making the sound rotate. Here only four loudspeakers are necessary but they have to be placed in or near the four corners of the room or hall so that two are behind the listeners: this set-up allows rotation at various speeds and in both directions. Stockhausen also found that if he made the sound jump from, say, front left to back right and front right to back left it would appear to be moving in loops, and that to create the impression of flooding the hall with sound all he needed to do was to relay the same sound from all the speakers in rapid succession. But what he never anticipated, and indeed never mentions in his writings about the work, is that if you stand at an equal distance from all four speakers you sometimes experience the illusion that the sound is looping in a vertical as well as a hor-

Stockhausen at the sound control desk for his Helicopter Quartet in 1994.

izontal plane. How this comes about is anyone's guess, but the sensation is like suddenly, unexpectedly, being whirled away on a fantastic roller-coaster ride.

The sounds themselves are some of the richest and most diverse ever created in an electronic studio, and yet all come from the same source – a series of impulses. The machines needed to produce the wealth of sounds were an impulse generator, a filter, a reverberator, a ring modulator and a tape

recorder with its heads placed in the order play-back–erase–record rather than the usual erase–record–playback. The fact that the whole piece stems from a simple sequence of impulses meant that he was able to show that pitch, timbre and rhythm are closely related and not independent, as they usually appear to be when listening to music. At one point, a high note comes zooming towards us from the distance, zig-zagging down through space and gradually changing into a pulse. The effect is not unlike a giant bee slowing down its wing beat to come into land. But the pulses continue to get slower until eventually, with the help of a reverberator, they become recognizable as a pitch again – now a low, steady E.

The tape is entirely self-sufficient, though Stockhausen always intended it to be accompanied by piano and percussion. In fact the piano responds to that low E with an E of its own, transforming the unfamiliar electronic sound into something familiar and 'real world'. This is why Stockhausen called the work *Kontakte*. As in *Gesang der Jünglinge*, he wanted to make a 'contact' between the unfamiliar and the familiar, except that in this case the familiar sounds are live. The audience is not just listening to a tape played through loudspeakers but has something to look at, in the shape of the players, who are placed at either side of the platform and from time to time move to the centre to play a tamtam and a gong. At one stage an amusing drama develops out of this movement. We already know that the tape can produce piano- and percussion-like sounds, but it has never responded directly to what the players have been doing (in the main, in fact, it has been the other way round). Now the players, it seems, make an effort to force a response. The dramatic incident builds up as the pianist and percussionist successively play overlapping crescendos on cow-bells and hihat (from their places), then gong and tamtam (in the centre); each crescendo is louder than the last, and when the pianist's tamtam reaches fortissimo, the percussionist caps its sound by striking his gong at triple forte. Suddenly the tape responds. From it come sounds that closely resemble the tamtam and gong, and these too are loud. The 'unknown and nameless' has made contact.

Stockhausen carried through the idea of making contact with unknown worlds lying 'out there' in several pieces, most notably in *Kurzwellen*, a piece he created in 1968. Here the strange sounds are not those he himself devised and fixed on tape, but the sounds picked up and emitted by shortwave receivers – atmospherics, bits of morse code, snatches of music and strange mumblings going on out there in real time as the work is performed. There are six players on the platform listening to the signals and modifying them in the various ways that Stockhausen has determined in advance. Shortwave signals, he believes, 'come from utterly different worlds – worlds beyond speech, beyond reportage, beyond music, beyond morse codes'. But the instruments transforming the signals – piano, electronium, tamtam with microphone, and viola with contact microphone – are themselves transformed by electronics. In other words, they do not produce the familiar sounds that everyone expects, but have themselves ventured out into uncharted regions. It is perhaps significant that in 1968 everyone believed that the space age had dawned. Men were orbiting the earth and were about to land on the moon. In that year, Stanley Kubrick released his film *2001: A Space Odyssey*, which culminates as the hero, David Bowman, zooms off through space on his odyssey into the unknown and is finally transformed into a 'star-child'.

Most composers would say that composition itself is, metaphorically, a journey into the unknown. But if their subject is the exploration of what is physically unknown, then electronics are the best medium to convey the strangeness of the world they have entered. This realization is certainly behind the approach of the Australian composer David Lumsdaine (born 1931) in *Aria for Edward John Eyre* (1972); this hour-long piece concerns the explorer who in 1840 set out to find a suitable droving route from Adelaide in the south to grazing grounds in the north of Australia, but was ultimately forced to make the first crossing of the Great Australian Bight to Albany in the west without provisions and with only an Aboriginal boy for his companion. The piece is scored for soprano, two narrators, an amplified double bass, and an ensemble of three clarinets, horn, trumpet, trombone, harp and two percussion. As well as two tapes, one containing electronically modified material sung by the soprano, the other modified material played by the ensemble, there are also live

Birtwistle's *The Mask of Orpheus*, as staged by English National Opera in 1986.

electronics controlled by an operator sitting at a console. Lumsdaine's purpose is not simply to give an impression of the vast emptiness of the Great Australian Bight and the unnerving sounds that can sometimes be heard there, he also wants to convey what happens deep inside Eyre's own world. The work is concerned with spiritual as well as physical discovery.

The genesis of *Aria* was a reading of Patrick White's novel *Voss*, which draws on Eyre's diary of the journey. In the novel Johann Voss carries with him the constant thought of his secret passion, Laura Trevelyan, as he leads his expedition across the continent. A spiritual communion binds them together, so that from her home in Sydney she suffers what he suffers on the journey, and as betrayal and mutiny whittle away Voss's power to endure hardships, so her presence and his attachment to her grow stronger and stronger. Lumsdaine also draws on Eyre's diary and has the first narrator read, in a matter-of-fact tone, selected excerpts from it; they relate how the route north was blocked by a great salt lake, how his overseer was murdered by the

Aboriginal bearers who then fled with the provisions, and how he and the Aboriginal boy endured the remaining 850 miles of the journey by themselves. The second narrator echoes the first, but in a disjointed manner, so that we get a glimpse of Eyre's inner feelings. His deepest emotions are reserved for the soprano singing her long, potentially endless aria. Eyre had no Laura to sustain him on his journey, and the aria being shaped in the depths of his mind comes from his mystical union with the desert itself. It celebrates both the inner and the outer landscapes.

Concerts involving electronic equipment are not easy to mount. The machines can be temperamental when moved. It takes time to set them up and achieve a good balance, much longer than it takes to set up and balance a symphony orchestra. Furthermore, technology develops so rapidly that what was once considered standard equipment soon goes out of production. Quadrophony never took off commercially and it is now difficult to find the four-track tape recorder needed for *Kontakte* and extremely difficult to assemble the number required for Birtwistle's *The Mask of Orpheus*. Another difficulty is the shape of concert halls and opera houses, and the inflexibility of their fixtures. For the standard repertory the best shape is that of a shoe-box. But this is totally inadequate to the performance requirements Boulez lays down for *Répons*, the work that has been preoccupying him ever since the late seventies. Like *Kontakte*, *Répons* needs a square hall with movable seats that can be arranged to suit the disposition Boulez insists upon for the instrumental and electronic forces. This is why when the second version of the work was performed in London in 1982 it had to be given at the Royal Agricultural Hall rather than the Royal Festival Hall or the Royal Albert Hall. On a raised platform in the centre of the space is an ensemble of nine woodwind, seven brass and eight strings with a conductor. In front of the conductor are the principal electronic instruments – a powerful 4X computer, a less powerful PDP 11/55 computer, and a halaphone, a machine invented to control the diffusion of the sound in space with maximum richness and minimum interference. The six soloists (piano 1, piano 2 (doubling organ), harp, cimbalom, xylophone (doubling glockenspiel) and vibraphone) are situated on rostrums placed in a circle round the walls of the hall. Each

Schoenberg's designs for a set of playing cards.

soloist has a small loudspeaker producing what Boulez calls 'wallpaper music' when required, and between the soloists are six large loudspeakers relaying the 4X computer's transformation of what they have been playing. The audience sits in the circular space between the central platform and the soloists.

Boulez has been the director of the Institut de Recherche et de Coordination Acoustique / Musique (IRCAM) since it first opened in 1977, and in fact it owes its existence to him. It was therefore inevitable that he should want to compose a work that would make use of the research undertaken there, especially in the field of computers. *Répons* differs from the electronic music produced by Stockhausen and others in the fifties and sixties in that here the electronic machine responds to the live instrumentalists, whereas in earlier works it was the live instrumentalists who responded to the machine. This, of course, was only made possible by the rapid advances in computer technology during the intervening fifteen or so years. The 4X computer was produced by one of IRCAM's engineering teams and is capable of performing 200 million analytical and transformational operations per second. As well as transforming the soloists' material in accordance with one of the programs Boulez has had stored in its memory, it is also responsive to manual control. Boulez does not want the new technology to overrule spontaneity. Among the computer's functions are the modification of timbre, the enrichment of harmonic colour, the instant transposition of pitch by means of a frequency shifter, and a delay system. The last is designed to project a sound through time and space by creating multiple echoes which can be rhythmized.

The entrance of the soloists occurs after six and a half minutes

Nadia Boulanger said that the first thing she noticed about Boulez, which was very scary, was that if you played the note G, he would hear not only the note G, but the whole harmonic series around it, all the possibilities of the note. His ear was so acute that he was hearing a multiplicity of things that no one else could hear.

The first of Boulez's piano *Notations* from 1945 . . .

of music played exclusively by the instrumental ensemble in the centre, without electronic modification. This opening ensemble could be considered the equivalent of the music that precedes the entrance of the prima donna in a nineteenth-century opera, in that it prepares the ground and builds up the audience's expectations. As well as establishing a pattern of call and response, it even introduces, in a primitive way, some of the procedures the computer will undertake later. In one passage, for instance, the brass anticipate the delay system by rhythmizing a series of sustained notes. But, with the entrance of the six soloists, we are suddenly plunged into the action proper. The entrance is slow and measured. An air of magic is created by six huge arpeggiated chords, the first merely amplified, the second transformed by frequency shifting and a 'delay system', which projects the sound in space like a multiple echo. A series of longer sections follow, each characterized by a specific instrumentation, texture and transformation technique. Boulez calls one the 'Balinese section' because of its similarity to gamelan music, the central ensemble having a semiquaver *moto perpetuo*, the six soloists' eight arpeggiated chords each sustained by even longer 'delays'. Another he calls the 'funeral march' or 'Scriabin section', a slow movement containing a long crescendo, which gradually fills the whole sound space, setting it alight just as Scriabin had done in *Prometheus: The Poem of Fire*.

This 'Scriabin section' was originally the last. Since then two more versions have appeared, the latest lasting forty-five minutes, more than twice as long as the first version introduced in 1981. In fact Boulez originally planned the work to last for a whole evening, and still thinks of it as a 'work in progress'. Computer technology is advancing in such an exciting way, he says, that he wants to incorporate the new discoveries into *Répons* without having to embark on something new. It is essential, therefore, that the work should be kept 'open'. In fact building up a piece section by section or movement by movement is nothing

The orchestral *Notations* not only colourizes the 'black and white' piano version, but puts it through the most sophisticated kaleidoscope.

. . . and his orchestral expansion of bars 4 and 5.

'Arches of light': Santiago Calatrava's exquisite bridge in Barcelona.

unusual for Boulez. *Pli selon pli* also emerged and was performed in stages. He also likes to go on working at pieces long after everyone else thinks they are finalized. In 1977, when he was commissioned to write something for the Orchestre de Paris but was still busy trying to establish IRCAM, he reworked four of his twelve *Notations* for piano, which he had composed as a student in 1945 when he was still experimenting with the twelve-note system. To discipline himself, he had restricted the twelve pieces to twelve bars each. They were nuggets, but eminently suitable for expansion. The reworkings of the four he selected were not unlike the treatment the 4X computer would later make possible. The original twelve bars are still recognizable, but the pieces are lengthened and scored for a large orchestra, and consequently contain a range of timbres, harmonic colours and spatial depth only hinted at in the earlier version.

The development of minute quantities of material into works of substance appears to be a characteristic of those composers who work with computers at IRCAM. In 1982 the Finnish composer Kaija Saariaho (born 1952), after attending a computer music course there, stayed on, initially to write pieces built out of just six seconds' worth of sound. Her main interest is in the analysis and transformation of sounds made by traditional instruments – the cello, for instance. All she needed for such a work was a recording of a cellist playing a single note, at first with a normal bow stroke so that the sound was as clear and pure as possible, and then with increasing bow pressure so that it became scratchy and full of noise. She next devised computer programs to analyse and transform the sound. Out of these operations came *Lichtbogen* ('Arches of light', 1985) for nine instruments and live electronics, and *Nymphéa (Jardin secret III)* (1987) for string quartet and live electronics. These works are quite different from each other, but they both focus the listener's attention on timbre, harmonic colour and space; so although the process of devising programs for the computer was analytical and linear, the listener's attention has to be holistic and non-linear. In other words, the music demands that the listeners enter a state of consciousness which differs fundamentally from the one they inhabit while carrying on their normal activities in the everyday world. This may well be the closest music has come to Schoenberg's concept of *Klangfarbenmelodie*. 'How high the development of spirit that could find pleasure in such subtle things,' he said. Well, yes – but perhaps all it really takes is the willingness to submit oneself to sound *per se*.

Chapter 5
Three Journeys through Dark Landscapes

Throughout most of the nineteenth century, when the Italians and French dominated opera and the Austrians and Germans instrumental music, composers from other countries had to turn to folk music if they wanted to find an individual voice and establish a national identity. Glinka knew this as early as the 1830s, and although the dominance of the western Europeans waned as the twentieth century approached, folk music continued to have this function right up to the First World War. Since then composers have usually found their voice by identifying themselves with a particular movement – expressionism, neo-classicism, serialism, minimalism – rather than a particular country. But in the political dictatorships which have figured so largely in the twentieth century, composers who failed to conform to the narrow dictates of the authorities and went their own way often found that their music was likely to be banned. This is what happened to Shostakovich in Russia and Lutosławski in Poland. Stalin's decision to make all cultural and scientific institutions ideologically uniform after the Second World War resulted in both composers' being condemned as formalists: according to the authorities they had put form above content and their music had little or nothing to do with socialist realism. Bartók would have suffered a similar fate had he not got out of Hungary before Hitler took over in 1944. The charge levelled against him, however, would have been cultural bolshevism.

Bartók was eclectic by nature, so that even when he had established his own style he was always open to new ideas. As a student he fell under the influence of Wagner and Liszt; then, when he heard *Also Sprach Zarathustra* in 1902, Strauss became his ideal. His symphonic poem *Kossuth*, based on the life of Lajos Kossuth, the revolutionary Hungarian leader of the abortive War of Independence against the Austrians in 1848–9, was modelled on *Ein Heldenleben*. It contained a *csárdás* and the kind of Hungarian material Liszt had popularized. But in 1905 when Bartók befriended Kodály and began to take a professional interest in

If music and politics were ever truly separate, then in the twentieth century musicians were to lose their innocence forever. In Eastern Europe music can be used as a kind of map to trace the psychological profile of a whole era. Truths can be expressed in music which, if written in words, would have cost the authors their lives.

Béla Bartók in the 1920s.

Judith demands the keys to the seven locked doors in Bluebeard's castle and, as each is opened, she discovers his torture chamber, his armoury, his treasure and his secret garden. Each of them shows traces of blood.

the collection of folk music he discovered that what had passed for folk music in Liszt and Brahms was in fact composed music of the kind that gypsy musicians played in restaurants and inns. The *csárdás*, for instance, was a dance that had been in vogue only between 1850 and 1890. Unlike Kodály, who was interested only in Hungarian folk music, Bartók collected material from all over eastern Europe, his collection of Romanian folk music being particularly outstanding. By the time he had completed his field work in 1918, he had noted over 10,000 songs and dances, many of which would not have survived had it not been for him.

The influence of folk music on Bartók's own compositions began when he and Kodály harmonized twenty Hungarian folksongs for publication in 1906. The piano pieces *For Children*, which Bartók wrote in 1908–9, are also basically folksong harmonizations, the first volume consisting of material collected in Hungary, the second of material from Slovakia. Several, however, are more than mere simple settings. One of the most adventurous is 'Mourning Song', which ends the second volume. It illustrates a procedure that was to become fundamental to Bartók's style – the use of several modes or scales within a piece for expressive as well as structural purposes. He called the procedure 'polymodality'. The melody of 'Mourning Song' is in the Dorian mode transposed to E (E–F♯–G–A–B–C♯–D). It is played three times, but the harmonization is through-composed. It starts with a piano introduction that sounds as if it were in C major. In the middle Bartók makes use of one of the traditional formulae which composers employed in tonal music to symbolize death: a slowly descending chromatic scale. Then at the end he brings back his introduction setting it against the repetition of the song's last phrase: A–B–G–E–D–E. At the very end only the notes G–E–D are supplied so that at the close the song seems to hang in mid-air. In this context the piano's introduction sounds as if it belongs to the Phrygian mode (E–F–G–A–B–C–D), which means that the harmonic colouring has been transformed.

By using four different scales and modes (the diatonic and chromatic scales plus the Dorian and Phrygian modes) Bartók has structured the piece so that about two-thirds of the way through the mourning has become a cry of grief, and at the end a memory drifting away into uncertainty.

The most famous and frequently performed work of all Bartók's short piano works from before the First World War, the *Allegro barbaro* (1911), is based on music which is original but nevertheless has all the flavour of genuine dances found in Hungary, Romania and Slovakia. The derivation of the first dance is Slovakian. Half the melody is built from a four-note mode used by various peoples in central Asia (E–G–A–B♯), the remainder from an old Hungarian pentatonic scale (A–B♯–D–E–G). The accompaniment, however, is chromatic. All the chromatic notes apart from A♯ are present, and the passage has to be interpreted as a combination of the Phrygian mode on F♯ (F♯–G–A–B–C♯–D–E–F♯) and the Lydian mode on F♯ (F♯–G♯–A♯–B♯–C♯–D♯–E♯–F♯). In other words, Bartók had at his disposal all the advantages of total chromaticism while preserving what he deemed to be the vitality of the old modes.

Although Bartók had no difficulty in making use of the folk idiom in fairly short piano pieces, integrating it into longer pieces based on the forms of art music caused problems. His First String Quartet of 1908, for instance, quotes part of a pentatonic folk melody from Transylvanian in its finale and includes a melody of Hungarian type in the first movement, but it owes much more to Wagner and particularly to late Beethoven than to folk idioms. The same must be said about his one-act opera, *Duke Bluebeard's Castle*. This dates from the same period as the *Allegro barbaro*, but its sound world and symbolism owe much more to Debussy than to anything from the plains of Hungary. Like Debussy's *Pelléas et Mélisande* its story concerns the need to preserve secrets and mysteries. Once Judith, Bluebeard's new wife, has unlocked the seven doors of his inner self and learned his secrets, her love for him is shattered and she has to suffer the fate of his

Duke Bluebeard's Castle: Judith opens the fifth door to reveal Bluebeard's kingdom. From David Alden's 1991 production of the opera for English National Opera.

other wives – become a shadow, his memory of what might have been. The influence of Debussy also extends to Bartók's use of *parlando*, vocal lines based on the natural speech inflections of his native language. Kodály, in his review of the opera when it was eventually produced in 1918, regarded this as being of particular significance: 'This is the first work on the Hungarian operatic stage,' he said, 'in which the singing is consistent from beginning to end, speaking to us in an uninterrupted Hungarian way.'

Hungarian is a Finno-Ugric language related to Finnish, Estonian and certain minority languages in Russia such as Cheremis. Its stress and intonation patterns have been of great interest to linguists trying to find a connection between speech and music. One salient feature of Hungarian is that there are no articles, and first syllables are automatically accented, sometimes quite heavily. This is why rhythms such as a stressed short note followed by an unstressed long note are such a feature of Bartók's music, and why it is immediately recognizable. *Duke Bluebeard's Castle* opens with the lower strings playing a pentatonic tune based on the notes F♯–A–B–C♯–E, in equal note values without any accents at all. As yet the stage is still in darkness. But when a new tune cast in thirds appears on oboes and clarinets in a strange exotic mode we sense that Bluebeard and Judith are about to enter. The distinctive feature of this tune is the accented mordent on the first note of every phrase. The unfamiliar mode (F♯–G–A–B–C–C♯–D♯–E) makes the passage sound rather sinister, reflecting Judith's sense of foreboding and disquiet; in this threatening atmosphere she longs to open all the doors to let the light in. But in its stress and intonation patterns the melody carries different connotations: according to the linguists Ivan Fónagy and Klara Magdics, who have studied and written about such patterns in Hungarian, the outline of the melody typifies someone expressing tenderness and longing. In other words, the mode represents the atmosphere, the melody Bluebeard's emotions.

At the end of the opera, when Judith has

Bartók at the piano in the 1920s.

joined the other wives behind the seventh door and Bluebeard is left alone on stage to sing 'Henceforth all shall be darkness, darkness,' the opening music comes back and reference is also made to the crucial scene where the sixth door is opened and Judith's doubts about Bluebeard's love are raised by the sight of the lake of tears. That scene is centred on A and Bartók switches from one mode to another to underline the increasing tension between Bluebeard and his wife. It opens with a descriptive passage in A minor (A–B–C–D–E–F♯–G♯–A) in which the mordent is extended into a quiver to indicate both the shimmering of the light on the water and the horror Judith experiences on seeing it. She knows instinctively what the mysterious water represents, even though she ingenuously keeps asking Bluebeard for an explanation. To make the tone of her voice seem innocent Bartók casts her questions in a simple pentatonic mode (A–C–D–E–G), her vocal line being a series of falling fourths (C–G–A–E). For Bluebeard's reply, 'Tears, Judith, tears,' Bartók uses a series of falling minor thirds. He places them against a lamenting melody on low strings cast in the plaintive Phrygian mode transposed to A (A–B♭–C–D–E♭–F–G–A). This too emphasizes falling minor thirds. But as Bluebeard's longing for Judith intensifies, this lament is transformed into a passionate tune on high strings in a pentatonic mode centred on D♭ (D♭–E♭–G♭–A♭–B♭). In other words, by using Judith's pentatonic colouring Bluebeard indicates that he has opened himself up to her. He is now prepared to reveal to her all his secrets. It is this passionate tune that Bluebeard recalls at the end of the opera, as a memory of what might have been. And to underline his despair, the opera closes with his falling minor third (C–A) placed in conflict with Judith's falling fourth (now F♯–C♯). F♯ and C♯ were the notes that began the opera. There they heralded the possibility that the mystery of love would be preserved; here they seal the fate of that illusion.

Duke Bluebeard's Castle dates from 1911 and was more or less contemporary with Schoenberg's *Pierrot Lunaire*, Berg's *Altenberg Songs* and Webern's *Rilke Songs*. But it would appear that Bartók became aware of what was happening up the Danube in Vienna only after the war, because it was then that he wrote a series of works which, although they continued to make use of folk music to a certain extent, abandoned polymodality

The Gilau mountains south of Cluj Napoca in Transylvania.

and veered strongly towards atonality. The first of these works was *The Miraculous Mandarin* (1918–19), a bizarre pantomime about a beautiful girl who lures men to a den so that they can be robbed by three ruffians. One of these men is a Mandarin who is so inflamed with passion for the girl that he continues to live even after the robbers have stabbed him repeatedly. He dies only after the girl has satisfied his desire. Bartók thought it one of the best works he had composed. But the other works in the series, the Three Studies for piano (1918), the *Eight Improvisations on Hungarian Peasant Songs* for piano (1920), and the two violin sonatas (1921 and 1922) are less successful. In fact, they are generally felt to lack direction. Bartók must also have felt this, because when he had completed the Second Violin Sonata he changed tack, abandoned atonality and wrote a very mild *Dance Suite* (1923) to celebrate the fiftieth anniversary of the union of Buda and Pest.

Between 1923 and 1926, Bartók spent his time touring as a concert pianist and helping to establish the International Society for Contemporary Music. He therefore became familiar with

everything that was happening in the contemporary musical
world and, being an eclectic, inevitably got caught up in the
'objective' styles that had emerged in the early twenties. His
concert programmes began to include more and more Bach, and
when he resumed composition in 1926, the works he produced
outstripped everything his contemporaries were doing in the
objective manner. He returned to polymodality and proved that
the folk idiom, when given a harder, more percussive edge, was
perfectly suitable for the long, developmental forms he had previously found so difficult. He devoted 1926 to piano music.
Among the pieces he composed were his one and only Piano
Sonata, the suite *Out of Doors* and his First Piano Concerto. He
also began work on *Mikrokosmos*, his monumental set of graded
pieces for the piano. 'The neutral character of the piano has long
been recognized,' he said. 'Yet it seems to me that its inherent
nature becomes really expressive only by means of the present
tendency to use the piano as a percussion instrument.'

The following two years were given to music for strings, the
two Violin Rhapsodies and the Third and Fourth String Quartets. It was these that established Bartók as the natural heir to
Beethoven in the field of quartet writing. He was not himself a
string player but had regularly accompanied Jelly d'Arányi,
Zoltán Székely and Joseph Szigeti, and had made himself an
expert on what was possible in string playing. As a result he was
able to make use of techniques that had never previously been
employed in works for string quartet. In the second subject of
the Third Quartet, for instance, the two violins are asked to play
on or very near the bridge to produce a
glassy sound. The first note of their tune
requires them to throw the bow on the
string to produce a controlled spiccato,
while the last two notes have to be connected by a glissando.

The structure of the Third Quartet
consists of four movements rolled into
one in a very unusual way. It is played
without a break and starts with what
could be considered the exposition of a
first movement (moderato). This leads to

a scherzo (allegro) serving as a kind of development. Then follows a highly varied recapitulation of the opening moderato; but this gets slower and slower so that it takes on the role of a slow movement. To bring the work to a close, there is a short, brilliant finale. The Fourth Quartet is also unusually structured, being in the form of an arch, *A–B–C–B–A*. But when he talked about it Bartók drew his analogy from nature: 'The slow movement is the kernel of the work,' he said, 'the other movements are, as it were, arranged in layers around it. Movement four is a free variation of two, and one and five have the same thematic material.' This analogy may have a bearing on his remark that 'we always follow nature in composition'. Indeed, the slow movement, 'the kernel of the work', seems to say that man and nature are not necessarily divided but can be shown to be at one.

The movement is based on two types of melodic material: one has its roots in the recitative-like Romanian 'long song' (*hora lunga*), the other in bird song. It opens with the 'long song' played by the cello, accompanied by drone-like chords on the other three instruments, alternating between non-vibrato and vibrato. The most characteristic feature of the song is the sudden burst of short notes that enlivens the very long note at the beginning of each of its three strophes. In the second and third strophes the pitch becomes successively higher and the mood more and more impassioned. As soon as the long song is finished the first violin begins a melody based on bird song, and it immediately becomes apparent that the structure of the two songs is virtually the same. After variants of the long song and bird song alternate several times, the movement ends with the essential elements of the two being brought together to form a unity.

Bartók was not alone in wanting to 'follow nature in composition'. This is exactly what Webern, Varèse and very many more twentieth-century composers considered they were doing in their different ways. The analogy between folksong and bird song in the Fourth Quartet is unique in Bartók's work. What interested him far more was the analogy between natural forms and music, the bilateral symmetry of leaves, the rotational symmetry of rosettes, the way natural growth conforms to the ratios of the Golden Section. The reason why Bartók cast the Fourth Quartet in five movements was simply because the central movement functions as a vertical axis of symmetry. In this instance the symmetry is not exact: the last two movements are far from being mirror images of the first two, but their contents and proportions balance each other. In music the most frequently encountered symmetries are those around a horizontal axis. The most obvious of these is the bilateral symmetry found in a pentatonic scale, say D–F–G–A–C. Here the intervals (measured in semitones) are 3–2–2–3 and the axis of symmetry is G, the central note. But there can also be bilateral symmetry around an axis that is only notional. This happens in the octatonic scale, a scale which Bartók used as frequently as Stravinsky or Messiaen. In the one starting on D (D–E–F–G–G♯–B♭–B–C♯) where the intervals (again measured in semitones) are 2–1–2–1–2–1–2, the axis lies between G and G♯. The basic motif of the Fourth Quartet which is very prominent in the first and last movements, B–C–D♭–C–B–B♭, has its horizontal axis of symmetry lying between B and C. Later composers discovered that if chords, however dissonant they may be, contain notes that are arranged symmetrically around a central axis there is no need to

Bartók transcribing folk music in the 1930s.

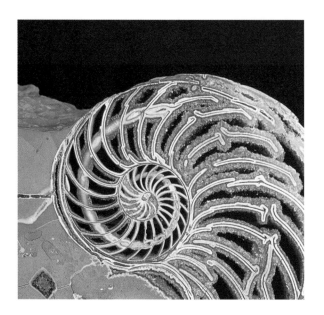

The successive chambers of the cephalopod Nautilus are proportioned according to the Golden Section.

resolve them. They sound absolutely stable. This discovery has played a crucial role in the way harmony has been handled in the second half of the twentieth century. Bartók, even though he was acutely conscious of horizontal symmetries, always resolved his discords in the traditional manner. The chord that reverberates in the ear at the end of the Fourth Quartet is C major. From a harmonic point of view, there is no need to state it explicitly because at this stage C has become the axis of symmetry and this alone would create stability; but Bartók must have wanted the resonances of the triad itself to be present to provide a conclusive sense of closure. Symmetric procedures are most obviously in evidence in the fugal first movement of the *Music for Strings, Percussion and Celesta*, which Bartók composed in 1936 for Paul Sacher and the Basel Chamber Orchestra. The scoring is for two string orchestras symmetrically arranged on either side of a group of percussion and non-bowed instruments, among which are a piano and harp. The first movement (Andante tranquillo) has as its subject a melody in four phrases, entirely confined to the eight chromatic notes spanning the fifth from A to E. A is the tonic, but to make it also the horizontal axis of symmetry Bartók devises a number of schemes. The first is to transpose successive entries of the subject to every degree of the chromatic scale, taking the starting notes in turn from a half-cycle of rising fifths (A–E–B–F♯–C♯–G♯–D♯(E♭)) and a half-cycle of descending fifths (A–D–G–C–F–B♭–E♭). This places the original version starting on A at the centre, from which the subsequent versions fan out above and below: A–E–D–B–G–F♯–C–F–C♯–B♭–G♯–E♭. However, the subject is open to variation and, as the second part of the sequence indicates, there is sufficient inconsistency in the order of the entries to ensure that they are never completely predictable. Once the cycle has been completed the music pushes forward to a climactic E♭, pounded out in octaves. To return to A, Bartók simply reverses the order of the keys. The subject is shortened in various ways and, most importantly, inverted. When this cycle is completed, the original and its inversion are played in full at one and the same time.

In the late 1940s, the Hungarian musician Ernõ Lendvai pointed out that this fugue is one of several movements by Bartók based on the proportions of the Golden Section (the division of a line so that the ratio of the shorter segment to the longer segment is equal to the ratio of the longer segment to the whole). The Golden Section is fundamental to the rate of growth in organic matter and is the standard for most of the proportions in the art of the Hellenic and Roman empires. Roughly speaking, the division falls about two-thirds along a line, but it can be more accurately calculated by means of the 'Fibonacci series'. This is named after Leonardo of Pisa, 'son of Bonaccio', a thirteenth-century Italian mathematician. In the Fibonacci series every member is equal to the sum of the two preceding numbers: 1, 1, 2, 3, 5, 8, 13, 21, 34, 55, 89, 144, etc. The higher the numbers the closer they get to the exact ratio of the Golden Section. Lendvai discovered that the ratios 21 : 13, 34 : 21 and 55 : 34 represent the number of bars in each important section and subdivision of Bartók's fugue. It is no coincidence that the climax

German tanks move into Budapest in March 1944.

occurs in bar 55 and that, if the usual whole-bar rest is added at the end, the total number of bars is 89. Other musicians believe that Bartók, like earlier composers, had no knowledge of the Fibonacci series and that his proportions were purely intuitive, based only on what was artistically appropriate. Nevertheless, the Fibonacci series was widely used by composers after Bartók's death, probably as a result of Stockhausen's analysis of Bartók's Sonata for two pianos and percussion, where it is particularly in evidence.

However, as far as the listener is concerned, it is not the symmetries or the proportions that make *Music for Strings, Percussion and Celesta* so gripping, it is the vitality of the work, and the way the fugal subject comes back transformed in the finale. When it is first announced, the theme is played pianissimo and sounds muffled and distant. The players have to use mutes, and in order to produce the ice-cold quality that most conductors ask for they usually play without vibrato. Later, as the music moves towards the climactic E♭ octaves, the mutes are removed and the sound becomes fuller and warmer. In the following section, when the music returns to A, the mutes are replaced and the sound reverts to the original etiolated quality. What the listener does not know as yet is that in the finale Bartók will cap the expansiveness he achieves at the climax of this first movement; but to dramatize the return, he must make the fugue subject sound even more pallid when it appears in the intervening movements. In the lively second movement, three of its four phrases come back at the beginning of the development section. They are difficult to detect because Bartók has them played in a percussive, brittle manner by the piano and by the violins and violas of the first orchestra plucking their strings so violently that they slap against the fingerboard. In the following Adagio, all four phrases are present, but they are totally isolated from each other and give the impression of being just a thin, faded memory. When the fugal subject returns in all its full-blooded vigour at the climax to the finale Bartók casts it in a new form: instead of the original chromatic scale A–B♭–B–C–C♯–D–E♭–E, he now uses what he called the 'acoustic' scale, which is derived from the first eleven overtones of a fundamental – in this case C: C–D–E–F♯–G–A–B♭–C. The melody is played forte and *molto espressivo* by all the strings, the sonority being enhanced by a pedal C on double basses and timpani.

The last work Bartók composed before leaving for America in 1940 was his Sixth String Quartet. In this the finale drifts away into uncertainty just as the 'Mourning Song' had done thirty years earlier. Bartók had found the political situation in Hungary, and in central Europe generally, since the end of the First World War and the break-up of the Austro-Hungarian Empire increasingly distressing. In 1919, during the short-lived Communist Republic of Councils, he was given an official position on the Music Directorate. But the republic lasted only five months before it was ousted by Admiral Nicholas Horthy, the representative of the armed forces. He conducted a 'white terror' against the communists, disenfranchised the peasants and virtually wiped out liberalism. Aided by the notorious Arrow Cross movement, he ran the country as a semi-fascist dictatorship until the advent of Hitler in 1944. When the Nazis invaded Austria in 1938, Bartók knew that the alliance between Hungary and Germany, which Horthy had concluded, would be strengthened, and that if the Nazis took over he would be declared *persona non grata*. His music had not been blacklisted in Germany because he had not allowed it to be played there during the Nazi regime. He loathed the Nazis so much, he told friends that when they came he would throw in his lot with the Jews though he was not Jewish.

In the five years he spent in America between 1940 and his death in 1945, Bartók completed only two works, the Concerto for Orchestra (1943) for the Boston Symphony Orchestra and the Sonata for unaccompanied violin (1944) for Yehudi Menuhin. His Third Piano Concerto, written for his wife Ditta, was unfinished when he died, and the orchestration of the last seventeen bars had to be undertaken by his friend Tibor Serly. The Violin Sonata, which Bartók knew would be presented as a companion piece for one of Bach's sonatas or partitas for unaccompanied violin, has the intellectual rigour and tonal invention to match its distinguished predecessors. The two concertos, on the other hand, are unashamedly populist.

Like all the composers who fled to America to escape the Nazis or the war, Bartók felt obliged to modify his voice to

Bartók in the late 1930s.

comply with American taste, at least in the public arena. Schoenberg went back to writing tonal music; Hindemith, once the most sardonic of composers, became solemn and weighty; Kurt Weill abandoned art music altogether and devoted himself to Broadway musicals; Benjamin Britten courted success with what amounted to a musical about the American folk hero Paul Bunyan. Even Stravinsky, whose name was on everyone's lips after the release of Walt Disney's *Fantasia* in 1940, felt he had to adjust his tone: after completing his Symphony in C, which he had begun in France, the first work he composed in America was a tango, which he hoped would be taken up by American dance bands. Bartók was not prepared to go as far as this. The bulk of the Concerto for Orchestra makes use of folk music from Hungary and the Balkans in his usual manner. It includes a two-part chromatic melody from Dalmatia, which he had discovered in an American library. However, in the development section of the finale, where he wanted to show off the Boston Symphony's brass, he transformed what might have been a Hungarian folksong into something unmistakably American – not the 'folksy' America Aaron Copland celebrated in *Our Town*, but the exuberant brashness of the big East Coast cities, which Bartók had visited. If the poignant finale of the Sixth Quartet represents his farewell to the Old World, this must surely be his tribute to the New.

Shostakovich in the 1960s.

One unusual feature of the concerto is Bartók's use of parody. Although he was not averse to making fun of himself – as in the finale of his Fifth Quartet, where a vehement passage assumes an air of false innocence on its return – he had never mocked another composer. But here he mocks the way Shostakovich turned a passage in his 'Leningrad' Symphony into what sounds like a Viennese cabaret song. Bartók was astonished that Shostakovich should introduce something so cheap and tasteless into a work about the suffering and heroism of the people of Leningrad. So after quoting the offending passage in the fourth movement of the concerto, Bartók added a raspberry in the form of strident trills. But it seems he was completely mistaken. Late in his life Shostakovich said that the Seventh Symphony was planned before the war and had nothing to do with Hitler's attack. 'I have nothing against calling the Seventh the Leningrad

Symphony,' he said, 'but it's not about Leningrad under siege, it's about the Leningrad that Stalin destroyed and that Hitler merely finished off.' All Shostakovich had been doing was to use the ludicrous to distance himself from the horrific fate of his native city. And Bartók did precisely the same thing in the second and third movements of his Sixth Quartet, a march and a burlesque. He composed them between August and November 1939 – that is to say at the time Hitler invaded Poland. They turned out to be the most sardonic movements he ever produced.

In contrast to Bartók, Shostakovich experienced no difficulty in finding his own voice. This was partly because he had inherited a strong tradition, which he could either embrace or react against; and partly because in the twenties, when he came to maturity, young Russians had a clear vision of what the Revolution stood for and were eager to make its ideals succeed. In those years, Leningrad and Moscow, far from being cut off from what was happening outside Russia, were two of the liveliest and most cosmopolitan artistic centres in the world.

As the symphony Shostakovich composed for his graduation at the Leningrad Conservatory in 1925 makes clear, he chose to react against tradition rather than conserve it. His teacher was Maximilian Shteynberg, Rimsky-Korsakov's son-in-law, a disciplinarian who gave him a rigorous training but did not succeed in arousing his respect for the achievements of the 'Mighty Five' (Balakirev, Borodin, Cui, Musorgsky, and Rimsky-Korsakov). As a child of the Revolution, Shostakovich had no time for folk music and the cultivation of the exotic. He belonged to the generation that had rebelled against the past. Communism was an international movement, which spurned the individualistic, bourgeois values of the Romantics. Shostakovich was able to hear all the latest pieces by most of the advanced composers of the time – Bartók, Berg, Hindemith, Krenek and 'Les Six', as well as Prokofiev and Stravinsky, the 'foreign' Russians; and while none of them had a direct influence on his style, he was nevertheless deeply in sympathy with the 'objective' and frequently satirical nature of the music they were producing.

Shteynberg called the compositions Shostakovich submitted to him during his student days 'grotesque', and this was the word that Shostakovich himself used to describe the first two

Red Square in Moscow, 1932.

movements of his graduation symphony. But even at the time the description must have seemed far-fetched: at best they are no more than jaunty. Yet they might have sounded grotesque to someone of the old school, who believed that at least the first movement of a symphony ought to be a serious affair, capable of establishing a dialectic. In all probability, Shostakovich was merely being ironic; his jauntiness could be interpreted as a criticism of the pomposity encountered in the symphonies of the Rimsky school. Irony was a weapon he always had at his disposal, and in later works it can darken into biting satire, which at times does indeed deserve the description 'grotesque'. On these occasions, however, it is nearly always levelled against political or social conditions. Shteynberg's pomposity merited only mild mockery. Eventually, in the last two movements, the First Symphony does become dramatic and serious. The drama stems from a short fanfare figure, first introduced by the trumpets in counterpoint with a long melodic line near the beginning of the third movement. This gradually develops until in the last movement it explodes: the orchestra is silenced to allow the timpani to pound out the figure in its inverted form as loudly as possible. The effect is like the heralding of a momentous event. Within seconds the mood changes to one of triumph, and the listener might be left wondering whether Shostakovich was referring to the guns of the cruiser *Aurora* firing to support the Bolsheviks in 1917. If this is so then the First Symphony is not as abstract as is usually thought. It could well be as Revolutionary as the Second and Third symphonies, which were written to celebrate (respectively) the tenth anniversary in 1927 of the October Revolution and the May Day celebrations of 1929. Both works end with Revolutionary choruses and begin with satires. But the satire is not directed against musical convention: the victim is the tsarist regime, which, according to the view commonly held by communists in the twenties, had been in a perpetual state of chaos.

Musicians were not alone in trying to express this view. An example in another art form may be found in a series of illustrations by the constructivist painter El Lissitzky for a children's book, *The Story of the Two Squares*, published in 1922. A black square and a red square are hurtling through space towards a red circle containing a host of geometrical shapes in total disarray. The black square proves powerless, but the red square crashes into the circle, scatters all the shapes, and eventually puts everything in order. In both the Second and Third symphonies chaos is represented by a dissonant instrumental prelude, containing none of the thematic development usually associated with the symphony, order by a rousing chorus for the triumphant Revolutionaries in a straightforward diatonic style. In both works the instrumental prelude leads straight into the chorus; in the Second Symphony the section leading to the entrance of the chorus begins with a trio of solo violin, clarinet and bassoon playing ungainly lines that are melodically, harmonically and rhythmically quite independent of one another. Gradually more and more instruments join in with equally independent lines to create even more dissonance. At the climax, a factory whistle sounds, the jangle of noise is silenced, and the chorus sing: 'O Lenin, you forged freedom from our torment . . . Nobody will ever deprive us of the victory over oppression and darkness . . . May the name of this victory be October.'

Shostakovich's two operas, *The Nose* and *The Lady Macbeth*

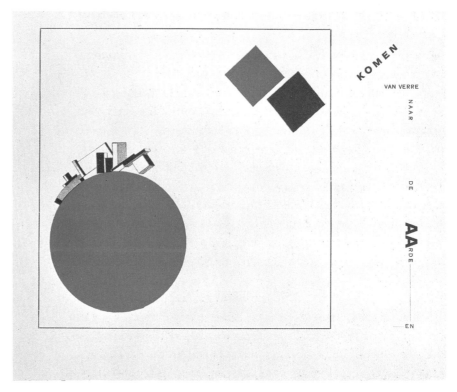

KOMEN
VAN VERRE
NAAR
DE
AArde
EN

El Lissitzky's illustration to *The Story of the Two Squares*, 1922. The red and black squares fly through space to attack the red circle.

of the Mtsensk District, the most important works he composed in the late twenties and early thirties, also satirize the old regime. But both texts are based on nineteenth century stories, so neither work can end with a rousing Revolutionary chorus. Shostakovich's concern is with the sufferings of particular characters. Whereas Sergei Einsenstein, in his film *The Battleship Potemkin*, could depict the misery of the masses, such large-scale themes are beyond the scope of opera, for in opera the main interest lies in the voices of individuals. Musorgsky's *Boris Godunov* may open on a crowd scene, where the wretched citizens, attacked with whips by the police, cry out for pity, but ultimately it is Boris himself – murderer and tyrant though he is – who becomes the focus of our sympathy.

The Nose is based on Gogol's farcical story about the nose of a civil servant which gets detached from the face of its owner, Major Kovalyov, and takes on a life of its own, strolling about the streets of St Petersburg in uniform, only to be chased by the police when the major starts the hunt for it. Eventually the police capture and beat it to death, willed on by the crowd shouting 'Take that, take that, and that!' It is undoubtedly the most 'grotesque' piece Shostakovich ever composed, not only in terms of its action but also its music. And yet in his *Testimony*, written near the end of his life, he maintained that what he wrote was essentially serious. '*The Nose* is a horror story, not a joke,' he said. 'How can police oppression be funny?' Shostakovich was only twenty-one when he began composing the opera and it may be thought that he deliberately set out to shock; but in fact his main concern was not so much with the outrageous behaviour of St Petersburg society in the first half of the nineteenth century, as with the plight of the nose and its owner. What started out as farce, ends up as tragedy.

No such transformation characterizes *The Lady Macbeth of the Mtsensk District*, however. From the moment the curtain rises it is clear that the action will begin and end tragically. Shostakovich intended this to be the first of three operas about the position of women in Russia. He chose to base it on Nikolai Leskov's story of the same title because, although he had to alter the plot to present the heroine more sympathetically, he believed it to be the best portrayal he had found of the plight of a woman in pre-Revolutionary Russia. The essential thing, he believed, was to treat the subject from a Soviet point of view. The tragic heroine is Katerina Ismailova, a vivacious young woman, whose life is stifled by the narrow, bourgeois world into which she has

Valerii Todorovsky's 1994 film of *Katia Ismaïlova*, from Leskov's story of *The Lady Macbeth of the Mtsensk District*.

been thrust. Her husband is a pompous bore, she has no children, and Boris, her lecherous father-in-law, lusts after her but cannot speak to her without shouting. The only light in her life is Sergei, a dashing young clerk whom her husband has engaged. When he is mercilessly flogged on Boris's orders, Katerina murders her father-in-law with rat poison. Later, when Sergei and she are interrupted in their love-making by her husband, she assists Sergei to strangle him. Eventually the two are tried and deported to Siberia, but on the way Sergei abandons her for another woman prisoner. Katerina's last act is to drown the woman and then herself.

Shostakovich said that as far as the musical language was concerned everything he wrote for Katerina was designed to attract our sympathy. 'She has a great deal of soft, warm lyricism, sincere and intimated grief, and much joy in her happy moments. All of her music has as its purpose the justification of her crimes.' The other characters, on the other hand, are satirized, even distorted – not least Sergei, whom Shostakovich considered 'a cruel and hideous criminal who oozes the future kulak'. The kulaks were 'enemies of the state', those peasants whom Stalin ordered to be liquidated in 1929 because they resisted collectivization. Shostakovich not only considered Sergei to be the model of a kulak, he also called Boris 'a typical master kulak'.

When the opera was performed in 1934, first in Leningrad and two days later in Moscow, it was immediately recognized as a masterpiece wholly in line with Soviet policy. Ivan Sollertinsky, the leading Soviet music and theatre critic of the twenties and thirties, said 'The staggering realism, the broad scope of its historical theme, the scale of the satirical unmaskings, and its tragic sweep, more Shakespearian than Leskovian – all this is on a plane unprecedented in Soviet music.' However, when Stalin attended a performance at the Bolshoi on 26 January 1936, he and the government delegation attending him walked out after the third of the four acts. A few days later an article appeared in *Pravda* entitled 'Muddle instead of Music', utterly condemning the opera and ending with the threat that unless the composer changed his ways 'things could end very badly'. A fortnight later there was an equally vitriolic attack on Shostakovich's ballet *The Limpid Stream* about life on a collective farm. Everyone assumed that the articles were written by Stalin himself, but in all likelihood they were the work of a journalist writing on Stalin's instructions. Stalin probably felt that there was an urgent need to condemn *Lady Macbeth* and have it removed from the stage because the third act contains a satirical attack on the police; as he had lately ordered the police to carry out purges following the assassination of Sergei Kirov in December 1934, anything that might undermine their authority was to be suppressed. The opera was therefore a 'cacophonous, a pornographic insult to the Soviet people'. Shostakovich was hauled in front of a special conference of the Composers' Union and vilified. 'From that moment on,' he said, 'I was stuck with the label "enemy of the people", and I don't need to explain what that label meant in those days.'

Rather than give in to despair, Shostakovich turned to the completion of his Fourth Symphony, which he had begun the previous year. But during the rehearsals by the Leningrad Philharmonic in the autumn, rumours circulated to the effect that he had defied the criticism and written an extremely complex work which was 'chock-a-block full of formalism'. On the orders of the Composers' Union, Shostakovich was obliged to withdraw it, and it was not performed until December 1961. Yet, had the Composers' Union not intervened in 1936, Shostakovich would almost certainly have been liquidated. The rumours were true, and if the work had been performed not even his friend, Marshal Mikhail Tukhachevsky, one of the Red Army's most senior and highly respected officers, could have saved him. The official policy set out at the 1930 Congress on Proletarian Art, held in Kharkov, was that art should have a political and social purpose. It was a 'class weapon'. It should not be concerned with what artists felt as individuals. All petit-bourgeois attitudes, all remnants of individualism should be eliminated. As if in direct defiance of this diktat the Fourth is Shostakovich's most Mahlerian symphony, huge in both its dimensions and its scoring, teeming with ideas, full of self-mockery, very volatile and

Shostakovich in 1943, at the time of composing the Eighth Symphony.

The end of the Fourth Symphony reminds me of Shostakovich's words at the end of *Testimony*. In one of the bitterest closings to an autobiography I've ever read it says, 'I wanted to put this down in order to save future generations from the bitterness which has turned my whole life grey.'

highly personal – personal in the sense that its satire is not directed against some social folly but against ideas he himself initiates in the music. During the course of the work, however, the lampoons and distortions become less biting and more light-hearted, and at the end – as in Mahler's *Das Lied von der Erde* – the music drifts away into the silence. What Stalin required, by contrast, was optimistic, easily digested music to spur the workers on in their battle to turn Russia into an industrial power and fulfil the second five-year plan.

After the symphony's withdrawal, Shostakovich had three options: he could give up composition altogether; he could capitulate to Stalin's demands; or he could play a game of double bluff – appear to conform with official policy, but beneath the surface allow his capacity for irony free rein. When the Fifth Symphony was first performed in 1937 it seemed he had chosen the second option. It is all of a piece. Apart from an affectionate parody of a Mahlerian *Ländler*, satire is eliminated, there are no dislocations to disturb the even flow, and the mainly diatonic material can be easily assimilated. The phrase 'a Soviet artist's reply to just criticism' was coined by a journalist, but Shostakovich let it stand and it is always quoted as if he had said it himself. What in fact he did say was, 'The theme of my Fifth Symphony is the making of a man. I saw man with all his experiences in the centre of the composition, which is lyrical in form from beginning to end. In the finale, the tragically tense impulses of the earlier movements are resolved in optimism and joy of living.' It could be argued that Shostakovich would have adopted an easier style even if Stalin had not intervened. Most composers modified their styles in the mid-thirties. There was a turning away from the hard-edged, parodistic objectivity that had been the fashion during the twenties and early thirties. Composers felt the need to integrate themselves more closely with tradition. This was certainly Bartók's approach in the *Music for Strings, Percussion and Celesta*. But Bartók

Alisa Poret's painting of Shostakovich and the grotesque.

modified his style gradually, whereas Shostakovich appeared to make a sudden reversal. Perhaps this was what the Russian musical public wanted, for the first performance of the Fifth proved to be a huge success. Perhaps they felt relieved that Shostakovich was prepared to toe the line. But how many, it might be wondered, detected the hollowness of 'the optimism and joy of living' in the closing pages. Shostakovich himself admitted that the rejoicing was forced, 'created under a threat as in *Boris Godunov*', he said. 'It's as if someone were beating you with a stick and saying, "Your business is rejoicing, your business is rejoicing" and you rise, shakily, and go marching off muttering, "Our business is rejoicing, our business is rejoicing."'

The rejoicing in the finale of the Sixth Symphony, which Shostakovich completed in the summer of 1939, is even more forced. The symphony lacks an opening allegro, and because the slow movement that stands in its place is longer and much more weighty than the scherzo and finale put together, the work has been called lopsided. Normally a symphony's first movement gives us hints of what we are likely to encounter in the following movements. This is why first movements are usually so varied: they present material that could easily turn into a slow movement, a scherzo and a finale. But here the opening slow movement seems to have no connection whatsoever with what follows. Its deeply private introspection gives no hint of the 'demonic energy' of the scherzo or the 'flippant hilarity' of the finale, as one of Shostakovich's biographers has so aptly put it.

Shostakovich said that when he was writing the first movement he had in his mind the summary execution of his friend Marshal Tukhachevsky in June 1937, and the events following the attack on him in *Pravda*. In the eighteen months that separated those two events he felt that he had lost control of his life. 'My past was crossed out,' he said, 'my work, my abilities, turned out to be worthless to everyone. The future didn't look any less bleak. At that moment I desperately wanted to disappear, it was the only way out.' The movement is dominated by the interval of a minor third. It starts with a lengthy paragraph which soon reaches a climax. At first the overall mood is far from gloomy or despondent. But after a lyrical second subject and a series of ominous trills there follows a long, sad tune on

The conductor Kurt Sanderling says of Shostakovich, 'If the music smiles, don't trust it for a moment.'

Around this time, for fifteen or more years, Shostakovich had a bag packed by the front door of his flat, waiting for the call in the middle of the night.

the cor anglais over a march-like rhythm, which has all the hall-marks of a Mahlerian funeral march. From that point on, apart from a moment of consolation when the first subject returns for the recapitulation, the music becomes increasingly more inward and despairing.

When he was at his lowest ebb during 1936–7, Shostakovich remembered the advice of his friend Mikhail Zoshchenko, the popular humorist: 'A beggar stops worrying as soon as he becomes a beggar, and a roach isn't terribly upset by being a roach. Life goes on.' Perhaps this dictum partly accounts for the dramatic change of mood between the first and second movements of the Sixth Symphony. But does it explain why, after the 'demonic energy' of the scherzo, Shostakovich should want to end with a finale that is so blatantly brash and vulgar? Apparently it was encored at the first performance in November 1939. In August of that year, Stalin had signed a non-aggression pact with the Nazis, and a few weeks later a treaty of friendship. Henceforth no one was allowed to speak ill of Hitler. Stalin ordered that he was to be referred to as 'our sworn friend'. The threat of war had receded. There was therefore cause for celebration, but only those who were musically insensitive could have failed to hear the grotesque irony in Shostakovich's work.

If Shostakovich thought the authorities had been placated in 1937, he was mistaken. In February 1948, he had to weather an even greater storm. A decree issued by the Central Committee of the Party accused Shostakovich, Prokofiev, Shebalin and Khachaturian, among others, of having 'formalist tendencies'. They were dismissed from their teaching posts, deprived of a regular income and had their music proscribed. The decree was one of a number issued on Stalin's instructions after the war. The first was directed against the writers Anna Akhmatova and Mikhail Zoshchenko, who were accused of 'bourgeois degeneracy' and effectively deprived of a living. Other decrees were directed against film directors, theatre producers and playwrights. Eventually virtually all the intelligentsia, including scientists and doctors, were purged. At a specially convened conference of the Composers' Union, Shostakovich was forced to read a repentance speech written by union officials and to pronounce himself willing to write for the people and follow party directives. From then until the death of Stalin in 1953, his public work consisted of film music and simplistic pieces such as *The Song of the Forests* celebrating Stalin as 'the great gardener' who had converted the steppes into forests. He was able to get his Twenty-Four Preludes and Fugues (1950–51) performed, but most of the music he wanted to write was confined to a drawer. Among the pieces he had hidden away were his Fourth and Fifth string quartets (1949 and 1952), and a satirical piece for four basses, choir and piano called *Rayok* (The Peepshow). This came to light only after his death. Shostakovich kept it hidden because it satirizes speeches made by Andrei Zhdanov and Dmitri Shepilov at the convocation set up in January 1948 to look into 'formalism' in music.

Rayok is modelled on a satire of the same name by Musorgsky, which pokes fun at four members of the music profession in the 1860s and 1870s: a professor who confuses music with theology and sings in the style of Handel; a critic who worships Adelina Patti; a critic who confesses to being the enemy of all innovation; and a boring composer who thinks himself a Titan. Shostakovich, however, confines himself to lampooning three eminent musicians of his day: Onesy, Twosy and Threesy – that is, Stalin, Zhdanov and Shepilov. Using Stalin's favourite tune, *Suliko*, Onesy keeps on repeating the words 'Popular composers write realistic music, anti-popular composers write formalist music.' Twosy begins with vocal exercises to prove that he is a singer and then when he has warmed up launches into 'Music without harmony, music without melody, unaesthetic music, antipathetic music, can be compared to a dentist's drill. It is utter balderdash.' Threesy embarks on a folksong used by Glinka in *Kamarinskaya* and urges his comrades to follow what the classic Russians: 'Glinka, Tchaikovsky and Rimsky-Korsakov,' he calls out, 'you are marvellously melodic. The very fibres of our being tremble when listening to you.' Finally the president of the assembly and the chorus warn composers to be vigilant because, if they are not, they can expect a lengthy spell in a labour camp. The satire is hardly subtle, but then neither is Musorgsky's. It was simply a means to let off steam in private.

Musorgsky was the only member of the 'Mighty Five' that Shostakovich revered. As well as reorchestrating *Boris Godunov*

Andrei Zhdanov, author of the 1948 decree against formalism in music.

Shostakovich with his son, the conductor Maxim, in 1972.

in 1939, and editing and reorchestrating *Khovanshchina* for a film in 1958, he also orchestrated *Songs and Dances of Death*. He said that working with Musorgsky's music clarified something important for him in own work. *Boris* lies behind his Seventh, Eighth and Eleventh symphonies; *Khovanshchina* behind the Thirteenth and the cantata *The Execution of Stepan Razin*; the *Songs and Dances of Death* behind the Fourteenth. The Fourteenth Symphony was composed in 1969. Shostakovich called it a symphony, but it is really a song cycle for soprano, bass, string orchestra and percussion. The texts are mostly translations of poems by Apollinaire, Lorca and Rilke, which deal with the cruelty and finality of death. In the last song, when the two soloists sing of all-powerful death keeping watch even in the hour of happiness, the peremptory sound of a woodblock suggests that death is already knocking at the door. There is no escape, nor is there any consolation: for Shostakovich death is not the beginning of an afterlife. Shostakovich said that everything he had written up to then merely served as a preparation for this work. At times it may be macabre, even gruesome, but unlike most of his earlier music, it is totally devoid of irony or satire. Death cannot be mocked.

The only Russian poem in the set is by the early nineteenth-century Estonian poet Wilhelm Küchelbecker, who was facing death along with his friend Anton Delvig, to whom the poem is addressed, after the failure of the December revolt in 1825. Both were members of a society of officers who had been calling for increased constitutional liberties and some form of representative government. For three weeks after the death of Alexander I in 1825 there was no monarch on the throne and the Decembrists saw this as an opportunity to establish a national assembly. But they had made no adequate preparations, had no plan of action and were brutally crushed by the forces of the future Tsar Nicholas I. Five were hanged, the remainder deported to Siberia to meet their deaths there. 'But', asks Küchelbecker, 'why the persecutions? The satires of Juvenal made tyrants tremble, but what is the reward for poets and those who have lofty ideals now? The only things that can never die are their sweet poetry and inspiring deeds. There is a union between those who follow the muses. Free, proud and joyful, it will always remain firm.'

Shostakovich must have felt that he too was of this fraternity, for his setting of the text is one of his most passionate and intense utterances. He places it at the climax of the cycle, where it follows a poem by Apollinaire, based on a painting by Efimovich Repin that depicts a group of Zaporozhian Cossacks sentenced to death for writing an insulting letter to the sultan of Constantinople. But as Shostakovich has explained, and the setting makes clear, the nature of their crime is not a cause for amusement: his music is his personal protest 'against those butchers who execute people'.

Lutosławski in 1953.

Russian composers were not the only ones to find their music proscribed as a result of the 1948 decree. In May of that year, at the Second International Congress of Composers held in Prague, the Polish delegation decided to follow the Russian example and insist that Polish composers should conform to 'socialist realism'. Witold Lutosławski (1913–1994) was then thirty-five; the First Symphony, composed between 1941 and 1947, had just been performed at Katowice and was about to be given again at the Kraków Festival. Fortunately for him, those who had the power to proscribe the work were not present. But they were when it was given in Warsaw eighteen months later. The vice-minister of culture said that Lutosławski ought to be thrown under a street-car; the work was declared formalist and banned.

Like Bartók, it took Lutosławski some time to discover his own style. Poland offered little in the way of a musical tradition, and the volatile political climate was devoid of idealism to provide an external stimulus. The only composers of any distinction in the thirties, Karol Szymanowski and Witold Maliszewski (Lutosławski's teacher at the Warsaw Conservatory), were writing in styles that had no potential for future development. For his early works, Lutosławski had no models other than those he

There is something shining and glittering and flying about Lutosławski's best work. He says, 'I would like to make music that carries the plus sign, not the minus sign.'

149

Lutosławski at the time of the world première of *Livre pour Orchestre*, 1968.

found in early Stravinsky and French composers such as Debussy, Ravel and Albert Roussel (1869–1937), whose Third Symphony and Sinfonietta for strings were of particular value when he came to write his Symphony.

Lutosławski's first important work was a set of Symphonic Variations completed in 1938, where the influence of Stravinsky and Roussel is particularly evident, especially in the brilliant scoring. It contains two features of significance for Lutosławski's future development: one is the contrast between the diatonic, simple, folk-like theme and the chromatic, kaleidoscopic and highly sophisticated variations; the other the isolation of three of the theme's notes, G#–A–E (a rising semitone followed by a falling fourth), to provide a point of focus as the music unfolds. They illustrate the fact that, however complex Lutosławski's music may be at times, there is always something very clear and memorable to hold on to. In the First Symphony, where the harmony is often atonal, he provides other versions of those easily recognizable intervals at focal points. In the first movement, they are a falling semitone and a rising fourth (F–E–A); in the slow second movement the fourth is expanded into a tritone (F–B–C); and in the finale, after a great deal of scurrying activity, the harmonic tension of the whole symphony is resolved when the semitone becomes a whole tone (A–E–F♯). Lutosławski thinks of intervals as having their own physiognomy, colour or 'atmosphere'. He describes the atmosphere created by perfect fifths, fourths and major seconds as being pure and serene, while that produced by semitones and tritones (augmented fourths and diminished fifths) is tense.

The proscription of the First Symphony was effectively the second occasion when Lutosławski's music had been banned. During the war, when the Nazis occupied Poland, no Polish music of any kind was permitted to be performed, including that of Chopin. Musical performances took place only in cafés, where Lutosławski scraped a living as a pianist. He and his keyboard partner, Andrzej Panufnik, managed to give the first performance of his Variations on a Theme by Paganini (1941) for two pianos at one of these café concerts in 1941; but this was the only work he had performed, other than his arrangements of pieces by Bach, Brahms, Schubert, Tchaikovsky and the like. After the banning of his symphony, Lutosławski made his living mainly from writing songs for children, many of them based on folksongs. 'Piosenka o złotym listku' ('Song of the golden leaf'), the second in a set of four songs published in 1951, has a simple diatonic melody in E minor, set off by a chromatic accompanying line beginning and ending on B and built entirely from semitones and minor thirds. This procedure is not unlike what Bartók had done in 'Mourning Song', except that here, instead of polymodality, the emphasis is on the consistency of the intervals in the accompaniment.

Despite the fact that Bartók's most interesting music – the music he composed in the twenties and thirties – was also declared formalist by the authorities, Lutosławski was familiar with it and it influenced him profoundly. It was through Bartók that he ultimately found his voice. In his Overture for strings, composed in 1949, the basic motif is a tight cell consisting again of two intervals, in this instance tone and semitone (B–A♯–G♯–A). In characteristically Bartókian manner, Lutosławski immediately inverts the motif (C–D♭–E♭–D). But instead of varying the intervals by transposing the motif to other modes, as Bartók would have done, Lutosławski preserves the intervals and uses the motif as a consistent point of reference. A similar procedure informs his Concerto for Orchestra, completed in 1954, but in this case the points of reference are mostly phrases or melodies rather than tight cells. All the tunes are diatonic or modal, and at least one is a genuine folksong. The work is indebted to Bartók's Concerto for Orchestra in that both are virtuoso pieces designed to have popular appeal. Lutosławski's is cast in three movements, two fairly short ternary movements and a long third movement: the third is longer than the other two put together and moves purposefully to a climactic chorale, which recalls the chorale in the second movement of Bartók's concerto.

The Concerto for Orchestra made Lutosławski's name, won him prizes in Poland and eventually led to the lifting of the ban on the First Symphony. But far more important for the development of his style was *Muzyka żalobna* ('Musique funèbre' or 'Music for mourning'), the third of the pieces indebted directly to Bartók. The work was written to mark the tenth anniversary of Bartók's death in 1955, but was not completed until three years later. *Music for Mourning* takes the first movement of Bartók's *Music for Strings, Percussion and Celesta* as its model, but because Lutosławski divides his tribute into four sections ('Prologue', 'Metamorphoses', 'Apogeum' and 'Epilogue'), it comes out at more than double the length of Bartók's movement. As in the Bartók, each string part is divided into two sections, but because a dramatic dialogue would be unsuitable for a memorial the players sit in the usual semi-circle.

The whole piece is based on the intervals of a semitone and a tritone, and this pairing not only underpins the structure but helps to create a consistent harmonic colour. Out of the two intervals – and for the first and only time in his life – Lutosławski made a twelve-note row (F–B–B♭–E–E♭–A–A♭–D–D♭–G–G♭–C). This row and its inversion are presented in the 'Prologue' not in the form of a fugue, as in Bartók's work, but as a series of canons, in two, three, four and finally six parts. Lutosławski said that his purpose was to create a harmony entirely devoid of thirds and

The Concerto for Orchestra's note row.

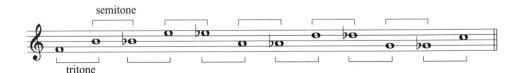

sixths, an 'open sonority' suitable for the act of mourning. The climax of the 'Prologue' consists of the notes F and B being pounded out in four different rhythms. In the 'Metamorphoses' the row is transposed through the cycle of fifths, as in Bartók's fugue, but here it is used as a frame for an increasing number of added notes so that the repetitions get longer and richer as the section unfolds. The metamorphoses also involve the note values, which make the music get faster and faster until eventually a climax is reached in a huge twelve-note chord. As might be expected in a work designed as a tribute to Bartók, this climax (the 'apogee') occurs at the

In 1968, examining sketches.

dividing point of the Golden Section that underlies the structure. Gradually the chord is reduced to a single note, at which point the whole orchestra plays in unison the twelve-note melody that began the work. The effect calls to mind the sonorous transformation of Bartók's fugue in the finale of *Music for Strings, Percussion and Celesta*, except that here the mood is more sombre. To bring the work to a conclusion, Lutosławski follows Bartók's example by placing his canons in reverse order, until only a single cello is left to carry the music into the silence.

To all intents and purposes Lutosławski's musical identity was now established, but a further key element remained to be added – the use of 'aleatoric' or chance operations. He was introduced to these in 1960, when he heard on the radio a performance of John Cage's Concerto for prepared piano and chamber orchestra (1951). The fact that he could even contemplate making use of the avant-garde techniques current in the music of the West is an indication of a change in the political climate in Poland in the fifties. After the death of Bolesław Bierut, the Stalinist first secretary of the Polish Communist Party in February 1956, there was a perceptible thaw in the attitude of the Polish authorities. Within a matter of months the Polish Composers' Union had organized the Warsaw Autumn Festival of Contemporary Music, which took place in the October of that year. During the next few decades, this festival was the one and only place where the composers of the Eastern bloc could hear what was – and what had been – happening in the West; at the first festival, for instance, *The Rite of Spring* was performed for the first time in Poland. By the mid-sixties, after experimenting with virtually every avant-garde technique developed in the West since the beginning of the century, Polish composers such as Zygmunt Krauze, Krzysztof Penderecki and Kazimierz Serocki had become some of the most progressive in Europe, and a steady stream of composition students from the West were going to Poland to complete their studies.

In the spring of 1950, Cage drew up a series of large charts on which he could plot rhythmic structures. The following year, when he came to write the Concerto for prepared piano, he decided that instead of composing music according to his own taste he could compose according to arbitrary moves on the charts. He followed the concerto with *Music of Changes* where all the procedures are the result of the tossing of coins. Lutosławski, however, never wanted to forfeit control over pitch. All he wanted was a way of loosening his control over rhythm. He realized that in passages which did not need to be rhythmically tight the texture would be richer and less predictable if the players had the freedom to play the notes in their own time and independently of one another. For example, instead of writing out those canons in *Music for Mourning* he could have left to the players to produce a canonic texture; the counterpoint would not have been strict but the texture would almost certainly have been unexpected.

The first of Lutosławski's works where the instrumentalists have this freedom is *Gry weneckie* ('Jeux vénitiens' or 'Venetian games'; 1961), a work in four short movements scored for chamber orchestra. The first movement is in eight sections, the odd-numbered ones being active, the even-numbered ones somewhat passive. In the odd-numbered sections seven woodwind instruments play *ad libitum* the same nine motifs in different orders and slightly different rhythms, so that the likelihood of them all playing the same motif in the same way at the same time is very small indeed. The harmony consists of two superimposed twelve-note chords symmetrically arranged around a horizontal axis. But not all the notes in this huge twenty-four-note chord sound at the same time, so that the harmony is never stable. The even-numbered sections consist of eight-note semitone clusters

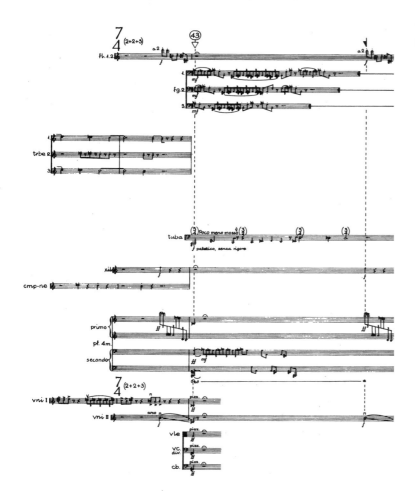

The freely independent lines of
the Third Symphony, 1983.

played quietly by the strings; as the section progresses the clusters are slowly transposed, so here the harmony does change. Each section begins with a loud, percussive signal which occurs without warning. The effect is like one of those children's games where, on a given signal, the players have to switch from one movement to another like clockwork; those who fail to respond immediately are out. In the fully notated third movement, where the piano supplies a simple melodic background for a long tune on the flute and a simultaneous elaboration of the tune on the harp, the texture is very close to heterophony – the simultaneous performance of the same melody in different ways by different instruments. All traditional African and Asian

He said once that he wished he could wake up in a new Renaissance time and find that all the music that was being played was contemporary music. 'Nowadays,' he said, 'we feel like the mustard at the great feast of music, and you know everybody dreams of being beefsteak sometimes.'

music for ensembles of instruments is based on heterophony, the most familiar being the music of the Indonesian gamelan, where a basic or 'nuclear' melody, played slowly and without embellishment, is elaborated by different instruments, each playing in a way suited to its range, speed of 'speaking' and tone quality.

Later, in works such the Preludes and Fugue for thirteen solo strings (1970–72), Lutosławski made the heterophony easier to follow. The first subject of the fugue, for instance, is played by a viola and two cellos. The nuclear melody, like the basic melody in *Music for Mourning*, consists only of semitones and tritones, but the three instruments play it in different rhythms. Lutosławski specifies the note values, but there are no bar lines and the instruments need not be rigid in their interpretation of the values. What the listener hears is a subtle counterpoint produced by three versions of the same tune. When the next fugal voice enters it too is presented in heterophonic fashion by three instruments, and so on. This means that when all four voices of the four-part exposition are playing there are not four lines of counterpoint but twelve. The fugue has six fugal expositions, each one having a subject of a different character: *cantabile*, *grazioso*, *lamentoso*, *misterioso*, *estatico* and *furioso*. In the section leading up to the climax, all six reappear in stretto (that is, they follow each other in quick succession). But because they are clearly differentiated and Lutosławski had such a wonderful ear, the texture, although palpitating with life, never feels cluttered.

The work is the longest Lutosławski composed. The idea of basing a work on the standard prelude and fugue (which we have come to associate most strongly with Bach) stemmed from his long preoccupation with bipartite structures, the first part being introductory, the second tightly constructed and containing the climax. His interest in this kind of structure can be traced back to the Concerto for Orchestra. Of course, the standard prelude and fugue is too short for a major work, so Lutosławski extends the structure to seven preludes, lasting over a quarter of an hour, and a fugue with six subjects lasting another quarter of an hour or more. This basic two-part structure also underpins the Third Symphony, which Lutosławski composed in 1981–3 for the Chicago Symphony Orchestra. Here, part one consists of an introduction and first movement, part two of the main movement plus an epilogue and coda, the two parts being played without a break. To articulate the structure, Lutosławski makes use of a peremptory signal, a very rapid rat-tat-tat-tat on the note E, played initially by clarinets, trumpets, trombones and xylophone. It functions very much like the signal in the first movement of *Jeux vénitiens*, but the context here is far from playful. Every time the signal occurs the music has to change or make a new start. It is as if events were being controlled by some dictatorial authority, who has only to rap on the table to command obedience from his minions. Had the work been written by an American or a Westerner, one might have thought the composer had borrowed the rat-tat-tat-tat from the law courts or the school classroom; but knowing that it was written by someone from eastern Europe, at a time when his country was under martial law, a more sinister interpretation might enter the listener's head. Lutosławski insisted that when he was composing he lived in an internal world that had nothing in common with the world in which we live. But it is hard to avoid the conclusion that, like Bartók and Shostakovich, his work was touched from time to time by the harsh realities of politics and oppression.

Chapter 6
America

During the second half of the nineteenth century most American music was under the influence of German culture. Most orchestral players were German as were most conductors. But in 1902 the pianist and composer, William Mason, could say in his book *Memories of a Musical Life*:

Enormous progress in the art and science of music has been made in America since I began my studies in Germany in the year 1849. There are now teachers of the piano of the first rank in all of our principal cities, who secure better results with American pupils than foreign teachers do, because they have a better understanding of out national character and temperament. Our country has also produced composers of the first rank, and the names MacDowell, Parker, Kelley, Whiting, Paine, Buck, Shelley, Chadwick, Brockway, and Foote occur at once to the mind.

Yet most of the composers Mason lists had, like him, to go to Germany for their training. The exception was Arthur Foote, who received his grounding in academic harmony and counterpoint at Harvard, where John Knowles Paine (1839–1906) had been teaching since 1862. Harvard eventually appointed Paine America's first full professor of music, and in his inaugural lecture he made it clear that, although he disapproved of some of its contemporary music, the German tradition was the only one he could relate to. 'Wagner, Liszt and their adherents', he said, 'have become so extremely involved and complicated, both in composition and performance that there must soon be a healthy reaction. The only hope for the present and future is the adherence to the historical forms as developed by Bach, Handel, Mozart and Beethoven.'

The first composer to break away from the German style and create something specifically American was Charles Ives. He gave notice of his intention when, as a lad of seventeen, he wrote a comic set of variations for organ on the tune known as *America*, which lampooned the Germanic seriousness of Paine's Concert Variations for organ on the Austrian national anthem.

It's tempting to think of American classical music as just one rugged individualist after another. In truth it's essentially a dialogue between different cultures thrown together at great speed.

If European art was a very long marinated casserole, then American art is the fastest, most brilliant stir-fry.

Just about all the various types of academic counterpoint are parodied; on several occasions the tune is cast in rhythms more suitable for down-town taverns than the organ loft; and to cap it all, he even includes passages in several keys.

Unlike their European counterparts, American composers had no indigenous folk tradition to make use of. Immigrants had brought their own folk music with them, but it belonged to the old country and identified national groupings within America, not the country as a whole. The music which took the place of folk music for most Americans was popular music. The editors of *Harper's New Monthly Magazine* knew this when writing about the music of Stephen Foster in 1854: 'The air is full of his melodies. They are whistled, and sung, and played on all instruments everywhere. Their simple pathos touches every heart. They are our national music.' Later the spiritual songs of the African slaves took on this role, and at the end of the century, Gospel hymns, ragtime and the marches of Sousa were added to the corpus of music thought to be characteristically American.

In the twentieth century, jazz and the blues joined the canon.

The 'folk music' that Ives drew on was the music he got to know as a boy in a small New England town and later at Yale – the songs of Stephen Foster, Gospel hymns, ragtime, university fraternity songs. Typical is the material he uses in his Orchestral Set no. 2 (1915). The first movement, 'An Elegy to our Forefathers', consists of fragments of 'plantation' songs by Stephen Foster – mainly snatches of two of Foster's best-known songs of mourning, *Old Black Joe* and *Massa's in de cold, cold ground* – placed in a highly evocative polytonal context. The title of the second movement, 'The Rockstrewn Hills Join in the People's Outdoor Meeting', is a reference to the revivalist services that took place in the open air, where the hymn singing was totally uninhibited, with none of the constraints imposed by the confined space of a church. To convey the spontaneous, unbuttoned atmosphere of these services, Ives casts two revivalist hymns, *Bringing in the sheaves* and *I hear Thy welcome voice*, in ragtime. He was not being sacrilegious. For Ives, the religious and secular could be equated: what mattered was 'the feeling behind the notes', the realization that in spirit the singing of revivalist hymns at a camp meeting was fundamentally no different from improvising ragtime in a tavern. And this apparent incongruity is carried over into the third movement, which opens with a verse and a half of the *Te Deum* ('We praise Thee, O Lord'), and then goes into a heartfelt version of *In the sweet by and by*. Ives called this movement 'From Hanover Square North at the End of a Tragic Day, the Voice of the People again Arose'. The day in question was 8 May 1915. At 9.30 that morning New Yorkers heard about the sinking of the SS *Lusitania* by a German torpedo, with the loss of 1198 lives, including 114 Americans. The event made a deep impression on Ives, not only because of its implications for the future, but because of the sense of unity he witnessed that day as he went home from the insurance office where he worked.

Charles Ives.

I remember, going downtown to business, the people on the street and elevated train had something in their faces that was not the usual something. Everybody who came into the office, whether they spoke about the disaster or not, showed a realization of seriously experiencing something. That it meant war is what the faces said, if the tongues didn't. Leaving the office and going uptown about six o'clock, I took the Third Avenue L at Hanover Square Station. As I came on the platform, there was quite a crowd waiting for the trains, which had been blocked lower down, and while waiting there, a hand-organ or hurdy-gurdy was playing in the street below. Some workmen sitting on the side of the tracks began to whistle the tune, and others began to sing or hum the refrain. A workman with a shovel on his shoulder came on the platform and joined in the chorus, and the next man, a Wall Street banker with white spats and a cane, joined in, and finally it seemed to me that everybody was singing this tune, and they didn't seem to be singing in fun, but as a natural outlet for what their feelings had been going through all day long. There was a feeling of dignity all through this, and the hand-organ man seemed to sense this and wheeled his organ nearer the platform and kept it up *fortissimo*, and the chorus sounded as though every man in New York must be joining in.

As a disciple of Ralph Waldo Emerson and the group of nineteenth-century writers known as the Transcendentalists, Ives was convinced that there is an intrinsic unity between men, though it may rarely be so evident as on that evening in Hanover Square station. This belief undoubtedly sprang from the need for the different groups of immigrants to find a common identity and live in harmony with one another. Indeed, the quest to find unity within the diverse and apparently incongruous is a feature of American culture as a whole. Ives reflected it even in early works such as the Second Symphony (1900–02), where he places excerpts from symphonies by Brahms cheek by jowl with quotations from Wagner's *The Valkyrie* to point out that, although the followers of Brahms and Wagner were at loggerheads, the music of the two composers was perfectly compatible and could even be juxtaposed with bawdy fraternity songs. The same principle lies behind *The Fourth of July* (1911–13) and *Decoration Day* (1912), pieces in which he remembers festive occasions of his youth, when he experienced the sound of different bands playing different tunes at the same time. On those boyhood occasions the noise may have been cacophonous, but in these composed pieces he makes sure that the tunes the bands play are related in some way. *The Red, White and Blue* and *The Battle Hymn of the Republic*, the principal tunes in *The Fourth of July*, for example, are strikingly similar in their second and third bars.

In fact, Ives never chose arbitrarily when he selected popular 'folk' material for his compositions: the tunes always have something in common with each other. An excellent example of the way he brings out such connections may be found in his First Piano Sonata (1902–10). This has five movements, grouped to form an arch, the outer movements being thematically related, as are movements two and four, while the central slow movement functions as the keystone. The first and fifth movements make use of the hymn tune *Lebanon* ('I was a wandering sheep'); the second and fourth the chorus hymns *Bringing in the sheaves*, *Happy day* and *I hear Thy welcome voice*. The borrowed material in the central movement is drawn from the hymn tune *Erie* ('What a friend we have in Jesus'), Stephen Foster's *Massa's in de cold, cold ground* and at the end *Lebanon* again. What unites all these tunes is a very simple three-note motif, built from the two intervals of the pentatonic scale, a whole tone and a minor third. In one form this may be, for example, G–E–D, in another E–D–B. The hymns Ives employs in the two ragtime scherzos are even more closely related, because they all end with the same five notes. But Ives does not supply these five notes until the end of the second scherzo. After a rousing version of the chorus of *I hear Thy welcome voice*, the music begins to dissolve in a characteristically Ivesian way, so that we hear the five notes as if they were fading away into the distance. Before the music disappears completely, Ives also gives us the closing notes of *Erie*, which were held back when the hymn was featured in the slow movement. The result is that we hear the motifs that unite the three central movements in gestures that poetically hover in the air.

Those who are familiar with ragtime only through the music of Scott Joplin (1868–1917), may find Ives's specimens a little wild. The first part of the second scherzo, for instance, contains rhythms as complex as two against three, five against four, five against three, and even ten against seven, as well as clusters of white notes in the right hand and black notes in the left. In comparison, Joplin's rags sound as if they were meant for the refined

environment of a middle-class drawing room. And indeed they were. When *Maple Leaf Rag* was first published in 1899, Joplin and his publisher decided that it should be called a 'classic' rag, so that the public would associate it with the classical piano repertory. He wanted his music to be played as if it were a Chopin study. 'The Joplin ragtime', he said, 'is destroyed by careless or imperfect rendering, and very often good players lose the effect entirely by playing too fast.'

Ragtime was a fusion of Afro-American additive rhythms and Euro-American formal principles, and throughout his life Joplin sought to express in this musical coming together the ideal of greater understanding between the black and white communities. The blacks, he believed, had to learn to accommodate to the whites, just as the whites had to learn to accommodate to the blacks. This is the gist of his opera *Treemonisha*, which was written and published in 1911 but not staged until the revival of ragtime in the seventies. Treemonisha is a young black woman, brought up by foster parents in a remote Arkansas plantation after the Civil War. She has been given a 'good' education, which sets her strongly against the conjurors, who are continuing to foster the superstitious beliefs of their African ancestors among the people. The conjurors kidnap her, but she is eventually rescued, and when she returns to her people she insists that the only punishment the conjurors should receive is a severe lecture on the need to conform to the civilized standards of the country to which they now belong. The opera ends with 'A Real Slow Drag', a celebratory dance in which ragtime becomes the very epitome of stateliness and grandeur.

What Joplin did for ragtime, the bandleader Paul Whiteman later did for jazz. In the twenties he tried to subdue its wildness and spontaneity and turn it into something serious and

Even the name 'ragtime' gives us an idea of the spiciness of the music. It's a mixture of two things: one is ragged time – syncopation – the beats within the beats, and the other is the idea of 'ragging', teasing.

(*From left*) George Gershwin; Du Bose Heyward, the librettist of *Porgy and Bess*, and lyricist Ira Gershwin, in 1935.

Eubie Blake said that the piano was the most popular instrument at the time, but seized on by black musicians because it was the instrument most able to imitate African instruments. They did not use the pedal, or subtle gradations of loud and soft. They made the piano into a startlingly percussive instrument, and it was this that appealed to Stravinsky, the fact that the pianists used no pedal.

respectable. Whiteman and his band, however, were white, and unlike Joplin their motives were commercial. They made their first recording in 1920 with a number called *Whispering*, which was arranged by Ferde Grofé to sound as if it were being played by a reduced symphony orchestra with violins playing the melody. Neither at this nor at any other time were Whiteman's musicians allowed to improvise in the style of the black bands of the time. By 1922 Whiteman had twenty-eight bands and was grossing over $1 million a year. But the highlight of his activities was a jazz concert he put on in New York's Aeolian Hall in February 1924, for which he commissioned George Gershwin's *Rhapsody in Blue*. Gershwin (1898–1937) had made his name with *Swanee* and other jazz-inflected songs such as *Fascinating Rhythm*, and Whiteman believed he had the talent to bridge the gap between Tin Pan Alley and the serious musical world with an extended jazz-influenced piece. Among those whom Whiteman persuaded to be patrons of the concert were Heifetz, Kreisler, John McCormack, Rachmaninov and Stokowski. 'My idea for the concert', said Whiteman, 'was to show sceptical people the advance which had been made in popular music from the day of discordant early jazz to the melodious form of the present.' So before Gershwin's *Rhapsody in Blue* and a specially composed Suite by Victor Herbert were played, the audience was given examples of 'discordant early jazz'. In the event, the Gershwin was a hit and has remained so to this day. But this is mainly on account of its melodies and the memorable clarinet glissando with which it begins. Gershwin lacked the technique to produce anything more coherent than a fairly loose sequence of musical ideas and relied too heavily on Lisztian tinsel. Nevertheless, by those who were unaware of what Ives had achieved, *Rhapsody in Blue* was hailed as the first distinctively American concert piece.

The paucity of well-trained composition teachers in America, who could provide young composers with the technique to overcome structural problems such as Gershwin encountered, meant that in some quarters during the twenties it was still thought necessary to study in Europe. But now, because Germany had been the enemy during the First World War, the Mecca was Paris, where Nadia Boulanger (1887–1979) taught. Aaron Copland (1900–1990) was the first to have lessons from her, and she continued to teach American composers almost until her death. In the twenties her students included Marc Blitzstein, Ross Lee Finney, Roy Harris, Walter Piston and Virgil Thomson; later Arthur Berger, Elliott Carter, David Diamond, Irving Fine and Harold Shapero, Easley Blackwood and Philip Glass were among those who sought her instruction. She was undoubtedly a brilliant teacher. 'At the period when I was her pupil,' said Copland, 'she had but one all-embracing principle, namely, the desirability of aiming first and foremost at the creation of what she called *"la grande ligne"* – the long line in music.' Her models were the neo-classical scores of Stravinsky, which meant that, while they were under her instruction, all her pupils had also to become neo-classicists. This was true of Copland even though his ballet *Grohg* (1922–5), which he wrote under her supervision, included a jazz number. Jazz was a corner of music, he said, which had somehow escaped Boulanger's notice until then: 'Before long we were exploring polyrhythmic devices together; their cross-pulsations, their notation, and especially their difficulty of execution intrigued her.' One of the movements of his Organ Symphony, which he wrote for Boulanger to play with the New York Symphony Orchestra in 1925, was inspired by jazz. So too were his *Music for the Theatre* (1925) and, particularly, his Piano Concerto (1926) which he himself played with the Boston Symphony Orchestra in 1927. According to Copland, jazz has only two expressions: 'the well-known "blues" mood, and the wild, abandoned, almost hysterical and grotesque mood so dear to the youth of all ages.' He therefore begins the Concerto with a 'slow blues' and continues with a 'snappy number'.

Copland abandoned jazz after 1929 mainly because between 1929 and 1935 jazz was forced underground by the Great Depression. Its carefree, uninhibited style was totally out of keeping with the sombre mood of the day, and the production of 'race records' – jazz recordings addressed to the black audience – virtually ceased for a while. Black musicians, in particular, found

The rising scale at the beginning of *Rhapsody in Blue* is really stolen from one of Bessie Smith's trademark wails, but after it what you hear is pure Jewish cantor music. This music smells as much of New York in the twenties as any Strauss waltz smells of nineteenth-century Vienna.

Bessie Smith.

Wayne Marshall as the soloist in *Rhapsody in Blue*.

it increasingly difficult to make a living. Sidney Bechet, for example, one of the finest clarinet and soprano saxophone players of the day, was forced to set up a shoeshine stand. Only the 'sweet' commercial bands, such as those of Guy Lombardo and Rudy Vallee, survived and prospered. Copland's immediate response to the change of climate was to write two of the tersest and most uncompromising pieces he was ever to produce, the Piano Variations (1930) and the *Short Symphony* (1933). The Piano Variations are particularly sinewy; yet though the material is reduced to essentials, the overall effect is one of great strength. The theme consists of five short phrases, each describing a motion from E to C♯; but the progress is always varied, and the C♯ is never allowed to sound conclusive until the very end of the work. Each of the twenty variations has its own distinctive character, but Copland never loses sight of Boulanger's *grande ligne*.

In 1933 President Roosevelt launched his economic and social reform programme known as the New Deal. Copland realized that, to fit in with its spirit, composers would have to abandon writing pieces that were 'difficult to perform and difficult for an audience to comprehend'. He had to 'say what he wanted to say in the simplest possible terms'. However, it took him several years to achieve this. In 1934 his ballet *Hear ye! Hear ye!*, a zany piece about a female night-club dancer on trial for murder, proved a failure and he never even tried to get it published. The work that did match the mood of the day and made a considerable impact, Virgil Thomson's opera *Four Saints in Three Acts*, had actually been written in Paris some time earlier, in 1927–8. Thomson orchestrated it in 1933 for a production early the following year in Hartford, Connecticut, with an all-black cast, stage direction and movement by Frederick Ashton and John Houseman, and cellophane décor by Florine Stettheimer. The production was then transferred to Broadway and Chicago and had a run of more than sixty performances.

Virgil Thomson (1896–1989) came from the southern state of Missouri and had gone to Paris to study with Nadia Boulanger for a year, mainly because of his fascination with the music of Satie and 'Les Six' (Auric, Durey, Honegger, Milhaud, Poulenc and Tailleferre). *Four Saints in Three Acts* was written in collaboration with Gertrude Stein, whom he met in 1926. Her libretto concerns day-to-day incidents in the lives of four sixteenth-century Spanish saints: Theresa, Ignatius, Settlement and Chavez. There is no plot, just counting, children's rhymes, and series of questions such as 'How many saints are there in it?' (that is, the opera), 'How many acts are there in it?' In the third act, when St Theresa, St Ignatius and St Settlement have a vision of the Holy Ghost, their response to it is 'Pigeons on the grass, alas', a phrase which became a watchword for silliness in the mid-thirties, even though, in context, it is very touching. Thomson derived his equally naïve music from Satie, the Baptist hymns he had learned as a child, chants that might well have come from the Anglican liturgy, and quotations from tunes such as *God save the Queen* and *My country, 'tis of thee*. The opera has never entered the standard repertory. Its initial success lay simply in the fact that its childlike innocence offered an escape from the oppressive events of the day.

Aaron Copland in 1986.

Gertrude Stein, in her typically off-centre manner, said that 'America is the oldest country in the twentieth century.'

Not all the composers who matured in the twenties were pupils of Nadia Boulanger. When Roger Sessions (1896–1985) approached her with a view to having lessons, she said that, as a pupil of the Swiss composer Ernest Bloch, he had no need of more tuition. Ruth Crawford (1901–1953), who in 1930 won a Guggenheim Fellowship to go to Europe for a year, met Bartók, Berg, Honegger and Ravel, but refused to study with anyone simply because, for the first time in her life, she had the financial freedom to devote herself to her own ideas in composition and because she had no time for contemporary European music, particularly the neo-classical works that Boulanger so admired.

Crawford belonged to a group of composers who wanted to create an American style that was independent of European influences, and did not require jazz, folk music, hymn tunes or quotations to give it character. They included the Californian Henry Cowell (1897–1965), Edgard Varèse and Dane Rudhyer (1895–1985) (a Frenchman, who, like Varèse, had immigrated to the States during the First World War), Carl Ruggles (1876–1971), and Charles Seeger (1886–1979), whom Crawford later married, and who is now better known as an ethnomusicologist. All were members of the Pan American Association of Composers, which Cowell and Varèse had founded in 1927. Ives was also a member, but by that time he had retired from both composition and business: his contribution to the association was (anonymously) to finance its publishing and concert-giving activities out of the fortune he had made as one of America's leading insurance agents. Ruth Crawford joined the association when she moved from Chicago to New York in 1930 and started to take composition lessons with Charles Seeger. Seeger had already formulated a theory of what an independent American style should consist of, but it was Crawford who refined it and put it into practice in the remarkable series of works she composed mainly on her trip to Europe. They include *Four Diaphonic Suites* (1930), Three Songs to poems by Carl Sandburg (1930–32), and a String Quartet (1931). The only works of substance she composed afterwards were Two Ricercare to poems by H. T. Tsiang (1932) and a Suite for Wind Quintet (1952). The smallness of her output may be one reason for her neglect, but more likely is that musicians and audiences have simply found her approach too uncompromising. Her works represent the most heroic and coherent attempt to create a style based on Americans' perception of their essential national characteristics, including the ability to co-exist without sacrificing their individuality.

The basis of Crawford's music is the highly individualized and independent melodic line. She avoids all tonal implications: no note is allowed to become prominent, and if a major or minor third does occur it is immediately followed by an interval that undermines its tonal implications. Various strategies are employed to generate the notes of a line and to ensure that it always remains highly characterized; one of the most pervasive is the use of musical shapes or contours which Seeger called 'neumes'. Seeger contended that the shape or contour of short motifs could play a much greater role in relating groups of notes and phrases than musical theory had previously admitted. Crawford demonstrated that by treating motifs as neumes she could create organic lines which could be varied and extended without any loss of integrity.

But the real interest of Crawford's technique lies in the counterpoint that results from putting together two or three organic lines. Traditionally counterpoint has to be concordant. In Crawford's music – as indeed in the music of Cowell, Ruggles, Seeger and Varèse – the harmony arising from the counterpoint is made as dissonant as possible, so as to ensure that the lines stand out from one another and preserve their independence. American composers, said Seeger, had 'to cultivate "sounding apart" rather than "sounding together" – diaphony rather than symphony'. Nevertheless, although each of Crawford's lines appears to be totally independent, she always ensures that there is a link between them, some subtle connection which indicates that at the deepest level they are not at odds but are mutually beneficial. The link may come from the sharing of a motif or neume, the consistency of the harmony they create between them, or perhaps, most effectively, the way they balance each other. Crawford was probably the first composer outside the Second Viennese School (Schoenberg, Berg and Webern) to make self-conscious use of rotational and bilateral symmetries in order to create balance in her music.

Nowhere are Crawford's efforts to forge links between

independent lines more successful than in her String Quartet (1931). As in traditional four-movement works, the first movement contains the greatest variety of material. The movement has six distinctive melodies, which develop quite independently of each other. It opens with two kinds of dialogue. In the lower register the viola and cello pass from one to the other a scurrying melody built from small intervals and containing irregular accents. Against this the first violin plays a slow-moving, singing melody with wide leaps; then, as if to express its opposition to such lyricism, the second violin interjects with melodic gestures that Crawford herself described as being strident and brusque. But the violin melodies are not quite as independent as they seem: they contain similar shapes and are therefore related in terms of their neumes. Later they are brought back to round off the movement, and here the relationship becomes even closer because the notes of one melody are played in the rhythm of the other. This means that although each melody has developed separately, in the long run they resolve their differences simply by a process of give and take.

The central movements of the quartet, a scherzo and a slow movement, have only one melody each, and this has to be shared between the instruments. Even though they are all contributing to the same task, Crawford still manages to give each instrument its independence. The slow movement is particularly interesting in this respect. Here the notes of the melody are passed from instrument to instrument one by one, but because the notes are sustained beyond their necessary duration, the resulting texture is four-part harmony rather than a single line. The independence of the lines comes from Crawford's use of dynamics. She called the movement 'a counterpoint of crescendos and diminuendos'. Each instrument is given its own pattern of 'hairpins', and at no time does the top of one instrument's crescendo coincide with any other.

The finale contains two lines, one for the first violin, the other for the three other instruments playing in octaves and muted.

The relationship may be likened to a contest in which the participants conform to the same set of rules but are fiercely opposed to each other. The rules are that each party should play a series of phrases divided by rests, the phrases getting successively longer by one note up to a maximum of twenty, or successively shorter by one note down to a minimum of one; the phrases that get longer get softer, and those that get shorter get louder. Once the process is completed and the first violin has reached twenty notes, the trio one, it goes into reverse, each part presenting the music it has already played, but now backwards and a semitone higher. The first violin's character is free and rhapsodic, that of the other three instruments constrained and regimented, in that they never have more than ten notes and are virtually confined to one duration – the quaver.

This description makes the affair sound like a mechanical game, yet in performance it is much more like a confrontation between people who are not prepared to compromise. While the non-symmetrical balance between the voices and the retrograde motion in the second half make the structure very stable, the most significant thing about the relationship is that neither part would

make sense without the other – they are mutually dependent.

Similar confrontations occur in the Two Ricercare, 'Chinaman, Laundryman' and 'Sacco, Vanzetti', which Crawford wrote in 1932 and which proved to be the last pieces she composed for twenty years. Here, however, the conflict conveys utter intransigence. Earlier that year the Seegers had joined the Composers' Collective, a radical group associated with the American Communist Party, the aim of which, said Seeger, was 'to connect music somehow to the economic situation'. Among those in the group were Blitzstein, Copland, Cowell and Wallingford Riegger. Although Crawford was never an active member of the collective, these songs were meant to express something of its concerns. The texts had appeared in the American *Daily Worker*; the first is the cry of a Chinese laundryman railing against the exploitation he is subjected to, the second a lament for the deaths of Nicola Sacco and Bartolomeo Vanzetti, who were electrocuted in 1927 for allegedly killing a paymaster in a Massachusetts factory hold-up. Liberal opinion considered them innocent, the victims of a witch-hunt against anyone who expressed radical, nonconformist or unorthodox views in the years following the Russian Revolution. In both songs the vocal lines are highly declamatory, the piano accompaniments, being constructed from ostinatos, highly regimented. The ostinatos in 'Chinaman, Laundryman' represent perhaps the brutish repetitiveness of the immigrant's work, those in 'Sacco, Vanzetti' something that proceeds with remorseless steadiness – the inexorable tread of justice perhaps, or the knell a prison bell would toll after an execution.

Shortly after completing these songs, Ruth Crawford began to feel that in the context of the Great Depression she could no longer go on writing music for a small élite; so she and her husband gave up composing to devote themselves to the collection and editing of Anglo-American folk music. The only work she composed between then and the completion in 1952 of her last work, the Suite for Wind Quintet, was a short, lightweight orchestral piece, *Rissolty, Rossolty*, based on three folk tunes, which CBS commissioned in 1939 for inclusion in a programme called 'School of the Air'. It was the kind of activity most composers had to undertake in the period of Roosevelt's New Deal. As Copland put it:

Suddenly functional music was in demand as never before. Motion-picture and ballet companies, radio stations and schools, film and theatre producers discovered us. The music appropriate for the different kind of co-operative ventures undertaken by these people had to be simpler and more direct. There was a 'market' especially for music evocative of the American scene – industrial backgrounds, landscapes of the Far West, and so forth.

In Copland's opinion, the composer who set the standard for 'how to treat Americana' was Virgil Thomson. His scores for the film documentaries commissioned by the Farm Security Administration of the US Department of Agriculture, *The Plow that Broke the Plains* (1936) and *The River* (1937), concerned the often tragic situations brought about by the Depression. The first tells how a once fertile land has been worked dry in an effort to produce food, the second how the Mississippi has been used and abused. The purpose was to publicize the progress of the various reclamation and conservation projects instigated by the federal government. Thomson's music for *The Plow that Broke the Plains*, quotes cowboy tunes such as *Goodbye, old paint* and *The streets of Laredo*, and uses blues-like material to convey, first of all, pathos and then, at the end, the defiant optimism of people determined to endure. The same mood of optimism brings *The River* to an end; here Thomson quotes music associated with the South: *Dixie*, *Hot time in the old town tonight* and *We won't get home until morning*, for instance.

Copland's contribution to Americana began with *The Second Hurricane* (1936), 'a play–opera for high school students', and then continued with a whole series of works celebrating the integrity of American individuals and, more particularly, American communities: the honest outlaw whose victims are the man who shot his mother and the man who cheated at cards (*Billy the Kid*, 1938); a comic version of life in the Wild West (*Rodeo*, 1942); birth, life and death in a small New Hampshire community (*Our Town*, 1940); the celebration of a marriage among the pioneers in the Pennsylvania hills (*Appalachian Spring*, 1943–4); and to cap them all *The Tender Land* (1952–4), an opera set in a Midwest farm in the thirties, which ends with the elder daughter leaving home, and her mother looking to the younger daughter to continue the family

Kurt Weill in 1930.

cycle, which is the whole reason for their existence.

What is significant about all these works is the total absence of political conflict. With the exception of *Billy the Kid*, the world they evoke is at peace with itself. Marc Blitzstein (1905–1964), on the other hand, took the view that political and social problems in contemporary society should be exposed in the musical theatre. He had been an active member of the Composers' Collective until it broke up had come under the influence of Bertolt Brecht, Hanns Eisler and Kurt Weill when studying in Berlin in the late twenties. The first of his full-length 'plays in music', *The Cradle will Rock*, dates from 1937 and its first production had Orson Welles as its director. The story centres on the difficulty of getting a trade union organized in Steeltown, USA. The action takes place in a night court, when the steel-workers are holding a late-evening rally to debate the foundation of a union, and members of the Liberty Committee set up by Mr Mister, the factory's owner and boss of just about everything in the town, are trying to disrupt it. Unfortunately for the members of the committee, the police arrest them on the mistaken understanding that they are the ringleaders of the rally. The plot unfolds in a series of flashbacks, cut into the central courtroom scene, during which the supposedly upright citizens of the Liberty Committee are exposed as being as corrupt as Mr Mister. It is they, not the workers, who are rocking (that is, threatening) the cradle of liberty. The play ends with the sound of the workers marching through the town united in their determination to form their union.

Blitzstein's music is clearly indebted to Weill's *The Threepenny Opera* and Eisler's *Die Massnahme* ('The [disciplinary] measure'), which also takes place in a courtroom and involves flashbacks. But it establishes an atmosphere that is entirely American. Blitzstein is particularly skilful in the way he makes the music move from speech into recitative into song and back again. As might be expected he made use of appropriate popular material, so that alongside passages that could have come out of a bravura piano concerto, his score includes ragtime and the inevitable Tin Pan Alley numbers intended to bring the house down – 'Nickel under the foot' for the leading lady (a prostitute) and 'That's thunder, that's lightening' for the company. It is hardly surprising, perhaps, that nowadays, when no one is interested in forming unions any more, the work sounds dated. But even at the time, it seemed out of step with people's concerns: in 1937 the public had no time for political theatre. The two most successful shows in New York that year were Richard Rodgers's *Babes in Arms* and Gian Carlo Menotti's *Amelia goes to the Ball*. Kurt Weill was certainly aware of the escapist mood of the American public in the late thirties, for his first Broadway musical was the light-hearted *Knickerbocker Holiday* (1938). It was only after the war that he was able to bring out musicals of a more serious tone; but even then he had to compromise to make them acceptable to the typical Broadway audience. His first post-war work was *Street Scene* (1946), based on Elmer Rice's play, a production of which he had seen in Berlin before he left Germany in 1933. For the musical stage he knew that certain changes had to be made: for a start the political element had to be toned down, and

Weill's *Street Scene*, 1946.

Leonard Bernstein
in the 1940s.

the love story between Sam and Rose made more passionate. 'Sam, instead of being the beaten Jew,' he said, 'will be the young poet trying to adjust to the world and to the hateful surroundings he is living in [the slums of New York] . . . His aria, *Lonely House*, is almost a theme song for the show; the house as a prison for the human spirit.'

Three years later, when he wrote *Lost in the Stars*, his last completed show for the musical stage, Weill felt he could be more open about political and social affairs. The work is based on Alan Paton's novel *Cry, the Beloved Country*, the story of a black clergyman who goes to Johannesburg in search of his sister and his son, only to discover that she has been forced into prostitution and he is on trial for the murder of the son of a white farmer. The story ends with the reconciliation of the clergyman and the farmer, who rises above the tragedy of his son's death by deciding to devote his efforts to helping the black community. It was this 'musical tragedy' that opened the way for Bernstein's *West Side Story* (1957), undoubtedly the most successful musical ever with a serious plot. This too, of course, ends in reconciliation, or at least in the strong probability that the rival gangs will heed Maria's plea and bring their feuding to an end.

While *West Side Story* may have been the first popular show to deal with ethnic conflict, abstract musical structures based on the ultimate reconciliation of apparently contradictory material had been a feature of American music ever since the early music of Ives. Ives had taken the traditional notion that a string quartet is an abstract conversation between four instrumentalists, and turned it into something more explicitly conversational. His Second String Quartet (1907–13), he claimed, is a 'String Quartet for four men who converse, discuss, argue (politics), fight, shake hands, shut up, then walk up the mountain to view the firmament'. From the tunes he quotes it is evident that the argument concerns the Civil War. And from the way he differentiates the instruments, it is clear that the person who tries to bring order to the proceedings is the second violin. In his manuscript Ives refers to the second violin as Rollo. Rollo is genteel, conservative and timid, so is given only 'nice' tunes to play.

This theatrical approach reappears in Elliott Carter's Second String Quartet (1959), which owes much to Ives's model, as well as to Ruth Crawford's quartet. Carter also casts the second violin as the person who keeps order, but in his score all four instruments are type-cast. Each, for example, has its own repertory of intervals. They all play major and minor seconds, but the first violin, whose temperament is 'fantastic, ornate, mercurial', is restricted to minor thirds and perfect fifths, the 'laconic, orderly and sometimes humorous' second violin to major thirds, major sixths and major sevenths, the 'expressive' viola to augmented fourths (or diminished fifths) and minor sevenths, and the 'impetuous' cello to perfect fourths and minor sixths. Their conversations are based on three kinds of relationship. Companionship prevails when all four instruments co-operate with one another and contribute equally to the musical conversation: this occurs in the opening and closing sections of the work. Discipleship characterizes the relationship when one instrument takes the lead and the others imitate it, each according to its own personality: this relationship forms the basis of the work's four main movements – the first violin leads the Allegro fantastico, the second violin the Presto scherzando, the viola the Andante espressivo, and the cello the rhapsodic closing Allegro. Separating the movements are cadenzas for the viola, cello and first violin, and these embody the third relationship – confrontation. Mockery greets the viola's expressive lament, insistence on strict time-keeping the cello's romantic waywardness, and stony silence the first violin's flashiness. But before the violin's cadenza is over, the second violin, viola and cello commence the final Allegro, where all are drawn into the sweeping arcs of the cello's accelerations and ritardandos. Gradually the conversation returns to the spirit of companionship.

Good companionship is one of the requisites for a successful performance of Terry Riley's *In C* (see Chapter 3), and in this piece it has to pervade from beginning to end. Given a collaborative spirit, anyone can take part – a whole community if they want to. The performers may play their melodic fragments as

Carter says that he wants to combine America's sometimes perplexing unwillingness to consider the past with its good-natured generosity and idealistic hope for the future.

Elliott Carter.

often as they like and at whatever speed they choose, but if the performance is not to fall apart, they must listen very carefully to each other and respond and react in close co-operation. In effect, the structure of the piece is yet another version of the American concern with individualism and social integration.

Terry Riley was born and bred in California and this may explain why he took such a radical approach to the issue. On the whole, composers from the East Coast have tended to affiliate themselves with Europe. Those from the West Coast, on the other hand, such as Henry Cowell (1897–1965), Harry Partch (1901–1974) and John Cage (1912–1992), have felt much closer to the cultures of the Orient. Henry Cowell's name has already been mentioned in connection with the Pan American Association and the Composers' Collective of New York. Yet he was born in San Francisco, the gateway for immigrants from the Far East, and as a child played with children from the Chinese community in the city and attended the Chinese Opera. During the First World War he became a pupil of Charles Seeger at the University of California at Berkeley; at that stage Seeger was still formulating his ideas about dissonant counterpoint, but by the time Cowell was introduced to them he had already published pieces that were radical as anything produced by Ives. Even as a fifteen-year-old he was experimenting with piano clusters. In *The Tides of Manaunaun* (1912), his very first piece, the right hand plays what could well be an Irish folk tune, while the left hand plays clusters of white notes, clusters of black notes, and clusters of all the notes lying between two specified pitches, sometimes one octave, sometimes two octaves apart. The right hand is notated in B♭ minor, the left hand in D minor, and for most of the time the sustaining pedal is down. Cowell's purpose must have been firstly to represent the tremendous tides sweeping to and fro through the universe before creation (which is what the title implies), but also to produce, by means of the overlapping reverberations, a

'I soon began to realize that whatever American character my music had would be the character of myself making music.' Elliott Carter.

sonority that seems to belong to another world.

As well as being the first to exploit tone clusters, Cowell also pioneered unorthodox ways of playing the piano. In the piece he called *Aeolian Harp* (1923), the pianist has to silently depress the notes of a chord on the keyboard with the right hand, and, inside the piano, sweep the strings for those notes with the left hand. *The Banshee* (1925) requires two players, one to sit at the keyboard and hold the sustaining pedal down for the duration of the work, the other to stand in the crook of the piano and sweep or pluck the open strings; the eery sound evokes the spirit who, in Irish legend, wails before a death in the family to which she is attached. While none of these invented sonorities is specifically oriental, they come together in a work that could not have been written if Cowell had not had the sounds of Chinese opera in his inner ear. It is called simply *Piece for Piano* (1924). In a mysterious passage just before the climax there are instructions for playing inside the piano in seven different ways. These are intended to produce sounds reminiscent of a Chinese orchestra, including the *yueh ch'in*, one of several kinds of plucked lute favoured by the Peking Opera.

Cowell's rhythmic innovations were all based on the principle of polyrhythms. The piano piece *Flights*, for instance, has $\frac{2}{4}$ as its time signature, but the three lines that run continuously through it move at different rates. The melody is in the middle voice, which divides each bar into five; the lower voice divides the bars into eight or nine; the upper voice into six or seven. Cowell was also the first composer to put forward the idea that there is a 'physical identity between rhythm and harmony'. He pointed out that both rhythmical and intervallic relationships can be expressed in mathematical ratios. The interval of a fifth, for example, which has a frequency ratio of 3 : 2 could imply a rhythm of three against two; a fourth (4 : 3) a rhythm of four against three; a major third (5 : 4) a rhythm of five against four, and so on. These cross-rhythms are by no means unusual in twe ontieth-century music. The last song in Mahler's *Das Lied von der Erde*, for instance, contains several specimens. However, the

polyrhythms to match more complex intervals, such as the tritone, which has a ratio of 45 : 32, can be realized only by a machine. The desire to use such complexities eventually prompted Cowell to ask the French inventor Lev Termen to construct a rhythm instrument, which they called the 'rhythmicon'. But in works such as his *Quartet Romantic* (1917) for two flutes, violin and viola, composed before he approached Termen, Cowell had to confine himself to chords with simple ratios. He began by writing a chorale in four parts, but listeners never hear the notes of the chorale: all they hear are the cross-rhythms based on the ratios of the intervals in each chord.

Like most composers during the Great Depression, Cowell abandoned these esoteric experiments in the mid-thirties and simplified his mode of expression. A good example is the series of Hymns and Fuguing Tunes for various ensembles, begun in 1943, which are based on the fuging tunes of the eighteenth-century Boston composer William Billings (1742–1800). (A fuging tune is a simple vocal piece in four-part harmony, in which the entries of the supporting voices are staggered.) The first work in his simpler style, the *United Quartet* of 1936, was intended to have universal significance. In this Cowell was following the example of Ives, who had always wanted to compose a 'universal symphony'. The idea of universal brotherhood was a central tenet of Transcendentalism, and Ives began to compose his symphony in 1911. The need for such a work became more urgent when first the Senate in 1919 and then the American people in the election of 1920 refused to endorse President Woodrow Wilson's proposal for a League of Nations. Ives felt that the refusal was a betrayal not only of the Transcendental ideal but of everything Americans had stood for in the past. It threw to the winds the idea that, given the will, people of different races and cultures could live in peace and harmony with one another. Undoubtedly, as one of Ives's greatest admirers, Cowell also sensed the dangers of isolationism, which may be why his *United Quartet* is written in 'a more universal style' than he had adopted hitherto. He believed that since it included elements from many places, peoples and epochs it would inspire listeners to think in terms of the whole world and not just their own particular corner of it.

Harry Partch had the same breadth of vision, but he was unable to express it until the fifties and sixties, by which time he had gathered a group of disciples around him to play the extraordinary instruments he had invented and on which his music depends. Born in Oakland, California, he spent much of his childhood in the Arizona desert, and was largely self-taught as a musician. Before he was twenty he had already become dissatisfied with 'both the intonational system of modern Europe and its concert system'. The music that interested him, he later claimed, was that of 'Yaqui Indians, Chinese lullabies, Hebrew chants for the dead, Christian hymns, Congo puberty rites, Chinese music hall (San Francisco), lumber yards and junk shops . . . *Boris Godunov*'. By 1928 he had written the first version of his book *Genesis of a Music*, in which he put forward what he called his 'new philosophy of music'. He rejected Western harmony and polyphony, insisting that music should go back to its roots – the single melodic line, conceived in terms of the human voice. He rejected the twelve-note tempered scale of Western music and replaced it with a 43-note scale derived from the pure intervals of just intonation. He also rejected the abstraction of Western music, holding that music was 'corporeal': as well as sound, it involved the physical motions of singing and playing; for him the visual was as important as the aural in a performance. This is undoubtedly why the instruments he invented over the years – 'blue rainbow', 'Castor and Pollux', 'cloud chamber bowls', 'diamond marimba' – are as beautiful to look at as they are to listen to.

However, those who reject the established ways of doing things cannot expect to get teaching positions or be employed by universities, and between 1935 and 1941 Partch was on the bread-line. Like tens of thousands of unemployed Americans, he was forced to become a hobo and 'ride the rails', wandering back and forth across the United States looking for work. Thereafter he existed mainly on grants, the income from research posts, and what he could earn with his group, the Gate 5 Ensemble. His experiences as a hobo are reflected in such works as *Barstow* (1941), the text of which consists of hitch-hikers' inscriptions seen on a hoarding while waiting for a lift, and *US Highball* (1943), his first dramatic work. He called this 'A

Chicago.

Musical Account of a Transcontinental Hobo Trip'. The text is chanted or intoned by a hobo named Mac, and consists of lists of railway stations, random thoughts and what he sees on hoardings. His aim is to get to Chicago, and Chicago is the word that ends his monologue. 'Instrumentally, what follows', said Partch, 'implies a tremendous letdown from the obstinately compulsive exhilaration of *getting* to Chicago. It implies bewilderment and that ever-dominant question in the life of the wanderer – what next?'

It is clear from his other dramatic works that Partch places the blame for the sense of homelessness, bewilderment and lack of direction at the feet of modern industrial society, his argument being that it has lost contact with its roots. Later on he turned to Greek tragedy, Japanese Kabuki and Noh plays for his models and texts. For *Oedipus* (1951) he used W. B. Yeats's translation of Sophocles' play; for *Revelation in the Courthouse Square* (1962), he himself adapted Euripides' *Bacchae*. In the latter Partch shifts the action from ancient Thebes to modern Hollywood, which he sees epitomizing the new, rootless forms of ritual that have become a substitute for living. For *Delusion of the Fury* (1969), his last dramatic work, he adapted a Noh play and dispensed with words altogether. The action is either danced or mimed, the chorus and vocal soloists singing only meaningless syllables. The whole affair, from its fantastic headpieces to the stylized movements of the musicians playing Partch's equally fantastic instruments, is nothing less than an attempt to give back to the world some of the magic which science and technology have taken away from it.

John Cage, by contrast, would have said that, provided you are prepared to open yourself up to the world, there is no need to be so extravagant to find what appears to be missing. 'Beauty is now underfoot wherever we take the trouble to look,' he said speaking of the painter Robert Rauschenberg, and then added, 'This is an American discovery.' Cage came from Los Angeles and was the son of an inventor. According to Schoenberg, with whom he studied at the University of Southern California in 1934, Cage was not a composer: he too was an inventor – an inventor of genius. Schoenberg based his judgement on Cage's lack of feeling for harmony, a lack which Cage readily acknowledged. It is certainly true that Cage relegated harmony, and

John Cage.

One of Charles Ives's credos was to hear what was actually there. It doesn't take very much to get from his inclusive ear to John Cage's experiments in silence. If you listen to silence it can very quickly become something deafeningly full of activity.

indeed pitch in general, to a secondary role in his music, and gave priority to rhythm and noise. 'Wherever we are,' he said in 1935, 'what we hear is mostly noise. When we ignore it, it disturbs us. When we listen to it, we find it fascinating. The sound of a truck at fifty miles per hour. Static between stations. Rain. We [composers] want to capture and control these sounds, to use them not as sound effects but as musical instruments.'

With one exception, this was an objective Cage continued to pursue all his life. The exception is the desire to control, which Cage gradually let go, especially after the late forties when he first came under the influence of Zen Buddhism. Later on he said that the composer should 'give up the desire to control sound, clear his mind of music, and set about discovering means to let sounds be themselves rather than vehicles for man-made theories or expressions of human sentiments.' In effect, Cage was putting into practice what Schopenhauer, who was also influenced by Buddhism, had been advocating a century before, namely, the abandonment of the will. But in abandoning the will he was also rejecting all that other composers have tried to do since the Renaissance. It is for this reason that Cage is considered by some to be the most radical and possibly the most influential composer of the century.

In 1937 Cage was lucky enough to find a job in the progressive dance studio run by Bonnie Bird in Seattle, where he accompanied the classes and composed for a percussion group. Later, after moving to New York, he worked with the choreographer Merce Cunningham. Thanks to these two associations, composing and devising music for dancing became a decisive factor in his output. Dancers think in terms of 'counts' when they are dancing; in 1939, when Cage was working on the percussion piece *First Construction in Metal*, he based just about everything in it on a count of sixteen. There are sixteen types of metal percussion instruments (including thunder sheets, brake drums and a piano with metal cylinders placed on its strings), sixteen sections each containing sixteen bars of $\frac{4}{4}$, and sixteen rhythmic motifs. To provide variety, the sixteen bars of $\frac{4}{4}$ are divided into phrases of $4:3:2:3:4$, and this series of numbers is also used for the circular permutations of the 16 rhythmic motifs. He afterwards thought that the piece resembled the structure of nineteenth-century music, but in performance it sounds much more oriental than European.

The following year, a talented student asked Cage to write music for a new dance of hers called *Bacchanale*. As there was no room for a percussion group in the dance theatre, he solved the problem by inserting bolts, wedges and large wooden screws between the strings of a piano, so that it became, in effect, 'a percussion orchestra under the control of a single player'. Later when Virgil Thomson heard Cage's 'prepared piano' he described it as being 'slightly reminiscent, on first hearing, of the Balinese gamelan orchestra'. At that stage in his development, Cage was thinking of musical forms as being 'empty containers', abstract structures made from proportional relationships, into which material – any material – could be placed. This approach is best exemplified by *Sonatas and Interludes* (1946–8) for prepared piano. The sixteen sonatas are in the classic two-part form of Scarlatti's harpsichord sonatas, both parts being repeated; but there the resemblance ends. Each sonata is based on a ratio – the proportions of the fifth, for example, are in the relationship 4:5. This ratio determines the relative lengths of the two parts, the number of bars in each part, the lengths of the phrases, and the lengths of the segments of each phrase. The content of the piece, the material Cage places in this 'empty container', is chosen simply to make these proportions clear: other material, other figurations, could have served just as well. As far as Cage is concerned, form and content are quite separate. The form is determined, the content hit upon by accident.

The success of *Sonatas and Interludes* enabled Cage to obtain a grant from the Guggenheim Foundation in 1949, on the strength of which he went to Paris, where he met and befriended Pierre Boulez. The two men both felt intellectually isolated in their respective environments, and each used the other to spark off new ideas. Cage was searching for new ways to organize rhythm, Boulez exploring the possibilities of total serialization. The friendship cooled only when Cage began to make more and more use of chance operations, and then ultimately renounced control altogether. Boulez, who was not averse to a certain element of chance in composition, believed that the composer should never completely abandon control.

As John Cage later said, all composers up to this point had heard music as if it was coming from the scrum in the middle of a football field.

Although Cage's decision was certainly due in part to a change of philosophical perspective, which came with his commitment to Zen, it also sprang from the need to find an antidote to the ultimate outcome of Renaissance thinking – the desire for total control. From then on his activities as a composer became secondary to his activities as a philosopher of indeterminacy and purposelessness. He considered his most significant piece to be *4' 33"*(1952), in which the pianist sits motionless and silent at the keyboard for the duration, and all the audience hears are the noises in the environment.

If Cage represents an extreme example of the West Coast frame of mind, the composer who may be seen as the extreme example of the East Coast mentality is Milton Babbitt (born 1916). For him, control is everything. 'I believe in cerebral music,' he says, 'in the application of intellect to relevant matters. I never choose a note unless I know precisely why I want it there and can give several reasons why it and not another.' Babbitt was trained as a mathematician and a composer, and in his *Three Compositions for Piano* (1947) he was the first composer to apply serial technique to durations and dynamics as well as pitch, thus anticipating Boulez by five years. But whereas Boulez derived his ideas from Webern and Messiaen (especially *Mode de valeurs et d'intensités* – see Chapter 3), Babbitt's came from Schoenberg, who had been in the States since 1933 and whose Fourth Quartet and Violin Concerto of 1936 had become more influential there than they would ever be in Europe. Babbitt saw in the Fourth Quartet the seeds of almost everything he was to do in the development of serial technique. Yet although this involved the application of the series to non-pitch components, he never lost sight of Schoenberg's insistence on a strong sense of line. Indeed, his lines can blossom into intense lyricism on occasions, as in his setting for soprano and tape (1964) of Ovid's story about Philomela. This tells of the girl who has her tongue cut out by her seducer, so that she can never tell the world about his conduct. Her plight arouses the pity of the gods, who transform her into a nightingale,

so that, as Coleridge put it, she can present her 'pity-pleading strains' in song. Babbitt transforms the language of her thoughts into the music of her song, partly through his dextrous use of a great variety of vocal articulations, partly by means of the extraordinary interplay of the voice and the electronic sounds he produced on the Mark II RCA Music Synthesizer.

Despite works like *Philomel*, however, Babbitt's rigour and intellectual complexity mean that for most listeners his music is impenetrable: he is a composer's composer not a music lover's. Babbitt acknowledges this, but is completely unwilling to compromise. In his opinion, advanced composers such as himself should withdraw from the public world and think of themselves as being like highly specialized research scientists, who work in the laboratory and accept the probability that the public will recognize the importance of their experiments only after a long lapse of time. Not long

after he made this observation it became a reality for dozens of American composers during the fifties and sixties who retreated to universities and wrote music which was unlikely to be heard by any but their colleagues and students. In the main they were highly competent pieces, composed for the university's resident string quartet according to the academically fashionable twelve-note method derived from Schoenberg. Even a long-established composer such as Roger Sessions took up the technique in the fifties, first in his solo Violin Sonata (1953) and then much more wholeheartedly in his String Quintet (1958). To break away from it, as George Crumb and one or two other university teachers did in the sixties, took a degree of determination and courage.

George Crumb (born 1929) was thirty-three when he broke away from what he now calls 'university music – the academic American style'.

I was teaching at the University of Colorado, and Cage came through to do one of his 'events'. I was taken with his totally refreshing way of challenging the basic things in music we had never questioned. He was a liberating influence for all kinds of composers throughout the world, even composers that one would not associate with his own very personal style.

Unlike Cage, however, Crumb was not prepared to abandon all control to indeterminacy, but discovered a personal language that was based on unusual sonorities. He found stimulation to explore these new sound worlds when he began to set the poetry of Federico García Lorca (1898–1936). Altogether he has composed nine works based on Lorca's verse, most of them written between 1963 and 1970. One of them was the work that gained him international recognition – *Ancient Voices of Children* for mezzo-soprano, boy soprano, oboe, mandolin, harp, electric piano and percussion; it won first prize at the 1971 International Rostrum of Composers in Paris, adjudicated by music producers from radio stations throughout the world. Its expressive yet readily accessible style ushered in a new era of simplicity in music worldwide, a simplicity that had nothing to do with the repetitiveness of minimalism.

The attraction of Lorca for Crumb was his sensual imagery, his awareness of lost innocence, and, says Crumb, the mysterious power that 'burns the blood like powdered glass' and 'rejects all the sweet geometry one has learned'. The five poems Crumb selected for *Ancient Voices of Children* are all about loss. The first few might lead the reader to believe that the primary concern is the physical loss of a child, but in the end it transpires that Crumb's subject is the loss of childhood itself: 'and I will go very far, farther than those hills, farther than the seas . . . to ask Christ the Lord to give me back my ancient soul of a child'. In the fourth song, after the words 'Each afternoon in Granada, a child dies each afternoon', which the mezzo sings pianissimo in Flamenco style over a drone, the pianist plays on a toy piano Bach's *Bist du bei mir* from the *Notebook* for Anna Magdalena; and in the last song, the oboe plays and elaborates the melody that opens Mahler's 'Der Abschied' in *Das Lied von der Erde*. But it is the sonorities that create the mysterious world of memories, dreams and half-focused reflections – the voice of the mezzo singing 'a kind of fantastic vocalise' into the lid of an amplified piano to produce 'a shimmering aura of echoes'; the sounds of a musical saw; a harp with paper threaded through its strings; Tibetan prayer stones; Japanese temple bells; a mandolin with one set of strings tuned down a quarter-tone to give 'a special pungency to its tone'; the occasional bending of the pitch on oboe and amplified piano; and from all the instrumentalists, whispers, murmurings and occasional shouts.

The essence of American music is its eclecticism. 'In composing *Ancient Voices of Children*,' says Crumb, 'I was conscious of an urge to fuse various stylistic elements. I was intrigued with the idea of juxtaposing the seemingly incongruous: a suggestion of Flamenco with a Baroque quotation, or a reminiscence of Mahler with a breath of the Orient.' The urge to fuse styles from different cultures was the inspiration behind most of the music discussed in this chapter, and indeed, given America's history and the diversity of its society, things could hardly have been otherwise. But we have also seen another side to American music, which is equally idiosyncratic, and that is the tendency to go to extremes. On one hand there are works such as Ives's Fourth Symphony (1909–16) and Carter's Double Concerto for harpsichord and piano (1961), which are full of activity and contain some of the most complex and dense textures ever com-

The 1986 film *True Stories*, directed by David Byrne of the rock group Talking Heads. 'The story is just a trick to get your attention. It opens the door and lets the real movie in.'

posed; on the other there are Cage's *4' 33"* and Philip Glass's opera *Einstein on the Beach* (1976), where virtually nothing happens. Ives and Carter are among those American composers who think of music as a discourse, a dialectic, in which the musically incongruous, and by implication, perhaps, the socially incongruous, can be reconciled; Cage and Glass are among those who consider that dialectics no longer have any place in music. The repetitive, minimalist music of *Einstein on the Beach* can only work when we consciously discard our dialectical expectations. Glass says that when listeners realize that nothing 'happens' in his music, they have to find another mode of listening – 'one in which neither memory nor antici-pation (the usual psychological devices of programmatic music whether Baroque, Classical, Romantic or Modernistic) have a place in sustaining the texture, quality or reality of the musical experience'. His hope is that listeners will be able 'to perceive the music as a "presence", freed of dramatic structure, a pure medium of sound'. This appears to be an attractive ideal, but in effect what the listener is offered is an escape from reality: there is no need to think when listening to minimalist music – the mind can simply switch itself off from rational activity and the capacity to feel. The danger of this, of course, is that music becomes a kind of drug. Fortunately, with the advent of composers such as John Adams (born 1947), minimalists have now become eclectics. In his opera *The Death of Klinghoffer* (1991), Adams says he was 'feeding on not just minimalism but Berg, Stravinsky, rock 'n' roll, doowop music, Arabic music and Jewish music. It makes it really fun to compose now, if you don't let those theoreticians get you down.'

John Adams.

Chapter 7

After the Wake: The Composer and Tradition

In the past, all composers, even the most innovative, built on tradition. Schoenberg built on the tradition he inherited from Brahms and Wagner, Stravinsky on the tradition that Rimsky-Korsakov passed on to him. It was the audible presence of tradition in their music that helped listeners to understand what they were saying. After the Second World War, however, there emerged a group of composers who decided that tradition must be jettisoned and that music should start again from scratch. These were the composers who attended the summer courses for new music held at Darmstadt after the war: Boulez, Stockhausen, the Belgians Karel Goeyvaerts and Henri Pousseur, and the Italians Bruno Maderna, Luigi Nono and Luciano Berio. All were born in the twenties and had lived under Fascism during their formative years. Like most young people at the time, they wanted to put the past behind them. But in their case, the decision was unparalleled. At no other time in the history of music had composers wanted to go to the extreme of completely abolishing the past. After the First World War composers had merely wanted to reject Romanticism, but in that war the authorities had not reduced music to the level of propaganda, as the Nazis did. Stockhausen said that he never wanted to hear a military march again. The ideal that the Darmstadt school had in mind was music that was totally objective and completely devoid of associations.

It was not until the early fifties, however, that this group of radical composers found a compositional method to realize their aspirations. In the intervening years, music was still in the hands of established composers, who were continuing to write as if the

'Revolutions have to be dreamt as much as engineered.' Pierre Boulez.

Warsaw in 1945.

195

Stravinsky conducting in 1947.

war had never occurred. Richard Strauss was then in his eighties and before his death in 1949 enjoyed a highly productive Indian summer. In a series of works culminating in his *Four Last Songs* (1948), he brought to its zenith the late Romantic style he had been pursuing since the 1880s. The songs are superb examples of the Romantic lied and bear witness to Strauss's extraordinary capacity to spin a long musical line. The last song, 'Im Abendrot', is through-composed, the principal line passing between the voice and the violins in one continuous sweep above slow-moving harmonies and the quiet, yet full, sonority of the typical Romantic orchestra. Being a valediction to Romanticism and Strauss's own farewell, it is fitting that it should end with a motif from his tone poem *Death and Transfiguration* (1889) – the one that is often described as representing 'the artist's ideology'.

The music that Stravinsky produced in the late forties was also backward looking. These were the years when neo-classicism, the style he pioneered in the twenties, reached its high point in his ballet *Orpheus* (1947) and opera *The Rake's Progress* (1947–51). Since 1920, he had taken the styles and mannerisms of such disparate composers as Pergolesi, Bach, Handel, Couperin, Beethoven, Rossini, Verdi and Tchaikovsky and made them his own by subjecting their formal gestures to his sometimes mischievous way of proceeding. In *The Rake* he took as his model eighteenth-century Italian opera, a genre whose very nature is the disruption of an ordered universe by a whimsical decision. Eighteenth-century Italian operas, whether serious or comic, are almost always set in motion by someone who decides to ignore reason and commonsense and act in a way that is bound to cause confusion. In Handel, the protagonist is usually a monarch or prince who falls in love with someone he cannot possibly marry, and as a result throws his court into utter confusion. In Mozart's Da Ponte operas, it is the action of a libertine that creates turmoil. Stravinsky based the plot of *The Rake's Progress* on the eight engravings by William Hogarth which trace the downfall of Tom Rakewell from the time he comes into his inheritance until he is committed to Bedlam as a lunatic. In Hogarth, Tom is clearly a rake by nature and so has only himself to blame for his fall; in Stravinsky's opera, he is simply a lazy but ambitious man, who becomes the victim of the devil in the guise of his servant Nick Shadow. The opera's libretto was written by W. H. Auden and Chester Kallman, but this alteration to the plot may have been suggested by Stravinsky himself. It brings the story into line with his belief that men can be victims of an irrational force over which they have no control. The music of *The Rake's Progress* consists of a series of set pieces divided by secco recitatives, but because the familiar forms and patterns are constantly being dismantled by Stravinsky's own mannerisms and gestures, the overall impression is one of affectionate irony. According to his amanuensis, Robert Craft, 'while composing *The Rake's Progress* almost the only music he would play on the piano and on his gramophone was *Così fan tutte*; the only opera performances he would attend were of Mozart, Verdi, and those epigones of the eighteenth century, Rossini and Donizetti'.

1951, the year in which the first performance of *The Rake's Progress* took place in Venice, also saw the première, in London, of Benjamin Britten's opera *Billy Budd*. This too is set in the eighteenth century and deals with the destruction of an innocent victim by the power of evil. But Britten's music, even though it draws on several models, including Stravinsky himself, avoids any direct reference to the eighteenth century or indeed to any other music of the past. Its prime aim is to draw audiences into the moral dilemma facing the protagonist, Captain Vere, whereas an out-and-out neo-classical composer would want to distance them from it. The style had therefore to be immediately comprehensible, the language expressive and easily grasped. Typical is the scene which came at the end of Act 3 in the original production. Vere, the captain of a warship on active service during the French wars of 1797, has to tell Billy Budd, one of his young sailors, that the drumhead court has sentenced him to death for unwittingly killing the master-at-arms, and that his execution is to take place in the morning. Vere looks on Billy as being 'the

Benjamin Britten and W. H. Auden in America in 1942.

mystery of goodness', and is afraid. 'Before what tribunal will I stand if I destroy goodness?' he asks himself. As captain of HMS *Indomitable* he is 'king of this fragment of earth, of this floating monarchy', but he is also 'the messenger of death'. Throughout his monologue, the accompaniment has rhythms associated with a stately funeral march. But as soon as he leaves the stage to deliver the verdict to Billy, the march gives way to a series of common chords which, by their scoring and by the nature of their relationship to one another, indicate first the mystery and terror implicit in the role that Vere is forced to perform, and then Billy's dignity and calm as he receives the news. The passage bears witness to Britten's belief that music is at its most effective when simple.

The success of *Billy Budd* was as nothing to the acclamation that had greeted Britten's first opera, *Peter Grimes*, which was hailed not only as the finest opera written by an Englishman since Purcell's *Dido and Aeneas* but also as a major landmark in English music generally. It was first produced in June 1945, just after the end of the war in Europe, and within three years it received a dozen international productions. English music was thus removed from its provincial backwater and cast into the open seas of worldwide scrutiny. The opera's setting, a fishing town on the East Anglian coast, is quintessentially English, as indeed are the characters who inhabit it. Peter Grimes, a fiercely proud, independent, yet deeply insecure, fisherman, arouses the animosity of his fellow townsfolk mainly because he is an outsider, someone who stands apart and has ambitions above his station. The action hinges on his treatment of his young apprentices. One has died at sea and the new boy accidentally falls to his death during the course of the story. The townsfolk blame Grimes for both deaths and on two occasions pursue him like a lynch mob. But on the morning after the second occasion, when Grimes goes out in his boat with the intention of drowning himself, and it is reported that there is a boat sinking out at sea, they continue to go about their daily work as if nothing had happened.

Britten said that when writing *Peter Grimes* he 'decided to reject the Wagnerian theory of "permanent melody" for the classical practice of separate numbers that crystallize and hold the emotion of a dramatic situation at chosen moments'. One of his chief aims, he said, was 'to try and restore to the musical setting of the English language a brilliance, freedom, and vitality that have been curiously rare since the death of Purcell'. But the influence of Purcell on him extended far beyond word-setting. It can be detected in some of the formal aspects of the score, such as his use of ground bass and the structure of one or two of the big set pieces. What distinguishes Purcell's use of the ground bass is the contrast between the rigidity of the bass and the freedom of the melodic line above it. Britten uses this model for the Passacaglia that forms the Interlude between scenes ii and iii of Act 2, where the action changes from the town's main street to the interior of Grimes's hut. Thirty-six repetitions of a ground bass underpin nine highly characterized variations of a viola tune, each of a different length. The bass is actually a continuation of the bass line in the quartet for four female voices which precedes the Passacaglia. The men of the town have just gone off in search of Grimes and the four women, convinced that men never grow up, sing what amounts to a lullaby for them. The audience is soon to discover, however, that the man who behaves most like a child is Grimes himself. The Passacaglia is a character sketch of him. The ground bass illustrates his obstinacy, the variations the volatile nature of his moods, the fact that he can be brusque and potentially violent at one moment, tender and dreamy the next. When the curtain goes up on scene iii Grimes is pushing the boy and urging him to get ready for a fishing trip. In its construction the scene is not unlike Purcell's dramatic song *The Blessed Virgin's Expostulation*, where a series of declamatory recitatives are separated by reflective songs. Here the declamatory recitatives, which draw on the Passacaglia's variations, are used for Grimes's rough, impetuous treatment of the apprentice and the boy's terrified reaction, the songs for Grimes's sudden lapses into introspection as he dwells on his memories, hopes and dreams.

Like Purcell, Britten was an outstanding song writer. Where his settings differ from Purcell's is in their accompaniments. Both composers tend to make use of a specific figure, but Britten tries to make the figure illustrative of the poem's central image, whereas Purcell's approach is more abstract. In this sense Britten is much closer to Schubert, who provides listeners with a figure that can immediately conjure up a picture – rippling water, galloping horses, the turning of a wheel. Typical is Britten's setting of Tennyson's 'The splendour falls on castle walls' in the *Serenade* for tenor, horn and strings (1943). The poem is one of the lyrics Tennyson included in his narrative in blank verse *The Princess* (1847). At one stage in the story three young couples climb a mountain and see the glories of a sunset. The lyric reflects their response to the sight, the 'castle' being a distant mountain, seen in the light of the dying sun. They imagine that on its turrets there might be a bugle, which, if it sounded, would echo round the peaks and call up the 'horns of Elfland'. In this situation, Britten needed two musical images, one for the splendour of the distant mountain castle, another for the bugle echoing round the peaks. A tight, stately, highly accented trochaic rhythm on the strings provides the first, while a fanfare of brilliant, echoing triplet figures on the horn, free and cadenza-like, is used for the second. The text giving rise to this second image is the refrain which closes each of the poem's three stanzas:

Blow, bugle, blow, set the wild echoes flying,
Blow, bugle; answer, echoes, dying, dying, dying.

In the third and final stanza, the last line is changed to 'And answer, echoes, answer, dying, dying, dying.' These words give Britten the opportunity to make the trochees 'bugle', 'echoes', 'flying', 'answer', 'dying' echo the much tighter trochees the strings played before. To bring the song to a close he reverses the procedure, the singer's 'dying, dying, dying' being echoed by the strings. It is a simple ending, but no better example could be found to illustrate Britten's attention to the inner meaning of a poem. By following the individual voice of the singer with the concerted voices of the strings, he finds a musical equivalent for Tennyson's transition from these particular echoes to those that perpetuate the human race and do not fade away.

O love, they die in yon rich sky,
They faint on hill or field or river:
Our echoes roll from soul to soul,
And grow for ever and for ever.

Michael Tippett's vocal music was also influenced by Purcell, and indeed *The Blessed Virgin's Expostulation* has often been cited as one of the models for *Boyhood's End*, a cantata for tenor and piano which was exactly contemporary with Britten's *Serenade*. The text comes from W. H. Hudson's autobiography of his childhood in Argentina, the extract Tippett selected coming from the section dealing with the writer's emotions on his fifteenth birthday, when he knew that he was growing up and would shortly lose the immediacy of his contact with nature. Although the word-setting is as brilliant and as Purcellian as anything Britten achieved, the work offers a vivid illustration of how the two composers differ. Tippett's accompaniments are closer to Schumann's than to Schubert's. He may begin with a descriptive figure, but as often as not he will develop and transform it so that its initial identity is changed. Essentially Tippett's thinking owes more to the classical symphonic tradition than Britten's. This is undoubtedly why the various sections of *Boyhood's End* are arranged to conform to the classical symphonic formula: introduction (recitative), allegro first movement (through-composed song), slow movement (recitative), scherzo and finale (linked to form another through-composed song). The similarities to *The Blessed Virgin's Expostulation* lie partly in the juxtaposition of declamatory recitative and song, but mainly in the free, seemingly spontaneous nature of the vocal line. As mentioned in Chapter 3, Tippett has that rare capacity to make his music dance, even when the rhythms do not appear very dance-like on paper. This means that he can imbue Hudson's recollections with an ecstatic lilt not present in the original text.

Michael Tippett.

By the time Tippett came to compose his opera *The Midsummer Marriage* in 1946, he had at his command a vocal and instrumental technique ideally suited to the project. Tippett relies on symphonic procedures to underpin almost everything. Although one or two of the set pieces, such as the huge aria for Sosostris in Act 3, are treated as separate numbers, most are absorbed into the symphonic context. The exultant recitative and aria which Mark sings near the beginning of the opera in anticipation of his marriage to Jenifer, for example, is simply a lyrical episode within an unfolding development section. The most unusual feature of the work, however, is the emphasis placed on dance, not as *divertissement*, but as ritual. Most of the opera's second act is taken up with three 'Ritual Dances', while a fourth brings the last act to its climax.

The relationship between Mark and Jenifer is the main issue. As is usual in comedies, they have to overcome the obstacles to their marriage – in this case not just the traditional ones raised by the girl's father, but their own illusions about themselves. To surmount these they have to undergo a process of Jungian individuation. They must learn to become aware of their real selves, and discover that love can flourish only when the self is transcended. Above all they must come to terms with the past and realize that their forthcoming marriage has its roots in the ancient ritual. Tippett makes this clear when Mark interrupts an ancient dance being performed by a group of mythological figures, and demands a new dance for his wedding; two guardians of tradition and the old knowledge tell him that if the ritual is abandoned there will be 'no point of rest, no grace, no beauty'. During the 'Ritual Dances' in the central act, Jack and Bella, a second couple preparing for marriage, witness three events that refer to their relationship: the hunting of the hare by the hound in autumn, the fish by the otter in winter, the bird by the hawk in spring. The fourth 'Ritual Dance' is initiated by Mark and Jenifer, after they have overcome all obstacles and appear within the petals of a lotus, transfigured as Shiva and Parvati, in mutual contemplation. Their dance celebrates voluntary human sacrifice: 'Fire in Summer'. Tippett relates this to the ancient fire festivities, which traditionally took place on Midsummer's Day, in remembrance of what may have been a primitive initiation ceremony. He has frequently been criticized for relying too heavily on Jung, Frazer's *The Golden Bough* and Jessie Weston's *From Ritual to Romance* for what he wanted to say about physical, spiritual and creative renewal in *The Midsummer Marriage*. But with their help he was able to give back to the musical theatre some of the magic it once had, and to draw attention to the value of tradition at a time when younger composers were abandoning it.

Among the composers active in the late forties were several who had embraced serialism before the war and had once been considered radicals. One of them was the Norwegian composer Fartein Valen (1887–1952), who, although he was familiar with Schoenberg's system, had invented his own form of serialism in the twenties. Valen permitted the repetition of a note before all the others had been sounded, a procedure that Schoenberg disallowed. His pursuit of serialism won him nothing but opposition in Norway, and when the Nazis invaded his country in 1940, he had to compose in total isolation. It was then that he must have felt the value of tradition and the necessity of upholding it. When, after the war, the Violin Concerto he had composed during some of Norway's bleakest days was performed at the 1947 ISCM Festival in Copenhagen, it was hailed as a landmark in the country's music, not only because it was elegant and lyrical, but because, like Berg's Violin Concerto, it ended with a chorale – in this instance *Jesu, meine Zuversicht* ('Jesus, my certainty').

Luigi Dallapiccola (1904–1975) is another composer who turned to serialism before the war and received recognition only after it was over. Success came with his *Canti di prigionia* for chorus, two pianos, two harps and percussion, given at the 1946 ISCM Festival in London. Unlike Valen, however, Dallapiccola was able to build on his success. During the First World War, he and his family were interned for a time by the Austrians, but it was not until 1938, when Mussolini announced that he was going to pursue the same anti-Semitic policy as the Nazis, that Dallapiccola decided to write a work about prisoners. *Canti di prigionia* is based on the last testaments of prisoners who are about to be executed: Mary Queen of Scots, Boethius and Girolamo Savonarola. The musical inspiration came from a performance of Webern's choral piece *Das Augenlicht*, which Dallapiccola heard in London in 1938. He had already begun to make tentative experiments with serialism, but it was some time before he felt able to commit himself to it wholly. As well as fragments of the *Dies irae* plainsong, *Canti di prigionia* contains two twelve-note rows, but his handling of them is very free and they are mainly confined to certain turbulent sections of the work; the nearest he gets to Webern is the inclusion of a canonic passage in Savonarola's farewell.

Dallapiccola maintained that the attraction of the twelve-note method lay in its melodic potential – a potential he was eventually able to realize in the *Liriche greche*, three sets of songs on ancient Greek texts composed between 1942 and 1945. After the first performance of *Canti di prigionia* in December 1941, he decided to cut himself off from what was happening in Italy and 'retreat into serenity'. The three sets of songs take as their texts Italian translations of poems by Sappho, Alcaeus and Anacreon. The six Alcaeus songs (the second set) were eventually dedicated to Webern after the war when Dallapiccola learned of his tragic death. The first song exposes the row and its retrograde, and forms an introduction. The other five are all based on canons, and make quite clear that Dallapiccola's interest in this strict form of counterpoint lies in its economy. In fact, as in Bach's exercise in canonic writing, *The Musical Offering*, he goes one step further by having the same melody run through all six songs. This is no coincidence: Dallapiccola's subtitle echoes Bach's '*Canones diversi*', and, like Bach, he begins with a 'canon perpetuus', a canon that returns to its beginning and is therefore potentially continuous. Bach also stands behind *Quaderno musicale di Annalibera*, the set of short piano pieces he composed for his daughter in 1952. In this instance, the model is Bach's *Notebook* for Anna Magdalena Bach. Annalibera was only eight, but Dallapiccola includes in his gift for her three formidable canons: the first consists of an arching melody shadowed by three different versions of itself, the second is a canon in contrary motion, the third a canon cancrizans (that is, a canon in which the second voice enters with the retrograde version of the melody).

Dallapiccola's main works, however, are dramatic pieces where high-flying contrapuntal textures have only a limited place. They include a ballet about Marsyas (1942–3) who was flayed alive by Apollo for daring to challenge the god to a musical contest, an oratorio about Job (1950) on whom God imposes terrible afflictions for no apparent reason, and a full-length opera about Ulysses (1960–68) who is searching for a meaning to his existence. *Ulisse* culminates in a scene where, after he has killed the suitors, Ulysses is alone at sea in a small boat. The night is starlit and brilliant, and as he looks up to the stars he suddenly realizes that he is at one with the god who has been the author of all his suffering. The same moment of revelation also brings Dallapiccola's two one-act operas to an end. It derives from the climax of Dante's *Divine Comedy*, where Beatrice leads Dante to paradise through the stars. The first of the operas, *Volo di notte* (1937–9), is based on Antoine de Saint-Exupéry's story about a pilot who decides to fly above a storm, knowing full well that his plane is running out of fuel and nothing can save him. As he ascends, the stars come into view, and suddenly everything about him seems to shine: his hands, his clothes, the wings of the aircraft. In the other opera, *Il prigioniero* (1944–8) the sight of the stars has a grim significance. The action takes place in a sixteenth-century Spanish prison and concerns torture by hope. The prisoner's gaoler has led him to believe that the political situation has changed and that he may be able to make his escape and regain his liberty. When the prisoner discovers the door of his cell left open he eventually finds his way into a garden. It is night and the sky is filled with stars; in his exultation he throws his arms round a tree. But from nearby comes the voice of the gaoler, softly repeating the word he had used to address the prisoner in his cell: 'brother'. It is none other than the Grand Inquisitor himself, and as the prisoner is led away to his death he murmurs to himself 'Liberty? Liberty?' Dallapiccola make use of three twelve-note rows in the opera, which represent prayer, hope and liberty. He also makes oblique references to operas by earlier composers. The chords that open the work, and are heard repeatedly throughout, for instance, are strongly reminiscent of those that open Puccini's *Tosca*. By referring to Puccini's opera, Dallapiccola is informing the audience before the action begins that his opera also is about deception.

The desire to retain strong associations with the music of the past during and immediately after the war was felt even by those who had been pupils of Schoenberg and were completely *au fait* with the twelve-note system. The Spanish composer Roberto Gerhard (1896–1970) studied under Schoenberg for five years in the twenties, but was never wholly committed to serialism until the fifties. As a republican Gerhard was forced to leave Spain in 1939 and seek refuge in Britain. Since Franco outlived him, he remained there for the rest of his life. But his roots were in Spain and he never forgot his inheritance. The slow movement of his Violin Concerto (1942–5), intended as a tribute for Schoenberg's seventieth birthday, is based on the row that Schoenberg devised for his Fourth Quartet (1936). But although the melodic material unfolds serially, the harmony belongs to an impressionistic world which Schoenberg would have shunned. And in the finale, where there are two enigmatic references to the *Marseillaise*, the dancing rhythms are eventually transformed into those of Gerhard's native Catalonia. It is almost as if the ghost of the great Spanish violinist Pablo Sarasate were hovering over the proceedings. Later, between 1945 and 1947, Gerhard wrote a comic opera based on Sheridan's play *The Duenna*; when it was eventually staged in 1992, it was considered, despite one or two dramatic flaws, to be worthy to stand alongside the two accredited comic opera masterpieces of the period, Strauss's *Capriccio* and Stravinsky's *The Rake's Progress*. Its ultimate success was due not only to the relationship of the various numbers to the song and dance forms of Spanish folk music, but also to the witty way in which Gerhard paces the music. His serial procedures are contained within an essentially tonal framework, which means that the listener can sense where the music is going and can be taken by surprise if the goal is delayed or the harmonic direction is changed.

In a musical culture where the twelve-note system was beginning to be accepted as perfectly compatible with music of the past, the ideas and music of the Darmstadt school of composers came as a shock. In the early days very little of their music was heard outside the confines of Darmstadt, but in May 1952 when Boulez published an article in *The Score* called 'Schoenberg is Dead', the musical world was left in no doubt that the aim of the avant garde was to reject tradition *in toto*. Most of that issue of *The Score* was devoted to tributes to Schoenberg, who had died the previous July. Ironically, the article that followed Boulez's was Roberto Gerhard's 'Tonality in Twelve-tone Music', one of the things Boulez attacked. Since the end of the war Schoenberg had produced some of his tersest and most widely respected scores: the String Trio (1946), *A Survivor from Warsaw* (1947), the Violin Fantasy (1949), two unaccompanied choral pieces, *Dreimal tausend Jahre* ('Three times a thousand years', 1949) and *De profundis* (1950), and the uncompleted *Modern Psalm* (1950). While acknowledging that Schoenberg

The bridge between the two halves of the Warsaw ghetto. Jews were not allowed to use the road that intersected the two parts, and were forced to use a footbridge.

Jewish children playing in the streets of the Warsaw ghetto.

had 'brought about one of the greatest revolutions that has ever taken place in music', Boulez maintained that the way he handled the twelve-note system,

left the way open to every sort of survival. For example, the persistent use of accompanied melody, of counterpoint based on principal and subsidiary (*Hauptstimme* and *Nebenstimme*). This, surely, is a most unfortunate inheritance from romanticism? It is not only in such outworn concepts, but also in the style itself that we can detect reminiscences of a discarded world. For stereotyped clichés abound with Schoenberg, clichés typical of a romanticism at once ostentatious and outmoded. I mean those continual anticipations with expressive stress on the harmony note, and those false appoggiaturas; also those broken chords, tremolos, and repetitions which sound as terribly hollow and deserve only too well the name 'subsidiary voices' which they have been given. Lastly there are the poor, and even ugly, rhythms, in which variations of the classical technique appear in the most disconcertingly simple way.

Schoenberg's grave in Los Angeles.

The article ends with the words of the title printed in capitals, 'Let us then, without any wish to provoke indignation, but also without shame or hypocrisy, or any sense of frustration, admit the fact that SCHOENBERG IS DEAD'. And by that Boulez meant all music from the past. The only music the avant garde revered was that of Webern, which was considered to be a precursor of their new pointillist style. From the pieces they were producing, it was clear that pointillism reduced music to its fundamentals: melodic lines, harmony, and consistent dynamics and attack had been eliminated, human feelings excluded, and all sense of the past or future eradicated.

As we saw in Chapter 3, the first piece to make music out of unconnected single notes was Messiaen's *Mode de valeurs et d'intensités* (1949). Its musical material consists of three overlapping twelve-note modes, the first covering the upper register of the piano, the second the middle register, and the third the lower register. By applying one of twenty-four different durations, one of twelve different types of attack, and one of seven different dynamics to each of the notes, Messiaen produces a repertory of thirty-six individualized notes. The order in which they appear seems to be arbitrary, and therefore the piece can in no way be called serial. But serial techniques could easily be combined with Messiaen's procedure, as Karel Goeyvaerts (born 1923) was to demonstrate in his Sonata for two pianos (1950), a piece which directly influenced Stockhausen's *Kreuzspiel* (1951) for oboe, bass clarinet, piano and percussion. As mentioned in Chapter 1, the piece that is now considered to be the *locus classicus* of integral, or total, serialism is the first piece in Boulez's first book of *Structures* for two pianos (1951–2). By using Messiaen's first twelve-note mode, with its associated scale of twelve durations, by increasing the number of dynamics to twelve, and serializing all four parameters, he produced, in the first section of the work at least, a style in which everything is reduced to 'absolute zero'. The only invention he allowed himself was the choice of register in which the individual notes should be placed.

Kreuzspiel was exactly contemporary with book 1 of *Structures*. Both were written immediately after a performance of Messiaen's *Mode de valeurs et d'intensités* at Darmstadt in 1951. Unlike Boulez, however, Stockhausen serializes only pitch and durations, and where Boulez makes these elements indepen-

Pierre Boulez in the 1950s.

dent, Stockhausen ties each duration to a specific
pitch class, so that all Cs are the same length, all C♯s
another length, and so forth. In *Kreuzspiel*, the interest lies in the 'cross-play', the way the pitches cross
from one register to another in the piano and woodwind, and the rhythmic patterns cross over among
the percussion instruments. The idea came from the
middle movements of Goeyvaerts's Sonata. Of particular interest is Stockhausen's introduction of an
entirely capricious element into his score. Whenever
notes coincide, which happens fairly often, the sys-
tematic course of the various processes is thrown
into momentary disarray. 'The note in some way or
another drops out of the series,' says Stockhausen,
'alters its intensity, transposes into the wrong register or takes a different duration from the one pre-
ordained.'

Although it cleared the ground for future innovations, pointillism soon had its day. All pointillist
pieces tended to sound the same. *Kreuzspiel* is one of
the exceptions, mainly because of the timbral variety
of the percussion instruments, particularly the two
finger drums (tumbas), which sound like the drums
in a classical Indian raga. One or two of
Stockhausen's colleagues, notably Boulez, accused
him of playing to the gallery by including them. But
perhaps this is the very reason why his music created
so much excitement at the time. Stockhausen always
has the listener in mind and has always been prepared to break the rules or the systems he devises in
order to make his music more approachable or more
dramatic. This is nowhere more vividly illustrated
than in the orchestral piece *Gruppen* (1955–7). The
work is actually scored for three orchestras, each
with its own conductor. One orchestra is on the audience's left,
another in front of it, and the third on its right. The fascination
of the piece lies in the way the three orchestras respond to one
another and, in the process, transform the material that is tossed
to and fro among them. In effect, Stockhausen makes the whole

Stockhausen's *Gruppen*
performed in Birmingham in
1996. The three conductors
are (*top to bottom*) John
Carewe, Simon Rattle and
Daniel Harding.

Long after a great deal of the music of the fifties has been forgotten, *Gruppen* will be left standing there, equally infuriating and magnificent.

affair sound as if a musical conversation is taking place on a gigantic scale.

As the title suggests, Stockhausen's interest has shifted from single notes to groups of notes – 174 altogether, and each highly individualized. None lasts for more than a few seconds, and they are usually but not always confined to one orchestra. Needless to say, most of the elements are serialized. Those that are not include the instrumentation of each group. The second group, for instance, is scored for solo violins, violas and cellos from the second orchestra. For the most part, all play in measured tremolo (on the bridge of their instruments). The serialized elements include pitch, tempo, the length of the group, the range of notes covered, and the way each of the violins and violas subdivides the regular minims played by the two cellos. The shape of the passage, however, may have been determined by the shape of the mountains that Stockhausen could see from his window when he was composing the piece in Switzerland. No sooner has this second group established itself than the third enters so that the two overlap. The third group is scored for the oboe, celesta, harp and tutti strings of the third orchestra, and it is immediately apparent that, although the two orchestras remain distinct, a rather amusing dialogue is taking place. The leader of the third orchestra, for example, plays fairly slowly a two-note figure similar to one that the leader of the second orchestra has just played in a far more lively fashion. Stockhausen transforms the imitation into a joke, however, by making the second orchestra 'correct' the leader of the third orchestra brusquely and dismissively, as if his hand were being smacked.

The humour of this passage comes from Stockhausen's imagination as a composer. In fact *Gruppen* is at its best when the self-imposed processes are relaxed and composition takes over. There are, for example, three large sections involving a number of groups in which the serialization of tempo and the range of notes is suspended and the music becomes dramatic and climactic. The first focuses on a solo violin line shared by the leaders of the three orchestras, the second contains plucked or struck sounds thrown from orchestra to orchestra, while 'to set the wild echoes flying' the third has muted and unmuted brass calls and a piano cadenza. This last culminates in the most intense climax of the work. Afterwards, with the eventual appearance of a *cantus firmus* on bells, harp, piano and vibraphone, the music gradually achieves more and more stability until it eventually fades into silence.

If Stockhausen suspends his schemes from time to time in order to create an effect, one or two of the Darmstadt fraternity had to do so for political reasons. Luigi Nono (1924–1990) showed himself to be at the forefront of avant-garde thinking in his *Polifonica–monodia–ritmica* in 1951, a piece which starts in a pointillist manner, though this eventually gives way to Italian lyricism in the work's central section. In 1952, however, Nono became an active member of the Communist Party, and henceforth his music had to be devoted to furthering its cause, which he did not through overt propaganda but by pointing out the evils of Fascism. As has already been mentioned, one of the basic tenets of the avant garde was that music should never seek to go beyond itself. This is why the avant garde found the setting of words so problematic in the early fifties. To get round this problem, composers began to split up words so that only phonemes, pure sounds devoid of extra-musical meaning, were discernible. While Nono was eventually to make extraordinarily effective use of this procedure, initially he was forced to accept that if he was to convey something of the misery that Fascism had inflicted on the world, he could not avoid using words and meaningful texts. Even so, in *Epitaffio per Federico García Lorca,* composed in 1952–3 to memorialize the sufferings of the Spanish people under Franco, words ultimately have to give way to music. The work is serial but intensely lyrical, and in the last of its three main sections draws on Spanish folk music. This final section consists of a setting for soprano, chorus and orchestra of Lorca's poem about the sacking and burning of a gipsy encampment during the Spanish Civil War by the Fascist Civil Guard. Most of the text is recited, so that the drama and pathos of the incident can be transmitted with absolute clarity; but at the climax, when the flames encircle the camp and the guardsmen ride away, Nono gives the chorus an unaccompanied melody, which is clearly derived from folksong. The line passes pensively from one section of the choir to another so that the text is not always easy to follow. It is the music that conveys the pity of it all: 'Oh

Stockhausen's
Helicopter Quartet.

One of Stockhausen's recent pieces is a string quartet in which each player has his own helicopter; it makes the logistical problems of *Gruppen* seem like child's play. But what matters in the end is how the music communicates, the visionary wildness of it all.

city of the gypsies! Who could see you and not remember you?'

Epitaffio is a powerful work, but its disregard for one of the avant garde's basic tenets must have worried Nono. It was not until 1956 that he resolved his dilemma in *Il canto sospeso*, a cantata for soloists, chorus and orchestra in nine movements, based on the last letters of those about to be executed by the Nazis. Some are very short, like the letter of a young Russian girl which constitutes the seventh movement: 'Goodbye mother, your daughter Lyubka is going down into the damp earth.' Others, originally longer, are cut down to a few salient sentences. One of these is the letter from a fourteen-year-old Polish boy, used for the fifth movement: 'If the sky were made of paper and if all the seas of the world were ink, I could not describe my sorrow to you or tell you what I can see all around me. Goodbye to you all. I cannot stop weeping.' The fourth movement combines selected sentences from three letters, all written by Greeks before their execution. But only the letters from the Russian girl and the Polish boy quoted above are presented so that listeners can follow their meaning reasonably clearly. The rest are virtually impossible to follow, either because Nono destroys the continuity by giving one word to the sopranos, the next to the basses, the next to the altos and so on, or because he reduces the text to a jumble of syllables. In other words, the music has returned to a form of pointillism, except that here the points are phonemes, which Nono sustains so that long lyrical lines emerge. At a performance of the work, listeners will doubtless have a copy of the texts in front of them, but what they hear is the cries of the victims transformed into music that transcends the written words.

Not all the members of the avant garde in the fifties were associated with Darmstadt or prepared to experiment with pointillism. The Greek composer Iannis Xenakis (born 1922), who had fought in the resistance during the war, knew personally what it was like to be imprisoned and condemned to death by the Nazis. 'In my music,' he said, 'there is all the anguish of my youth, of the resistance [the Greek anti-Fascist movement], and the aesthetic problems they posed, together with the gigantic street demonstrations or the rarefied mysterious noises, the mortal noises of the cold nights of December 1944 in Athens. Out of this was born my interest in masses of sound and, in turn, stochastic music.' Xenakis uses the term 'stochastic' to describe a musical situation in which the behaviour of individual elements within a broad band or mass of sound is random and unpredictable, but

Stockhausen's Helicopter Quartet. The Arditti Quartet's Graeme Jennings.

Keqrops by Xenakis: the overall sound is subtly calculated, the individual components are of less importance.

the behaviour of the mass itself can be predicted. Stochastic music, therefore, contrasts the clusters and contours of a mass of sound with the irrational behaviour of the details within it. Xenakis was an engineer and when he settled in Paris after the war he earned a living by helping the architect Le Corbusier with engineering and architectural calculations. Later he worked more closely with Le Corbusier and was asked to draw the plans for the convent of La Tourette and the Philips pavilion at the 1958 Brussels Exhibition. The model Xenakis used for the pavilion was the hyperbolic paraboloid, and he afterwards said that the idea for it came from the interlocking glissandos he had used in his orchestral work *Metastaseis* (1953–4), his first piece of stochastic music.

Later Xenakis went on to use a variety of mathematical models. *Pithoprakta* (1955–6), his next orchestral piece, makes use of information derived from the calculus of probabilities; *Herma* uses set theory and Boolean algebra; *Evryali* arborescent graphics. These last two are formidable piano pieces, dating from 1961 and 1973 respectively – formidable in the sense that they are extremely difficult to play but not necessarily to listen to. Despite the complexity of the concepts used by Xenakis to describe how he composed them, they are actually extremely vital and often very witty pieces. They exude the spirit of the Mediterranean rather than that of the study.

Equally opposed to pointillism were the young, avant-garde British and Commonwealth composers of the period. Most of them were born in the thirties, and were therefore younger than their continental contemporaries, so that Boulez, Stockhausen and Nono were composers they looked up to. But because the British Isles had never been invaded during the war and had never experienced Fascism, none of the young British composers felt any necessity to reject the past. They wanted their music to sound avant garde, yet they were not prepared to jettison tradition. Above all they were not willing to abandon the presence of line, though for them 'line' meant nothing so obvious as a melodic line, but a thread that ran unobtrusively through the piece: 'A line on which to hang things,' said one wag. What they did reject was the goal-orientated music associated with the tonal system. This is why medieval and Renaissance music became important for many of them, particularly music containing a cantus firmus.

The first to combine serial and medieval techniques in the same work was Peter Maxwell Davies (born 1934) in his short sextet for wind instruments, *Alma Redemptoris Mater* (1957). It is based on the plainsong Marian antiphon of the title, which the English composer John Dunstable (*c.*1390–1453) used in one of his most celebrated motets. In Maxwell Davies's piece the plainsong is absorbed into a ten-note row and heavily disguised, so that the uninformed listener is not likely to be aware of the work's connection with medieval music.

Twelve of Dunstable's motets are 'isorhythmic' – isorhythm being a means of spinning out a fragment of plainsong to make a cantus firmus long enough to span a motet of substance. The technique involves the superimposition of a repeating rhythmic pattern of a certain length (*talea*) upon a repeating melodic pattern of a different length (*color*) so that the beginnings of the two patterns coincide only after each of them has gone through several repetitions, the number, of course, being different for each pattern. When they do coincide, a larger cycle results, and that too can be repeated. Usually Dunstable started with a long cycle and then repeated it twice at successively faster tempos so that he ended up with three sections whose lengths were in the ratio of 6 : 4 : 3 or 3 : 2 : 1. Clearly this procedure was easily adapted to serialism, though, to comply with the proscription on repetition, methods had to be found to disguise the rotation of the cycles. One of the most original solutions occurs in David Lumsdaine's *Kellyground*, a half-hour-long, isorhythmic piano piece dating from 1966. Lumsdaine's *donné*, the idea which gave rise to

The opening of Stravinsky's *Agon*. The composer's 'pocket-sized history of music' and the title theme of *Leaving Home*.

Las Meninas by Diego Velasquez, 1656.

the *talea*, was the rhythm produced by two bells tolling in the ratio 4 : 5. To produce longer cycles he calculated the rhythms produced by three bells and then four bells ringing at different rates. These provided the equivalent of Dunstable's three large cycles, but Lumsdaine changes the cycles around so that the sequence is four bells, two bells, three bells. His *color* is a twelve-note row, permutated so that it too can be expanded into long cycles. At the end of the work the material is condensed into great bell-like chords so that the *donné*, the sound of clanging bells, is revealed.

The title *Kellyground* refers to Ned Kelly, the nineteenth-century Australian outlaw who was something of a Robin Hood figure and who might never have been captured had he not worn a heavy and cumbersome helmet on his last stand against the police, an image made famous by Sidney Nolan's series of paintings. Lumsdaine's piece centres on Kelly's last night in Melbourne gaol before his death by hanging – the bells that come to the surface at the end of the work being his death knell. The sequence of incidents leading up to his death suggest that Kelly ultimately finds peace within himself. Each rotation of the *color* relates to one of these incidents: Kelly's return to consciousness, his sight of the foothills of the Wombat Ranges, the clamour of bird song when the sun rises, and finally the moment when he takes the bird song into himself. By alternating very rapid rhythms of the bird song with slow almost static music, Lumsdaine creates the impression that we have entered Kelly's mind and are listening as intently as he to the songs of the birds. It is as if in the few moments before his death Kelly becomes fully at one with everything around him.

Although medieval techniques are not audible in *Alma Redemptoris Mater* or *Kellyground*, the young British and Commonwealth composers of the day were profoundly influenced by a work in which echoes of the medieval world can be clearly detected – Stravinsky's ballet *Agon* (1953–7), the score and recording of which were both issued in 1957. Most British composers of that generation still acknowledge their debt to it. *Agon* is one of a number of pieces that reflect Stravinsky's interest in Webern between 1952 and 1955, an interest which drew him closer and closer to serialism during the fifties until eventually he embraced it completely in *Threni* (1957–8), a choral work based on the Lamentations of Jeremiah. In *Agon*, however, serialism occurs only in parts of the score. The work is based on a set of French courtly dances of the seventeenth century, arranged into four groups of three and supplied with a very formal framework: the same fanfare opens and closes the ballet, and the same interlude appears between the four groups.

However, it is only the dance types that refer to the seventeenth century; the music, with its constant use of the Landini cadence and its strange orchestration, refers to earlier periods. Francesco Landini was a late fourteenth-century Italian composer and the cadence associated with his name moves to the final note from the minor third below, not, as is usual, from the note immediately above or below. It is consequently very distinctive and even those who are unfamiliar with the late fourteenth century will recognize it as being medieval in character. Stravinsky's orchestration, on the other hand, is a little less easy to pin down. He scores the work for a standard symphony orchestra plus mandolin and piano, but the sonorities he obtains are unique. One dance is scored for solo violin, xylophone and two trombones; another for three flutes, mandolin, harp, piano, timpani, solo viola, three solo cellos and two solo double basses, the double basses and two of the flutes playing harmonics throughout. Clearly combinations such as these bear no relationship to seventeenth-century ensembles, and these precise instruments would not have been found in the fourteenth century either. But in all probability Stravinsky had read Gustave Reese's *Music in the Renaissance* when it was published in 1954, and there he would have found lists of equally strange instrumental

George Balanchine was spot on when he said that *Agon* is a machine, but a machine that thinks. It is like a pocket-sized history of music. The orchestration has the wheezy quality of Renaissance music, but also the dubious smell of Renaissance sanitation.

Picasso's reinterpretation of Maria Augustina Sarmiento, one of the figures in Velasquez's *Las Meninas*.

groupings used in the Italian *intermedi*: one, for example, calls for four harpsichords, four viols, two sackbuts, two lutes, two tenor recorders, flute and a cornett.

The feature of *Agon* that appealed most strongly to Maxwell Davies was the Landini cadence. In 1961 Davies went to the major Picasso exhibition in London and was fascinated by the way Picasso had expanded or exploited in several of his paintings certain obscure details in Velasquez's *Las meninas* – the outline of a dog or a trick of perspective, for example. Taking this as his lead, he selected a detail from the 'Pas-de-deux' in *Agon* – a rising minor third on the violas decorated by the same minor third on a solo violin – and expanded it into a String Quartet lasting a quarter of an hour. For his note row he took a line from the tenor part of his carol *Ave Maria – Hail, Blessed Flower*, which contains a preponderance of minor thirds. For his structure he followed the example of Stravinsky's 'Pas-de-deux', dividing the work into two parts, the first consisting of a long Adagio, the second a series of shorter, faster movements, resembling the form of a sixteenth- or early seventeenth-century canzona. In the Adagio, the cantus firmus, decorated by melismas which the players can play freely in their own time, proceeds from beginning to end without a break; in the canzona, however, it is split up into shorter units and is varied in much the same manner as Monteverdi varies the plainsong in the canzona form that makes up the 'Sonata sopra "Sancta Maria"' in his Vespers of 1610 – that is to say, by changing the rhythm and context to produce a mosaic of different perspectives. One interesting feature of the Adagio is Davies's method of permutating the note row by using a traditional bell-ringing 'change' known as a Plain Hunt.

For Harrison Birtwistle the significant thing about *Agon* was its striking orchestration and Stravinsky's ability to 'invent an ancient world'. In *The Rite of Spring* Stravinsky did indeed create such a world, but Birtwistle believes that he also did so in *Agon* and one or two other works. The dances in *Agon* are so original and carry such conviction that they sound as though they are the source of early seventeenth-century music by composers such as Pierre Guédron. They seem to represent the dances of the *ballet de cour* in their first, vital but raw state, before they became refined. This being so, a circular process is implied: at any point a composer can initiate the historical process again, can start from the beginning. In other words, inventing an archaic world serves the same purpose as constructing an isorhythmic cycle – it suggests perpetual recurrence. The world that Birtwistle himself most enjoys inventing is that of the ancient Greeks – the raw, sensuous world that existed long before Socrates and the Republic. *Tragoedia*, the piece that established Birtwistle's name in 1965, returns to the tragic theatre as it might have been in its primitive days before Aeschylus. But it is a purely instrumental piece, scored for a string quartet and a wind quintet, with a harp to link them. All that is known about the ancient theatre is that it was a Dionysian festival, and that from out of the chorus which took part there gradually emerged one or two protagonists. In *Tragoedia* the protagonists are the horn and cello, the odd men out of their respective groups – the horn because it is the only brass instrument, the cello because it is the only instrument held between the knees. Their duets culminate in a soaring love song, after which they are absorbed back into the chorus, each, in effect, acknowledging that their individuality can flourish only in relation to the community to which they belong and to which they must ultimately return.

Birtwistle bases the sections of the work on the formal divisions of early tragedy – 'Prologue', 'Parodos', 'Episodion', 'Antistrophe', 'Stasimon', etc. – but never forgets that the word 'tragoedia' means 'goat dance'. And yet at the centre of the piece, in the movement he calls 'Stasimon', there is a period of Apollonian serenity singularly at odds with the Dionysian raucousness characteristic of so much of the work. It is around this moment of tranquillity that the whole work pivots; the essence of its structure is bilateral symmetry, not only about a vertical axis, but also, and much more significantly, about a horizontal one. 'This is what impels the music forward across the central "Stasimon" and into the second "Episodion",' says Birtwistle. 'Symmetry may be seen retrospectively as a static phenomenon; but incomplete symmetry, that is, symmetry in the process of being formed, is dynamic because it creates a structural need that eventually must be satisfied.' It should be noted, however, that none of Birtwistle's symmetries are exact mirror images: all of them are varied, so a much more accurate description of his aim, not only in *Tragoedia* but in all of his pieces, would be 'non-symmetrical balance'.

All Birtwistle's music contains a theatrical dimension and all his pieces are built on the notion of perpetual recurrence or cyclic return: *Tragoedia* returns to a version of the goat dance with which it began. But these aspects of his music can be heard even more vividly in *Ritual Fragment* (1990), composed in memory of Michael Vyner, the administrator of the London Sinfonietta. The work is scored for fourteen players, and the ten who can carry their instruments without too much trouble are requested to move in turn to the front of the platform, where they pay their tributes to the deceased. When they stand up and return to their seats at the back after their tributes, those who have accompanied them signal their approval by slight gestures, which Birtwistle has written into their music. In that the instrumentalists have roles to play in the solemn ritual, they resemble actors who cannot be themselves but have to play a part. Their tributes are based on the cyclic return of a melody which is varied to suit the nature of the instruments. The bass trumpet is hardly likely to play it in the same way as the agile flute, for example. The melody itself is never exposed, but is simply a frame for what must appear to be a series of improvisations. However, since Birtwistle has never embraced serialism, it cannot be a twelve-note row. As likely as not it will resemble a fragment of plainsong, but this can never be verified because his chromatic elaborations conceal what lies beneath. What can be confirmed is that Birtwistle thinks of his music as being monody, an unaccompanied melodic line. For those who have heard his music, and believe that its richness can come only from the interplay of several independent lines, this may seem strange. But when these lines are examined they turn out to be duplications at the fourth, fifth or octave of the monody or cantus firmus. Birtwistle's harmony therefore has its roots in twelfth- and thirteenth-century organum, and it is this that helps to give his music its elemental quality, the feeling that, like *The Rite of Spring* and a few works by Varèse, it belongs to an ancient world. The only way in which it differs from organum is that Birtwistle rarely uses perfect fourths, fifths or octaves; he nearly always distorts them by widening or narrowing the intervals, so that they become discordant and abrasive.

Birtwistle relates everything he does to a central organizing principle, which involves starting with an absolutely regular and uniform pattern of the simplest, most predictable kind, then superimposing upon it a pattern which is its extreme opposite, something utterly capricious. This is the principle that governs the growth, development and evolution of living things, but biochemists put it the other way around: organic life, they say, results from the perpetuation of purely accidental and unpredictable events by the necessity of chemical reactions. In Birtwistle's harmony the purely accidental and unpredictable events which distort and give life to the predictable nature of fourths, fifths and octaves, for example, come from computer-generated random numbers. Birtwistle applies the principle not only to harmony but also to just about everything he does in his music. Who could be more capricious than Mr Punch, the 'hero' of his first opera, *Punch and Judy* (1966–7)? Punch has his origins in the seventeenth century, and the work, with its host of separate numbers, is modelled on the kind of opera that became fashionable during the middle Baroque era – except that Birtwistle insists that his work is a 'source opera': although it is written after its seventeenth- and eighteenth-century models, it creates the impression that it predates the sophistication of Scarlatti and Handel.

The plot concerns the ritualized murders Punch perpetrates – his arbitrary slaughter of the baby, his wife Judy, the lawyer, the doctor and even Choregos, the showman, who manipulates the puppets and is, in effect, Punch's *alter ego*. Birtwistle also includes Punch's quest for Pretty Poll, an idealized doll on a stick, and his eventual outwitting of the public hangman. But, of course, the opera is an allegory: no sooner are the characters killed than they return to life; and in the end Punch wins his Pretty Poll. Given the folk origins and connections of *Punch and Judy*, it is surprising to find that the work that stands behind it – that shadows it, as it were – is Bach's *St Matthew Passion*. One reason may be that Birtwistle wanted the logical unfolding of Bach's masterpiece to be a reminder of how rituals usually proceed; another may be that he wanted to indicate that in its own way *Punch and Judy* is also a kind of Passion. Three of its many chorales are 'Passion Chorales'. There are also two 'Passion Arias', the more poignant being the one with oboe d'amore obbligato, sung by Judy after the ritual death of Choregos. Throughout the opera, Choregos, in the way he links and comments on the various episodes, is both chorus and Evangelist, a role emphasized by the expressive, *parlando* style of his delivery. The climax of the opera comes when Punch sings a serenade to Pretty Poll, only to have her dismissively brush him aside. Choregos, looking at him from the side of the stage, then sings the most expressive music in the whole opera, music not unlike that given to the Evangelist when he reports Peter's denial in Bach's Passion: 'Weep, my Punch. Weep out your unfathomable, inexpressible sorrow.'

Punch and Judy is one of the very few of Birtwistle's compositions related to a specific work from the past. Like most other British composers of his generation, Birtwistle finds the past useful mainly for the techniques it can supply. But in the sixties and early seventies an increasing number of composers throughout the Western world began to make quotations from other periods of music an integral part of their style. The reason varied with the composer and the work. In *Eight Songs for a Mad King* (1969) Maxwell Davies quotes arias from Handel's *Messiah* to bring out the pathos of George III's condition, and refers to the styles (though not necessarily to specific pieces) of a range of other composers. In his piano piece *Ruhe sanfte, sanfte Ruh'* (1978), David Lumsdaine made the last chorus of the *St Matthew Passion* the basis of an extended meditation as a memorial for the wife of a friend. In *Kurzwellen mit Beethoven* (1970) Stockhausen put together a tape consisting of a continuous stream of fragments from Beethoven's music, interspersed with passages from his letters, which a group of players transform according to Stockhausen's instructions, the aim being 'to hear with fresh ears musical material that is familiar, "old", preformed; and to penetrate and transform it with a contemporary musical consciousness'.

Such uses of quotation was not confined to western Europe. It was the late sixties when George Crumb produced his *Ancient Voices of Children*. A little later, in his fifteenth and last symphony (1971), Shostakovich quotes snatches of Glinka, Rossini and Wagner. The Fifteenth is an enigmatic work which makes sense only when it is realized that in his last years Shostakovich suffered from poliomyelitis, and that while he was composing the symphony his condition was getting worse. In essence, he was taking an ironic look at his public and private personas and preparing himself for death. The first movement parodies the satirical mask he wore all his life, and when he quotes (or rather misquotes) the opening bars of the famous melody from Rossini's *William Tell* Overture – which in Russia is associated with toy soldiers and in the West with the Lone Ranger – he makes the whole movement sound like a sham. In contrast, the melancholy second movement, where there are no quotations, must surely represent the dark, private side of his nature. The remaining movements reflect on mortality. For those familiar with the scherzo of Mahler's Seventh Symphony (discussed in Chapter 2), Shostakovich's scherzo can be nothing else but a dance of death. And for those who know *Tristan and Isolde*, the fate motif from *The Ring*, and an elusive song by Glinka, his finale can only mean that Shostakovich had come to believe he might face the horrors of death with equanimity and even, perhaps, with humour.

The composer who went further than anyone else in his use of quotations was Bernd Alois Zimmermann (1918–1970). Although he included himself among the post-war avant garde, he was older than Boulez and Stockhausen, and felt that he still had his roots in tradition. He therefore had no inhibitions about writing an opera in the late fifties and early sixties, even though his younger contemporaries spurned the genre – Boulez even proclaimed that opera houses ought to be blown up. In the event, *Die Soldaten* ('The soldiers', 1958–60) turned out to be the most important German opera since Berg's *Wozzeck*. Indeed, it owes a great deal to Berg's masterpiece in that each scene is based on a specific musical structure such as the chaconne, ricercare and toccata. Where it differs is in its simultaneous use of different locations and temporal dimensions. Although he eventually had to modify his plans, Zimmermann originally envisaged a stage with twelve acting areas, each with its own instrumental ensemble. This would enable the audience to see different events taking

Györgi Ligeti's own painting *The people who live in the clouds*, 1967.

place in different locations more or less simultaneously. At the same time, by his use of quotations, he could also achieve what he called 'rotated time', a sudden shift from the present to the past.

The plot is based on a story by the late eighteenth-century dramatist Jacob Lenz, who believed that drama should be devoted to strong, ruthless characters. As the title of the play suggests, the strong, ruthless characters in *Die Soldaten* are a group of army officers who deliberately set out to turn a respectable middle-class girl into a whore. The setting is Flanders 'yesterday, today and tomorrow'. In the crucial second act of the opera, when the girl's seduction takes place, Zimmermann has the organ play the *Dies irae* plainsong; trombones and tubas play the chorale *Wenn ich einmal soll scheiden* ('Be near me, Lord, when dying'), sung just after Christ has yielded up the ghost in Bach's *St Matthew Passion*; two of the stage ensembles play military marches in different tempos; and on top of all this, four high trumpets blaze out the chorale

Komm, Gott Schöpfer, heiliger Geist ('Come, Creator God, Holy Ghost').

Zimmermann had personal experience of how ruthless and cruel soldiers could be because he had served in the army during the war. He knew also that in a world where soldiers are masters, pity is at a premium. In the last interlude and final scene of *Wozzeck*, Berg pulled out all the stops to evoke pity not only for Marie and Wozzeck but also for their child. *Die Soldaten* ends with the last meeting of the violated woman and her father. She has been reduced to begging for her living and asks him for money. Not recognizing her, he refuses at first, then when he thinks of his daughter he relents, though he is still unaware of who the beggar is. The scene takes place against a visual and aural collage in the form of film footage, musical cross-references and pre-recorded tape. At the end, when the woman falls to the ground weeping, the theatre is filled with the sound of marching boots.

It was only later that Zimmermann equated his use of quotation with collage in art, his model being Kurt Schwitters, who assembled his works from discarded materials such as tram tickets, old shoe soles, feathers and dishcloths. Zimmermann's *Musique pour les soupers du roi Ubu* (1966), an orchestral piece he described as a 'ballet noir', consists entirely of quotations, 'discarded' pieces of Baroque, Classical, Romantic and modern music, placed within Renaissance dance tunes. The title of the piece refers to the 'strong and ruthless character' whom Alfred Jarry had conjured up in the closing years of the nineteenth century and 'celebrated' in several plays. Ubu is nothing more than an outrageous, overgrown schoolboy, who makes himself King of Poland in order to kill and torture everyone he comes across. He was meant to represent 'the eternal imbecility of man, his eternal lubricity, his eternal gluttony, the baseness of instinct raised to the status of tyranny'.

In one of his last works, *Requiem for a*

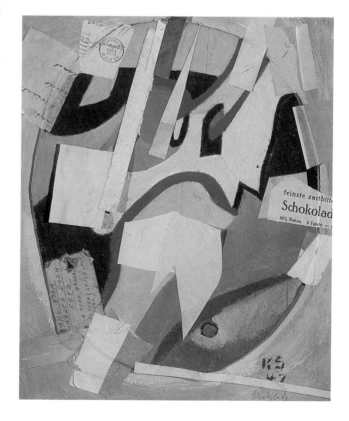

Kurt Schwitters' collage *Schokolade*, 1947.

Young Poet (1967–9), Zimmermann made extensive use of quotations from verbal texts as well as from music. His purpose here was to summarize the history of Europe between 1920 and 1970 from two perspectives, the public and the private. To represent the first, he selected sentences from speeches by Hitler, Chamberlain, Churchill, Stalin, Nagy, Papandreou and Dubček, among others; to represent the other he chose passages from certain literary texts, focusing in particular on the work of three poets who died young and by their own hands: Vladimir Mayakovsky, Sergei Yesenin and Konrad Bayer. He hoped that by juxtaposing the texts it might be possible to encompass the period as a totality and to reflect on its contradictions. The fragments are not presented in chronological order, so that during most of the work Zimmermann creates the impression that he is eavesdropping on someone's unfocused recollections. What holds the work together is a sung Requiem Mass going on in the background. The work is scored for soloists, speakers, three choirs, jazz band and symphony orchestra, and with these forces Zimmermann can include musical quotations from a great many different periods, styles and genres. Beethoven and Wagner rub shoulders with Messiaen, and Messiaen with the Beatles, at that time the representatives of the music of the future. For Zimmermann this was the essential feature of collage. It enabled him to draw attention to time – the issue that has preoccupied not only twentieth-century composers, but all those who want to escape from the goal-orientated philosophy of contemporary society. Zimmermann took his cue from St Augustine's observation that in God there is no before and after, only an eternal present. When men talk about past, present and future, St Augustine maintained, they are speaking loosely; we live only in the present, so can really only refer to 'a present of things past, a present of things present and a present of things future'. Zimmermann believed that his collage technique made this absolutely clear.

Luciano Berio (born 1925) has also built a piece from verbal and musical quotations, but refuses to acknowledge that it is collage. 'I'm not interested in collages, and they amuse me only when I'm doing them with my children,' he says; 'then they become an exercise in relativizing and "decontextualizing" images, an elementary exercise whose healthy cynicism won't do anyone any harm.' Berio had been much closer to the ideas of the Darmstadt circle than Zimmermann, but he arrived on the scene when pointillism was beginning to wane. By far the strongest influences on his music were his early contact with Dallapiccola and his marriage to the American mezzo-soprano Cathy Berberian. It was in writing for Berberian that he developed his interest in vocal techniques and performing gestures. *Circles* (1960), one of the most acclaimed of his early works, is a setting of three fragmentary poems by e. e. cummings for mezzo-soprano, harp and two percussionists. Practically everything in the piece circles, including the sounds derived from the consonants and vowels of the words, which are passed, often with great rapidity, from singer to instrumentalists and back again. It requires a mezzo of great dexterity and a wide range of vocal techniques. Among the other pieces Berio composed for his wife was *Sequenza III* (1966), one of several 'sequenzas' written to exploit the virtuosity of outstanding performers he admired. *Laborintus II* and particularly *Sinfonia* – the work where Berio's use of quotations reaches its zenith – were designed for the Swingle Singers, an extraordinary group of mainly French singers, who dazzled everybody in the sixties with their virtuoso performances of instrumental music by Bach. One of their most distinctive features was the vibratoless singing of the four female members of the group, a rare phenomenon in those days.

Laborintus II was commissioned by French Radio to celebrate the 700th anniversary in 1965 of the birth of Dante. The texts were compiled by the poet and Dante scholar Edoardo Sanguineti and drawn from the *Vita nuova*, the first nine cantos of the *Inferno*, and a passage on music from *Il convivio*. In addition eight actors recite, among other things, parts of a rambling and, in this context, meaningless 'catalogue' of Hebrew history, compiled by Isidore of Seville, along with a modern equivalent of it. Sanguineti's intention was to draw a parallel between Dante's journey through the labyrinth of the underworld, and the journey that he himself would have to take to escape 'the degradation of values' that characterizes the maze of modern society. The relationship hinges on Dante's condemnation of usury. But instead of using Dante's words, he quotes part of Ezra Pound's *Canto XLV*, which draws on Dante's condemnation to castigate the rampant commercialism of modern society. In the end, however, Sanguineti does discover something of value, in the harmonious effect of music on the soul and in looking at sleeping children.

Berio's music is concerned almost exclusively with the temptations the traveller encounters on his journey through the labyrinth, and his principal musical image is that of the three sirens in Homer's *Odyssey*, which James Joyce brought up to date in *Ulysses*, where they figure as prostitutes who ensnare men by offering their bodies in exchange for money. The bulk of the music is therefore given to two sopranos and a mezzo, who have to sing into microphones all the time. The work opens with their street calls and, indeed, throughout they represent the voices of temptation. Apart from introducing jazz to suggest the raciness of the modern urban world, Berio makes only one reference to other music – when Sanguineti says that he is beginning to see visions after accomplishing 'nine days of bitter anguish' in the labyrinth, and the three sirens beguilingly evoke the madrigal style of Monteverdi.

Virgil in his study, from Tom Phillips' illustrated translation of Dante's *Inferno*.

Like *Laborintus II*, *Sinfonia* represents a journey through a labyrinth, but on this occasion the labyrinth is of Berio's construction. It is put together from a host of apparently disparate events from the past and the present, and Berio's aim is to find a way out of the maze and discover a glimmer of hope for the future. The events he chooses include the two most significant of 1968, the year *Sinfonia* was composed – the assassination of Martin Luther King and the student demonstrations in Paris. These are juxtaposed with references to myths about the origin of water, which Claude Lévi-Strauss discusses in his anthropological study *Le cru et le cuit* ('The raw and the cooked').

Quite frequently Lévi-Strauss refers to the transformation of these myths in social cultures as resembling the transformations that take place in music. Berio uses fragments of some of the myths in the first of *Sinfonia*'s five movements, but none is developed, and at the end they are left hanging in the air. The second movement is a meditation on the name 'Martin Luther King'; its music comes back as the cantus firmus of the last movement, where Berio completes the myths abandoned inconclusively in the first movement, forges all the work's material into a synthesis, and creates a sense of unity.

The longest and most important movement is the third, which has the scherzo of Mahler's Second Symphony running through it. Berio likens this to a skeleton, 'a skeleton that often re-emerges fully fleshed out, then disappears, then comes back again'. But, he says, 'it's never alone: it's accompanied throughout by the "history of music" that it itself recalls for me, with all its many levels and references – or at least those bits of history that I was able to keep a grip on, granted that often there's anything up to four different references going on at the same time'. The references he speaks of are quotations from pieces by Bach, Beethoven, Brahms, Boulez, Berlioz, Debussy, Ravel, Schoenberg, Stravinsky, Strauss and Stock-hausen, which 'appear, disappear, pursue their own courses, return to the Mahler, cross paths, transform themselves into the Mahler or hide behind it'.

Set against this musical fabric are verbal quotations – odd remarks made by Harvard undergraduates, slogans written by the students on the Sorbonne walls during the Paris insurrection and a host of other odds and ends. At one stage, as if to fill in time, the audience has the names of all eight members of the Swingle Singers read out to it, and is then asked if it is enjoying the show. The only thing that holds these scraps together is the refrain: 'Keep going, keep going,' an injunction that comes from Samuel Beckett's novel *The Unnamable*. In fact quotations from *The Unnamable* can be heard throughout the movement; they function in much the same way as the Mahler

Samuel Beckett.

229

scherzo. But they paint a grim picture. The issue, as so often in Beckett, is the passing of time. At one point in the novel, the narrator wonders why time 'piles up all about you, instant on instant, on all sides, deeper and deeper, thicker and thicker . . . why it buries you grain by grain, neither dead nor alive, with no memory or anything, no hope of anything, no knowledge of anything, no history and no prospects, buried under the seconds, saying old things, your mouth full of sand'. Nevertheless, at the end, in a sentence which Berio uses to bring the third movement to a close, the narrator discovers a ray of hope: 'I'll never know, in the silence, you don't know, you must go on, I can't go on, I can't go on, I'll go on.'

Berio calls the third movement 'a voyage to Cythera'. He is doubtless referring to Baudelaire's poem *Un voyage à Cythère*, which also paints a grim picture yet ends with a glimmer of hope. It tells of a traveller who comes across the island where Venus, the goddess of beauty and sensual love, had her first shrine, and is riveted by the sight of vultures devouring a rotting corpse hanging from a gibbet. 'O Venus, in your isle I found nothing standing but a symbolic gallows, with my own image hanged upon it – O heavenly Father, give me strength and courage to contemplate my heart and body without disgust!' The hope lies in the fact that the poem represents a turning point in Baudelaire's life. In Berio's *Sinfonia* the third movement is the turning point of the journey through the labyrinth. From then onwards the music and the texts gradually move towards the desired synthesis, tentatively in the fourth movement, more surely in the fifth. The fact that this final movement is underpinned by the meditation on Martin Luther King, who came to symbolize the need for reconciliation in the sixties, suggests that the journey has indeed ended in a spirit of unity.

Berio's insistence that the third movement of *Sinfonia* is not a collage comes from the fact that the musical quotations in the third movement were suggested by Mahler's music itself. They are 'signals which indicate which harmonic country we are going through, like bookmarkers, or little flags in different colours during an expedition full of surprises'. However, in 1973, his colleague Bruno Maderna (1920–1973) produced an opera which was pure collage. It is based on Petronius's *Satyricon*, a satire about the decadence of Roman society in Nero's time. The events take place during a dinner party given by a couple from the *nouveau riche*. As well as including the most grotesque gastronomic absurdities, the plot involves a drunken brawl and two ghost stories. The sixteen scenes follow no logical sequence and may be placed in any order the production's director or conductor thinks fit. The decadence of the characters' behaviour, the lack of any moral centre to hold things together, have their musical equivalent in a score which also has no centre, for it consists almost entirely of quotations from popular classics and passages of pastiche. At the time, it was considered an indictment of modernism. Maderna's fellow composers, especially those he had been associated with at Darmstadt, believed it to be an attack on all they had stood for in the fifties and sixties. *Satyricon* can be seen as symbolizing the disintegration of those strong idealistic movements that distinguished the period after the war. After 1973 there were no flags to rally round. Everybody was alone, and one of the most fruitful periods in twentieth-century music had come to an end.

Chapter 8
Music Now

Although there are still those who wish to explore the extremes of complexity or simplicity, most composers since the early seventies have sought a less polarized position. Even those who have remained loyal to the advanced style they established in the fifties have softened their approach – not necessarily to conform to fashion, but simply because there is no longer any need to be so uncompromising. Boulez's *Rituel in Memoriam Maderna* (1974) is a much more accessible work than *Structures I* (1951–2), *Le marteau sans maître* (1954) or even *Pli selon pli* (1957–62). Carter and Birtwistle have also become more immediately approachable. Carter's *A Symphony of Three Orchestras* (1976) is still pretty formidable, but *In Sleep, in Thunder* (1982), his setting of poems by Robert Lowell for tenor and chamber ensemble, presents many fewer problems for the listener; and in his Oboe Concerto (1988), it seemed that he might even be returning to the neo-classical tendencies he had abandoned in the forties. Birtwistle doggedly sticks to the highly idiosyncratic procedures he forged for himself in *Refrains and Choruses* (1957), but his voice has been tempered too. He now takes much greater account of what he calls 'the sanctity of the context'. By this he means that he allows the material to find its own way out of a given situation; it need not conform to any pre-compositional plan he may have made. As *Gawain* (1991) and *The Second Mrs Kong* (1994), his two recent operas, bear witness, the cyclic procedures are now much less in evidence, so that his music flows more easily and has become richer and more expansive.

One of the great changes from the end of the nineteenth century to our own is the fact that heaviness was always considered profundity, and now, the idea of lightness – not lightness like a feather but lightness like a bird – is something we have learned to treasure in all the arts.

Many of the composers who have moved closer to the centre than Boulez or Carter have relinquished the style they established when they started out. The exceptions to this *volte face* are those whose music has always been rooted in modality. Xenakis's *Herma* and Lumsdaine's *Kellyground* may not have sounded modal to audiences in the sixties, but now

that both composers have produced works in which their modal thinking is more clearly exposed, one hears their earlier works in a new light. Xenakis has used modality most obviously in the incidental music for Euripides' *Helena* (1977) and *The Bacchae* (1993); Lumsdaine in pieces such as *A Tree Telling of Orpheus* (1991), where in the course of twenty minutes of music the harmony contains so few accidentals that it could almost be deemed a 'white-note' piece. Both composers continue to write richer and more complex music, but the modal elements are much nearer the surface than formerly. Listeners will have no problem detecting them in Xenakis's *Tetora* (1990), despite the plethora of note clusters the string quartet plays in the second half of the piece. The same may be said of Lumsdaine's *A Dance and a Hymn for Alexander Maconochie* (1988). This is a piece for chamber ensemble celebrating the occasion, during one of the blackest periods of the English convict system in nineteenth-century Australia, when the commandant of the Norfolk Island colony let his prisoners out for the day to roam, sing, dance, act plays, and generally do as they pleased. The musical material is generated by Lumsdaine's serial matrix, the highly versatile 'Gemini matrix' he invented in the sixties, but at no time does the serial technique obscure the modal nature of the harmony or the way the music ultimately 'discovers' its final.

The composers who have been unable to achieve the flexibility of Xenakis and Lumsdaine are those who returned to the tonal system, and in the seventies and eighties this meant a return to Romantic harmony. A prime example is Krzysztof Penderecki (born 1933), who came to prominence in 1960 with his *Threnody for the Victims of Hiroshima* for fifty-two strings. This is generally regarded as the apotheosis of textural music: the traditional workings of melody, harmony and metre are altogether absent, and the boundary between pitch and noise has been broken down. Most of the texture consists of note clusters, but Penderecki also calls for unorthodox string techniques such as playing between the bridge and the tailpiece or striking the sounding-board with the fingertips. It would seem that his purpose was to make noise expressive. But when he came to write a violin concerto for Isaac Stern in 1974, his quest for expressivity led him to cast aside noise and special effects and to embrace post-Wagnerian chromaticism. Later, in the Second Cello Concerto (1982) and *Polish Requiem* (1984) he returned to some of the effects he had exploited when he was younger, but they represent only fleeting glimpses of what was once prominent, and in no way challenge the dominance of his newly adopted style.

It seems now that minimalism has also found its destiny in Romanticism. This began to become apparent in 1980, when Philip Glass's second opera, *Satyagraha*, was produced. Although repetition is still the basis of the style, this work is much closer to conventional opera than was *Einstein on the Beach*, especially in terms of its highly lyrical vocal writing. But the work that confirmed the ultimate destination of minimalism was John Adams's *Harmonielehre* (1985). The title refers to Schoenberg's treatise on harmony which he wrote in 1911, around the time when he was abandoning tonality himself, but which seems to assume that tonal harmony would continue to be the basis of music in the future. By using the same title, Adams was presumably telling the world that he was taking up where Schoenberg left off and reinstating tonal harmony as if the intervening seventy or so years had been merely a temporary diversion in the history of music. The tonal aspects of his work are found not such much in its harmony as in its melody, though this does not become apparent until about a third of the way through the first movement. Until then the music is as mechanically repetitious as earlier minimalist scores; but when a melody does eventually emerge, it turns out to be a long meandering affair, which continues to unfold and develop right through to the end of the movement.

All three movements of *Harmonielehre* are based on dreams. The first one relates to seeing a submarine emerging from the depths of the sea. The second concerns what Adams calls the 'Amfortas wound'; this is a symbol for castration, which explains why the melody gets higher and higher and culminates in an orchestral scream. The last movement is more cheerful, being based on a dream in which Adams saw his baby daughter flying through the air on the shoulder of the great medieval mystic Meister Eckhardt, into whose ear she was whispering the 'secret of grace'. Here the melody, instead of growing and finding

Steve Reich's theatre piece *The Cave*.

its fulfilment in the closing bars, dissolves into minimalist repetitions again. Nevertheless, at the end the music resolves on a triumphant chord of E♭ major. The softening of the musical climate during the last three decades of the century has led to greater sympathy on the part of the musical establishment for composers who were neglected in the fifties and sixties simply because their styles were considered too Romantic for the prevailing taste. One of these is Nicholas Maw (born 1935), who objected to the post-Webern avant garde because their music had a completely different relationship with time from earlier music: it had forsaken all sense of narrative. In his opinion 'it was more like scintillating pieces of sculpture which you walked round rather than travelled through'. What disturbed him was not so much that it eliminated a sense of the future but that it obliterated a sense of the past. Memory was never brought into play because everything was new in the moment and nothing was ever repeated. As he has said recently:

That seemed to me to be the road to catastrophe. A lot of what has gone wrong with this century socially and politically has been the attempts by monsters like Hitler and Stalin to destroy whole peoples. Without being too apocalyptic, this music seemed to me to be a metaphor for the destruction of the memory of the individual and for the destruction of the imagination, for the only way the imagination can work is through memory.

The importance Maw attaches to memory was made evident by the fact that in the prevailing climate of the sixties he could still compose comic operas – *One Man Show* (1964, revised 1966) and *The Rising of the Moon* (1967–70) – comedy being absolutely dependent on the ability to remember and anticipate. But the work in which this ability is exploited as never before in the history of music is his huge, 100-minute orchestral work *Odyssey*, which he composed between 1972 and 1985. The work relates to Homer's epic only in so far as it always has an ultimate goal in view, even though the outcome of the journey is postponed by delays and digressions. Maw's *Odyssey* is in one continuous movement, but divides into an introduction, four parts roughly corresponding to the four movements of a symphony (the scherzo coming second, the half-hour slow movement third), and an epilogue. Its musical precedents are Schubert's *Wandererfantasie*, Liszt's B minor Piano Sonata and Schoenberg's *Verklärte Nacht*, which are also continuous structures concerned with narrating how a theme introduced at or near the beginning of the work eventually reaches its apotheosis at the end. The proportions of *Odyssey*, however, are more expansive than any of these forerunners. They are much closer to those of Bruckner, and it is Bruckner whom Maw cites when talking about the harmonic procedures in the work. Yet, though he refers to the 'great granite blocks of sound that crash into each other' as being Brucknerian, this does not mean that his music sounds like Bruckner. Its language is a continuation of the Romantic tradition as developed by William Walton, Berg and Jean Sibelius in his later years.

While Maw has never deviated from his commitment to the narrative style developed in the nineteenth century, Hans Werner Henze (born 1926) has embraced a great many styles in his lifetime. Lately his style has mellowed into a form of neo-Romanticism to which perhaps he has always been best suited. Henze's earliest music was heavily influenced by the neo-classicism of Hindemith and Stravinsky; then, when he went to Darmstadt in 1947–8 to have lessons with René Leibowitz, he turned to the twelve-note method. Later, in his Second String Quartet of 1952, it appeared that he had joined the avant garde. But the following year he decided to live in Italy, and thereafter a lyrical vein came to the surface. A lecture he gave at Darmstadt in 1955 about the supremacy of melody presaged his split with the avant garde, and when Boulez, Stockhausen and his friend Nono walked out on a performance of his *Nachtstücke und Arien* ('Night pieces and arias') at Donaueschingen in 1958 the split was opened beyond repair. 'The freedom offered by dodecaphony in earlier days is no longer felt as a refreshing impulse,' he said; 'it has become a vogue and a bore.'

In Italy, Henze devoted himself mainly to opera. The work he considers his best, *The Bassarids* (1965), concerns the triumph of

Nicholas Maw.

Castro and his guerillas in 1957, during the Cuban revolution.

the sensuous and elemental over the disciplined and rational; the first is represented by Dionysus, the second by King Pentheus, who goes mad when he comes face to face with the irrationality lying within himself. The choice of Euripides' *The Bacchae* as the subject of an opera undoubtedly had social as well as personal significance for Henze, for it could be construed that Pentheus symbolizes Germany under the Nazis – a culture which put too much faith in discipline and consequently lost touch with its inner world; as result it was taken over by a degree of madness such as the world had never seen before. When Henze approached W. H. Auden and Chester Kallman for a libretto, they told him that he would have to 'make peace with Wagner' before tackling the music. By this they meant that in order to cope with the transition from sanity to madness, the work would have to be symphonic in its construction. In the event, he produced a work cast in four symphonic movements that run without a break, so that he too was following in the footsteps of Schubert's *Wandererfantasie*. The slow movement of *The Bassarids* comes third, and in it Auden and Kallman included a comic intermezzo designed to illustrate the extent of the king's insanity by that stage. It gave Henze the opportunity to parody eighteenth-century conventions and to extend the range of quotations he includes in the work. After Pentheus has dressed himself as a woman, seen the secret rites and been torn apart by the Bacchae, the huge passacaglia that constitutes the last movement carries the action on to the point where the elemental, sensuous side of life reigns supreme and Dionysus ascends to heaven.

Shortly after the first performance of *The Bassarids* at the 1966 Salzburg Festival, Henze became increasingly involved with the activities of the New Left, and felt impelled to devote his energies to 'man's greatest work of art, the World Revolution'. The following year, Che Guevara was executed in Bolivia for attempting to rouse the tin-miners to rebellion, an event which Henze commemorated in *The Raft of the 'Medusa'* (1968), an 'oratorio volgare e militare' that made use of texts by the guerrilla leader. The title refers to the painting by Théodore

Géricault depicting the passengers of a frigate who have been abandoned on a raft by the ship's crew and left to die. At their helm is a heroic figure held aloft by his companions and waving his shirt as a flag. The reports of those who survived the experience make grim reading, but Henze must have thought that this figure represented the heroism the revolution required. He spent a year (1969–70) teaching in Cuba, where he conducted the first performance of his Sixth Symphony, which has woven into its texture fragments of the Vietnamese Liberation Front song *Stars in the Night* and Mikis Theodorakis's *Song to Freedom*. The work is scored for two chamber orchestras but all the players are treated as soloists. The idealism Henze brought to his music over the next few years reached its climax in *El Cimarrón* (1969–70), a seventy-six-minute 'recital' for an actor–singer, flute, guitar and percussion, about the life of a Cuban slave who becomes a revolutionary fighter after escaping from his Spanish masters. To achieve the bold, poster-like style he thought might appeal to a non-bourgeois audience, Henze sacrificed all the things that had distinguished his earlier music – rich harmony, fullness of textures, and, above all, lyricism.

These elements re-emerged in Henze's music after the fall of the Berlin Wall in 1989, when the idealism he had pursued for so many years also collapsed. His opera *Das verratene Meer* ('The treacherous sea') of 1990 and his Eighth Symphony of 1993 grind no political axes. He calls this symphony 'a summer piece' and says it relates to three episodes in *A Midsummer Night's Dream*. Although he fails to specify which episodes, from the nature of the music the first movement must relate to the scene where Oberon instructs Puck to fetch 'that herb I showed thee once' and Puck darts away to put a girdle round the earth; the second to the scene between Titania and Bottom; and the last to the fairies' blessing the rooms where the couples are asleep and Puck's wishing the audience good night. The music may lack the focus of Henze's earlier scores, but it reveals that he is at his happiest when writing in the voluptuous, Romantic idiom so admired by his one-time enemies, the bourgeoisie.

Although most of the composers discussed so far in this chapter have turned either partially or wholly to the middle ground, a pluralistic age is bound to have its extremes. There

Ernesto 'Che' Guevara.

One of the series of etchings called *Carceri d'invenzione* (1745–60) by Giovanni Battista Piranesi.

may no longer be any musical 'schools', but the last few decades have produced composers who represent on the one hand a 'new complexity' and on the other a 'new simplicity'. It so happens that the most extreme exponents of these tendencies, Brian Ferneyhough (born 1943) and John Tavener (born 1944), were both students of Lennox Berkeley at the Royal Academy of Music during the sixties. Berkeley clearly had the ability to draw out what was inherent in his students; he never imposed his own way of doing things.

After his Royal Academy days Ferneyhough went on to study in the Netherlands and Switzerland before settling in Germany and then the United States. His first major piece, Sonatas for string quartet, dates from 1967 and marked him out as someone who was always likely to make fantastic demands on both performers and listeners. It consists of twenty-four short sections of unequal length, and takes for its model the viol fantasias of Purcell, where strictly organized contrapuntal sections alternate with free sections. However, Purcell's fantasias are all relatively short (the longest is just over five minutes) and Ferneyhough had in mind a work of substance, in which the strictly organized and the free sections shared the same material but were nevertheless autonomous. He therefore began by writing two separate movements, one totally serial and automatic, the other informal, free and somewhat reminiscent of Webern's early atonal music. Not only do the two movements share the same material, but both place emphasis on specific types of articulation, such as pizzicato, glissando and tremolo. He then split up the movements into fragments and reordered them to form the twenty-four sections, making sure that the various types of articulation are all present in the first. As he said:

Like paths through a forest, the development of these elements [types of articulation] is *linear*; they run parallel sometimes, at other points disappear into the undergrowth, re-emerge later, wider or narrower, flow into one another and move apart again. Each of them has a part of the work in which 'its' main climax occurs, after which it withdraws once again into the background. There is, therefore, no *single* climactic section, and anyone looking for it will be grievously disappointed! Once one has grasped this essential point, the seemingly meandering course of the piece, as well as its length, will be more appreciable, I think.

In Ferneyhough's Sonatas, unlike a fantasia by Purcell, it is virtually impossible to hear when a strict section ends and a free section begins. The task of following the work becomes a little less formidable, however, if the listener bears in mind a remark that Ferneyhough once made in a casual conversation: 'The best way to approach my music,' he said, 'is to listen to it as if it were Elgar.' The advice was given in private and in a sense it defeats the purpose of his complexity, which is to allow listeners absolute freedom to choose how to listen for themselves, and how to discover their own way through the labyrinth of possibilities he offers them. But it is helpful advice – at least as far as Sonatas is concerned. A gesture high up on a violin can be related to one on the viola or cello, and when all the gestures in a particular passage are connected they do

Ferneyhough's response to Piranesi, from *Carceri d'invenzione I*, showing the extraordinary detailing that is characteristic of the composer's work.

indeed sound a bit like the sweeping, ornamented lines Elgar created, particularly in works such as the Violin Concerto. The problem is that, although this approach works for some of Ferneyhough's pieces, it is not valid for all of them. It fails miserably, for example, when one is trying to fathom his major work, the ninety-minute, seven-movement cycle *Carceri d'invenzione*, which he composed between 1981 and 1986.

The *Carceri d'invenzione* is a set of etchings by the Venetian architect Giovanni Battista Piranesi (1720–1778). The title means 'imaginary prisons', but the plates are really Romantic phantasmagorias, based on the intricate, overlapping, oblique perspectives used in Baroque opera sets. They are 'prisons' only in the sense that there seems to be no way out of the vast, maze-like interiors they depict. The attraction for Ferneyhough seems to have been the energy behind Piranesi's lines and the way they compete with each other for the attention of the viewer. The first of the three movements titled individually 'Carceri d'invenzione' (the second movement of the work as a whole) explores this spirit of energy and competitiveness: it is scored for sixteen solo instruments, each with its own independent, highly intricate, forceful line. The piccolo, trombone and piano enter first, playing their lines in a brilliant, vulgar manner. They are then joined by a group of seven woodwind and brass instruments, who are suave and controlled. A little later when all the wind and tuned percussion instruments have joined the mêlée, a string quartet enters, with instructions to be cold and metallic. Eventually, when all the instruments are playing, listeners have to cope with sixteen highly individualized and active lines, all demanding attention.

The other two 'Carceri d'invenzione' movements, four and six, are also for largish ensembles – respectively solo flute and a chamber orchestra of twenty individual players, and fifteen woodwind and three percussion players. Framing the cycle, as the first and seventh movements, are 'Superscriptio' for solo piccolo and 'Mnemosyne' for bass flute and tape (Mnemosyne being Memory, the mother of the Muses). The use of the related timbres of piccolo at the beginning, flute in the middle, and bass flute at the end is one of the ways in which Ferneyhough creates the sense that the whole work is indeed a cycle. Between the three 'Carceri' are two 'Intermedi' (movements three and five), one for solo violin, the other a twenty-seven-minute cycle of nine songs to texts by Ernst Meister and Alrun Moll for mezzo-soprano, flute, oboe, cello and harpsichord, called 'Études transcendantales'. Here Ferneyhough's concern was with 'questions of death, and what it is about a work of art that gives it a certain permanence, as against its ephemeral, immediate expressive capacity'.

Although one or two articles about the work have appeared in specialist magazines, these have tended to add obscurity to the work's complex and enigmatic nature rather than clarify it. However, they do reveal that Ferneyhough is still concerned with the relationship of the automatic and the informal, the piccolo's 'Superscriptio' being automatic, the solo violin's 'Intermedio' and the closing 'Mnemosyne' informal. The other movements, like the twenty-four sections of Sonatas for string quartet, are what he now calls 'synthetic'. What is absolutely clear is that once again Ferneyhough is challenging his listeners to find their own way through the labyrinth without much help from the composer. The present author finds that for him the best approach is to think of the lines as if they were bird song. This is certainly what the opening piccolo solo suggests – not an actual bird, of course, but an imaginary one that can sing with great sophistication and inventiveness. The 'Carceri' movements then become like dawn choruses in spring, and the song cycle the attempt of a human voice to imitate the bird-like songs the instruments suggest. There are times when the singer even tries to trill like a nightingale; that she cannot compete is made clear in the last song when she is reduced to speech, uttering only isolated phonemes and hitting claves.

Ferneyhough accepts the fact that his music is likely to appeal only to a limited number of people. He composes, he says, for active, collaborative listeners, who are prepared to jump between levels of texture and tolerate multiple meanings. Such listeners are hard to find in an era of easy listening. The music of his one-time fellow student John Tavener, on the other hand, reaches a much wider audience. His dramatic cantata *The Whale* was so successful at its first performance in 1968 that the Beatles issued the recording on their Apple label. In the early nineties,

243

John Tavener with the icons that are crucial influences on his recent music. On the left, *The Protecting Veil* (1987); above, *Mandelion* (1981, for solo organ); behind, *The Mother of God* (*Canticle*, 1976, for voices); right, *The Last Sleep of the Virgin* (1991, string quartet and bells); in his hands, the icon of the Saviour (*The Apocalypse*, 1994).

his cello piece *The Protecting Veil* went to the top of the CD charts: it was recognized, along with Henryk Górecki's Third Symphony and one or two pieces by Arvo Pärt, as being one of the most outstanding examples of the new simplicity. The popularity of this music has as much to do with its 'spirituality', its unequivocal affirmation of faith, as it has with the comparatively small demands it makes on the listener. Stylistically Tavener, Górecki and Pärt are quite disparate – the only thing that unites them is their desire to produce music that can speak to people immediately and directly. The doubts about meaning that Ferneyhough raises have no place in their work.

Tavener's early works reflect his leaning towards Catholicism; among the most important of these are the *Celtic Requiem* (1969), in which the liturgical text is dramatized by the interspersing of children's singing games associated with death (Ring-a-ring-a-roses, for example), the Crucifixion meditation *Ultimos ritos* (1969–72) and the opera *Thérèse* (1973–6). But in

244

1977 he converted to the Orthodox faith, and since then the ethos of his music, he says, has been that of Byzantine Greece. The Feast of the Protecting Veil celebrates the occasion in the early tenth century when Byzantium (Constantinople) was threatened by a Saracen army and the Mother of God appeared over the city with her veil spread out by a host of saints to keep the Christians from harm. Tavener likened his piece to an icon, 'a lyrical icon in sound'. He wanted, he said, to capture the almost cosmic power of the Mother of God. She is represented by the solo cello playing continuously throughout the work's forty-two-minute duration, the music of the accompanying strings being 'a gigantic extension of her unending song'.

The work falls into eight sections, the first and last representing Mary's veil, the central ones the crucial events in her life: her birth, the Annunciation, the Incarnation, her lament at the cross, the Resurrection, and her final sleep. Apart from the last, each section ends with an expressive and very Elgarian falling minor ninth (F–E) against an E low on the double basses. This motif contrasts with the sounds of bells, in the form of sharply accented chord clusters in the upper strings, which immediately precede it. At first there are only two bells, but in each successive section one more is added so that in the seventh section there are eight. The notes are those of a descending scale, the rhythm that produced by the bells of a monastery in Russia which Tavener had heard in a recording.

Bells clearly have great significance for Tavener because in one form or another they appear in virtually all his works. Arvo Pärt (born 1935), however, has gone further and based his whole technique on the sound of bells. He calls what he produces 'tintinnabulation'. As an Estonian, he too is of the Orthodox faith, though much of his music since the late sixties draws on texts from the Roman liturgy. His early works followed the approved Soviet models, but then when the music of the post-war avant garde began to filter through from the West in the early sixties he took up serialism. In retrospect this looks as if it was really an act of defiance, because in 1967 he came across plainsong and this proved a much more decisive influence on his work. Since then all his music has been based on his own version of plainsong – usually step-wise melodic progressions in a specific metre. Tintinnabulation involves placing these progressions against the notes of simple chords so that diatonic clashes occur. In the two-part opening of his *Missa sillabica*, for example, the alto voice sings a descending three-note scale (F–E–D) followed by a descending four-note scale (G–F–E–D). Against this, instruments play the notes of a D minor triad (D–F–A) not simultaneously but as separate notes. The result is that the G clashes with the A, the E with the F, giving an effect that is not unlike the clashes that occur in a peal of bells. The impression is intensified by the addition of other lines – almost invariably inversions of the basic line and the tintinnabulating figure. Pärt never modulates; each event represents a crystallized moment. In long works, such as his *St John Passion* (1981), a series of such moments accumulates to give the impression of a slow-moving, severely hierarchic ritual.

When Pärt wants to generate textures of greater complexity than those in the *St John Passion* he makes extensive use of the medieval technique known as a 'mensuration canon', in which the voices perform the same line but at different speeds. Typical is *Festina lente*, a piece for strings with optional harp, dating from 1988. The harmony is as simple as may be for it is entirely in A minor and there are no accidentals. All the interest lies in the way the melody, 'chanted' by the violas seven times in three different tempos, is filled out by the violins playing it at double speed and the cellos and basses at half speed.

Canons (though not mensuration ones) are also a feature of Górecki's Third Symphony, probably the most popular 'classical' work produced this century – for a time it was even in the popular music charts in some countries. During the late fifties and most of the sixties Górecki (born 1933) was the most 'advanced' of the avant-garde Polish composers. *Zderzenia / Scontri* ('Collisions'), in which one orchestral group clashes with another to cause musical chaos, shocked even the connoisseurs of modernism when it was performed at the 1960 Warsaw Autumn Festival. However, with *Muzyka staropolska* ('Old Polish music', 1969) for brass and strings, it became clear that he was rapidly moving away from his rebarbative early style. Even so, no one could possibly have anticipated the complete *volte face* that the Third Symphony represented when it appeared in 1976. Górecki called it a 'Symphony of Sorrowful Songs' and scored it for soprano, string orchestra and a piano that sounds like a quiet funeral bell. The texts are drawn from a fifteenth-century version of the Virgin Mary's lamentation, a prayer inscribed on the wall of a cell in the Gestapo's headquarters in Zakopane, and a folksong in which a peasant woman laments the loss of her son. In the first movement, the song is framed by long canonic textures, based on a twenty-four-bar cantus firmus in the Aeolian mode transposed to E. The movement starts with a canon on the double basses, the canonic texture expanding into eight-part polyphony as more and more instruments join in, each section playing the melody a fifth higher than the one before. The canon gives way to the soprano's song, then, when this is over, the procedure goes in reverse, so that the music ends where it began. The overall effect, both here and in the other two movements, is one of undeviating spiritual certainty. This comes across even in the second movement, where the prayer is that of an eighteen-year-old girl: 'No, mother, do not weep. Most chaste Queen of Heaven, support me always. Ave Maria.'

The one eastern European composer who has not abandoned the rigorous principles that characterized his early music is the Hungarian György Kurtág (born 1926). This may be because he has never been drawn to the comfort of religion. His first major piece, *The Sayings of Péter Bornemisza* (1963–8), which he calls a concerto for soprano and piano, takes its texts from sermons by a sixteenth-century Reformist pastor, who is obsessed by the traps that the devil may be laying for him and the conviction that man is nothing but a shadow. The only thing that gives him hope is that with God's grace his sins may be pardoned. But nothing is certain. All he seems able to rely on is the advent of spring, when 'those bleak, chilly, nippy, foggy, slushy, harrowing, wintry days are gone'. As the description 'concerto' suggests, Kurtág's songs make tremendous demands on both singer and accompanist. At first their virtuosity appears to be at odds with the black, guilt-ridden texts. But Bornemisza is not meditating inwardly, he is preparing sermons to be delivered in the grand rhetorical manner that Reformist preachers adopted in the sixteenth and seventeenth centuries. The striking thing about Kurtág's settings is that, although Bornemisza's tone changes

Kurtág's music sounds as if the notes had to be compressed to fit into a box small enough to hide their secret. It feels as though you're somehow eavesdropping on a private line of thought in a foreign language. The exact meaning isn't clear but the strength of the emotions is huge. He hints at Wagnerian proportions using Webern's language, telling a story as passionate as it is bleak.

when he talks about spring and the possibility of God's grace, Kurtág's does not. His music creates the impression that the hope Bornemisza is offering to his congregation is an illusion.

Kurtág took some time to find the style that suited him. He was well into his thirties before he produced his op. 1. His problem was the one that beset all Hungarian composers of his generation: how to follow Bartók. It was not until after a year spent studying with Messiaen and Darius Milhaud in Paris in 1957–8 that he found a *modus operandi* that was not a pale imitation of Bartók. In *The Sayings of Péter Bornemisza*, dating from 1963–8, Bartók's influence is discernible only to a limited extent. Much more noticeable, especially in the way Kurtág handles musical cells, is the influence of the early atonal music of Webern. What is not like Webern is Kurtág's penchant for supplying patterns in which a goal is implied: the music often expands outwards from a particular note in different directions to form a wedge shape (C–C♯–B–D–B♭–D♯–A etc.); elsewhere a note will be withheld from a phrase so that its eventual appearance sounds inevitable and cadential. In terms of texture, the omnipresent influence is the brilliance and resonance of the Hungarian cimbalom, an instrument Kurtág uses again and again in his music. Even when he is writing exclusively for piano, as in the Bornemisza cycle, note clusters, decorative flourishes, tremolos and sweeping glissandos all derive from the cimbalom's characteristic sounds and playing gestures.

Kurtág soon realized that he was at his best in short, pithy, highly characterized pieces. Since the String Quartet and the Wind Quintet, opp. 1 and 2, both composed in 1959, he has written nothing but sets of miniatures; the piano concerto that he has been promising for years to write has still not materialized. The most impressive of his works are those in the form of song cycles. Some are comparatively short, others last anything from half an hour to an hour. All are based on texts dealing with the dark side of life (loneliness, despair, degradation, hopelessness). And yet, like the song cycles of his great nineteenth-century predecessors, Schubert, Schumann and Mahler, Kurtág's music somehow manages to transcend the gloom. A combination of wit and a dead-pan approach somehow makes it bearable.

Kurtág's debt to the composers of Romantic lieder became

clear when he confessed that his working title for the song cycle *The Messages of the late Miss R. V. Troussova* (1980), for soprano and chamber ensemble, was *Frauenleben und -schicksal* ('Woman's life and fate'), after Schumann's *Frauenliebe und -leben* ('Woman's love and life'). The twenty-one poems are by Rimma Dalos, a Russian poet who lives in Budapest. They are arranged in three groups entitled 'Loneliness', 'A Little Erotic and Bitter Experience' and 'Delight and Grief'. Although, like the poems by Chamisso that Schumann set, the texts portray the feelings of a woman who has lost her husband or lover, they are far more outspoken and cynical. In the second group, where Miss Troussova recalls an episode of love-making, she can say, 'Why should I not squeal like a pig when all around are grunting?'; and in the third group, when she recalls the moment when her lover rejected her, the words she uses are, 'You took my heart in the palm of your hand, which you then carefully turned upside down.' Kurtág begins this last song with one of the most sonorous and colourful instrumental groupings he has ever devised: gentle flourishes on clarinet, cimbalom and vibraphone, a simple melody on harp and bells, a repeated harmonic on the viola, and the sound of gongs and tamtam stroked as softly as possible, as if in the distance. This sonority also forms the backdrop to the soprano's entry – 'You took my heart in the palm of your hand' – her notes being a decoration of a slowly descending whole-tone scale. When she reaches the words 'which you then carefully turned upside down', Kurtág manages to convey through the ominous stillness of the texture her powerless expectation of what is going to happen, and then, in a sudden and rapid movement, indicates that her heart has indeed been turned upside down. But the song does not finish there: it ends with a return to the calm and sonorous texture of the opening. This is done not simply to round off the form: its main purpose is to suggest that Miss Troussova believes her lover finds pleasure in destroying her. At the head of the song Kurtág places lines by the poet Alexander Blok: 'And there was a fatal joy in trampling on sacred things, an insane pleasure for the heart – a bitter passion, like wormwood!'

Although there is the vague outline of a narrative lying behind the Troussova songs, it is not decisive. Indeed the fifteen texts that constitute the third group could well have been placed in a different order. The precedent for this is Schubert's *Die Winterreise* ('The winter journey'), where the texts are in a different order from the one decided on by the poet, Wilhelm Müller. But this has little or no effect on the sense of the piece, because each poem describes a separate and unique event on the journey. The wanderer has no purposeful path to follow. 'There is a destination,' said Kafka, 'but no path to it; what we call a path is hesitation.' This is one of the lines that Kurtág sets in the biggest of all his song cycles, the hour-long *Kafka Fragments* (1985) for soprano and violin. The six texts leading up to it illustrate the nature of all thirty-nine:

There is no 'to have', only a 'to be', a 'to be' longing for the last breath, for suffocation . . . Coitus as punishment for the happiness of being together . . . My prison-cell – my fortress . . . I am dirty, Milena, endlessly dirty, that is why I make such a fuss about cleanliness. None sing as purely as those in deepest Hell; it is their singing that we take for the singing of angels . . . Slept, woke, slept, woke, miserable life . . . The closed circle is pure.

What holds these fragments together is the music. Each song has its own individuality and is autonomous, but they are linked – as Schubert's are linked in *Die Winterreise* – either by motifs, or by similarities in shape or rhythm, or because the harmony at the end of one song leads directly into that of the next. What is unusual about *Kafka Fragments* is the relationship between the singer and the violin. At times they compete with each other, like the mezzo-soprano and the instrumental ensemble in Ferneyhough's *Carceri* cycle. In the song addressed to Milena, the violinist has to use an instrument with its two bottom strings tuned down a tone (F and C rather than G and D); in response, the soprano keeps going down to the low F to compete with the violin's newly acquired range, so at the end of the song the violinist retaliates by tuning even lower. Throughout the cycle, as in the Bornemisza songs, virtuosity is the order of the day, the singer and the instrumentalist constantly trying to outdo each other in brilliance. In one song the singer is reduced to screaming when her attempts to imitate the violin fail.

As in his other cycles, Kurtág arranges the songs of *Kafka*

Fragments into groups. Here there are four. The first contains nineteen songs, the second one, the third twelve and the fourth eight. The single song of the second group is addressed to Pierre Boulez and entitled 'The True Path', the reference being to Boulez's contention that there was only one true path for post-war composers to follow, and that was his. The Kafka fragment reads: 'The true path goes by way of a rope that is suspended not high up, but rather just above the ground. Its purpose seems to be more to make one stumble than to be walked on.' Kurtág's song is like a chorale prelude. The violin plays slowly and almost continuously in double-stopping, mainly on its bottom two strings, producing little else but dirge-like sevenths and ninths; the singer, also in her lowest register, stumbles through the chorale, phrase by phrase, the dreariness of her line being relieved only near the end when Kurtág gives her a short cadenza in the totally incongruous rhythm of a siciliana.

Kurtág's style may have softened slightly over the years – his *Three Old Inscriptions* dating from the late eighties end in folksong style – but it has not changed as much as the styles of some of his Russian contemporaries have done since the sixties. Unlike Kurtág, none of the Russians were able to study in the West when young, and very few of them were able to attend the Warsaw Autumn Festival. Their first and for a long time only contact with the advanced serial techniques current in the West came through Luigi Nono, when he visited Russia in 1962. Edison Denisov (born 1929), Sofiya Gubaydulina (born 1931) and Alfred Schnittke (born 1934) were among the first to adopt serial techniques, and even though the works they composed were still related to tradition and were less radical than many of those produced in the West, they were nevertheless condemned by the authorities.

The clue to Schnittke's music may well lie in the fact that, although he was born and bred in Russia, his parents were of

One of György Kurtág's *Kafka Fragments*: 'I am dirty, Milena … '.

Celebrations on New Year's Eve 1989 on the Berlin Wall at the Brandenburg Gate.

German stock and German was the language he spoke at home. This dual cultural inheritance may explain why in all his works he pits one sound world against another. His Second Violin Concerto (1966), one of his first serial works, centres on a dramatic conflict between lyrical, sustained music given to the strings, and aggressive, percussive music given to the wind and (of course) the percussion. The work is in one continuous movement divided into six sections. The first is a cadenza for the solo violin and introduces the two sound worlds. In the second they are separated and developed by the orchestra. About half way through this section Schnittke introduces an 'anti-soloist' in the form of a solo double bass. Like the solo violin it plays lyrically, but its main function is to be the agent of destruction – every time it plays it ushers in an aleatoric passage of near anarchy for the wind and percussion. Order is restored only by the reappearance of the violin. The last time this happens is at the climax of the fourth section. But on this occasion the violin's response is so touching that even the brass section is moved. Instead of playing in their earlier percussive, staccato manner, the instruments sustain a long, very quiet chord. The implication is that aggression has been tamed, and this means that the solo violin now has the opportunity to realize its full potential. It can reappropriate, for example, the percussive rhythm it introduced in its opening cadenza.

Schnittke's predilection for drama and conflict in music was undoubtedly what led him to 'polystylism', the term he uses to describe his very idiosyncratic use of pastiche. His first steps in this direction were taken in his Second Violin Sonata of 1968, where brittle, very modern music is wittily contrasted with Romantic-sounding music based on the B–A–C–H motif, a four-note cipher based on the letters of Bach's name (in German B represents B♭ and H B♮). The tendency was more clearly manifested in his Concerto Grosso no. 1 of 1977 for two violins, prepared piano, harpsichord and strings. This was the work that made his name in the West. Here the main pastiche style is that of Corelli and Vivaldi. But for Schnittke, it is not enough merely to alternate between that and the modern style pitted against it. As in the concerto, there has to be an agent of destruction – in this case a sentimental popular tune, played at the outset by the prepared piano. The free chromaticisms and micro-intervals of the modern style dominate the first, third and fourth sections, the Baroque figurations the second and fifth. In the course of the fifth section, however, the figurations begin to resemble a sentimental tango. Since they can no longer maintain their integrity, the scene is set for the re-emergence of the popular song, which returns with devastating results, bringing about the disintegration of everything but itself: as the chromatic cells and Baroque figurations fall apart and fade away it seems that only the song's inherent vulgarity has substance.

While most of Schnittke's polystylist works use pastiche, some base the pastiche on specific models. In his Third String Quartet of 1983, for instance, Schnittke quotes a cadential phrase from a *Stabat Mater* by Lassus to represent Renaissance polyphony at its most

Chiat Day offices in Santa Monica, California. Frank Gehry designed the building and Claes Oldenburg the giant binoculars that stand in front.

serene, and the opening of Beethoven's 'Grosse Fuge' to represent the Classical style at its most dynamic and assertive. The first of the work's three movements is devoted solely to the serene, almost childlike nature of the Lassus; the second to the agitated, striving character of the Beethoven. The interest lies in which of the two will overcome. The third movement begins with the two contenders being presented in close proximity, but the case is decided when Schnittke brings to the fore a motif that has been alluded to from the very beginning of the quartet. Those familiar with Shostakovich's music will recognize it as the motif he used when referring to himself. Like the Bach motif, it is based on the German note names: in this case the initials spelt out are D–S–C–H (D–E♭–C–B♮), for 'Dmitri SCHostakovitch'. These notes are themselves a transposition of the four notes that open the 'Grosse Fuge', G–G♯–F–E. Shortly after the appearance of the full form of this motif, Schnittke introduces a pastiche of Mahler, the composer Shostakovich most admired. It is with Shostakovich and Mahler hovering in the background that Schnittke makes his decision to opt for the serenity of Lassus – or, at least, so the listener is led to believe. Lassus is certainly prominent in the coda, and towards the end Schnittke takes a variant of the phrase from the *Stabat Mater* higher and higher, as if it were ascending to heaven. But in the event, it is the Shostakovich / 'Grosse Fuge' motif that hangs in the air as the music declines into silence.

In 1985, after completing his Viola Concerto, the most Romantic of his scores, Schnittke had the first of several strokes, which have left him partially paralysed. Even though he had become the most frequently performed of all living composers at that time, the Russian authorities still disapproved of him. Favoured musicians in the Soviet Union were given luxury flats in the centre of Moscow and taken about in chauffeur-driven limousines; Schnittke and his family lived in a small, three-room flat in a run-down concrete block on the outskirts of the city, and because the lift rarely worked had to climb up five flights of stairs to get to it. When he was offered a teaching appointment in Hamburg, he therefore accepted it with alacrity. Since the mid-eighties his interest in polystylism has declined. The Piano Sonata he composed for his wife in 1990 makes no use of it

Anna Akhmatova.

whatsoever, but it does retain the contrast between modern-sounding music and simple diatonicism. Most of the material in the work's three movements is lyrical, but a distinctive feature of the two outer movements is the sudden shattering of the lyricism by something modernistic and disruptive – a rhythm, an explosive chord cluster, or a more extensive dissonant event. The most violent disruption occurs in the finale. No listener who knows that Schnittke has suffered several serious strokes can fail to connect this to what he has experienced. Indeed, what follows could well reflect his conviction that his survival represented a second birth for him. He brings back a theme from the central slow movement but harmonizes it with purely diatonic chords, so that it takes on a child-like quality.

The inclusion of diatonic, tonally centred music within a chromatic or even atonal context has featured in the music of several composers in the last two decades of the century. One of them is Schnittke's friend and compatriot, Sofiya Gubaydulina, who in the early nineties also settled in Hamburg. Like Pärt, Denisov and Schnittke, she too made use of serial techniques in the mid-sixties, most notably in her Piano Sonata (1965) and her cantata *Night in Memphis* (1968), a setting of ancient Egyptian mystical texts translated by Anna Akhmatova. Gubaydulina's decision to set translations by a discredited poet, revealing her deep religious commitment and interest in mysticism, only added to the weight of disapproval she suffered from the authorities. She had great difficulty in getting her works performed or published and had to turn to writing film music. Her fortunes improved when international conductors and performers such as Gennadi Rozhdestvensky and Gidon Kremer began performing her works in the early eighties. Her *Seven Words* for cello, bajan (a Russian folk accordion) and strings, indicates that by 1982 she was regularly adopting the practice of placing simple diatonic material within a much more abrasive modernist context. The 'seven words' are Christ's words from the cross, though they are never actually articulated. Throughout the piece the solo cello may be interpreted as representing Christ's agony and his fear that God has deserted him. The semitones and quarter-tones, clashing against sustained notes, the scrapings, distortions, tremolos and glissandos are all modern. But against them

Gubaydulina quotes and expands passages from *Die sieben Worte* (1660) by Heinrich Schütz, using the bajan to sound like a distant organ. The contrast not only highlights Christ's agony, it also affirms that behind and beyond it lies the eternal existence to which he will soon return.

Like so many twentieth-century composers, time is one of Gubaydulina's main preoccupations, as two of her more recent scores, *Stimmen . . . Verstummen* (1986) and *Figures of Time* (1994) make particularly apparent. She calls both of them 'symphonies' – but only in brackets. In her introduction to the latter, she talks about waking up one day 'with the powerful realisation that Time was re-orientating itself': when she was asleep it moved along vertically; when she woke up it returned to its horizontal progression. She goes on to say that the desire to convert 'the vertical time of timeless imagination into a linear form, the primordial moment of truth into an actual process,' is encapsulated in all works of art. By this, she is not necessarily referring to the timeless moment that mystics talk about, but to the fact that most works of art, whether visual, literary or musical, are conceived in what used to be called a flash of inspiration. Nowadays the experience would be put down to the right hemisphere of the brain functioning without any interference from the left – the right hemisphere being that side which specializes in holistic as opposed to linear thinking. In these moments, writers see the whole poem or novel before their eyes, composers the whole symphony or opera – not in detail, of course, but simply as an idea. How this idea is realized in time depends on the imagination and skill of the writer or composer. But once the idea has become a process, it exists solely in time; it cannot go back again to being the primordial moment. However, a sense of timelessness is of such importance to Gubaydulina that she always tries to suggest its presence in her music, even though it is ultimately no more than an illusion.

As we have seen in *Seven Words*, she achieves this by juxtaposing two contradictory types of harmony. The twelve movements that make up *Stimmen . . . Verstummen* (literally 'To tune . . . to become silent') vary in length from about half a minute to more than eleven minutes. The first movement consists of nothing but the chord of D major, passed fleetingly and delicately from section to section of the orchestra, so that an elusive, insubstantial atmosphere is created. The third, fifth and seventh movements also consist solely of a D major chord, but on each successive appearance the durations get shorter and shorter and its identity ever more elusive. The sequence suggests that the chord will also form the ninth movement, but by this time it has been reduced to silence. The conductor gestures for about a minute, but all that comes out of the orchestra are some low, inarticulate mumblings from the percussion. The even-numbered movements are longer. The second is chromatic and linear, and even though the lines are fragmented they culminate in a climax. This much more dynamic type of music returns to form the fourth, sixth and eighth movements, which in contrast to the D major movements, get progressively longer and become less fragmented. In other words, they gradually dominate the proceedings, incorporating passages of pure diatonic music centred on specific triads as they build up to dynamic climaxes. In the eighth movement the climax is so powerful that the linear music virtually collapses in its wake. After that comes the minute of silence. When the music resumes, the relationship between the two time-flows changes. From then onwards it is the static chord that dominates. In the last movement the D major chord is finally stabilized and held as if it could go on sounding for ever. Against it Gubaydulina places fragments of the linear music, but it is the motionless, timeless chord high up on the violins that prevails.

Stimmen . . . Verstummen represents a harmonic procedure that several composers have adopted in the eighties and nineties. It involves using diatonic triads or specific notes as points of reference – something the listener can hold on to – particularly in music that is otherwise dissonant or in a constant state of flux. But these diatonic elements rarely function in the way they do in tonal music, and they are not organized to generate movement towards a cadence.

The composer who makes the most frequent and effective use of a referential pitch is Wolfgang Rihm (born 1952), who numbers Stockhausen and Nono among his teachers. His harmony is basically atonal, pungent and hard-edged, yet when the situation demands repose he is prepared to go beyond simple points of reference and revert to tonality. Striking examples of this occur

Peter Greenaway's interpretation of *The Tempest, Prospero's Books*. The dancer Michael Clark plays Caliban.

in his opera *Jakob Lenz* (1980). A feature of his orchestral and choral music is his use of space, as in *Départ*, the nine-minute choral piece he composed for Stockhausen's sixtieth-birthday celebrations in 1988, on a text from Rimbaud's *Les illuminations*, which speaks of having had enough of 'visions, rumours and life's decrees'. The scoring includes both mixed chorus and speaking chorus, and throughout the piece Rihm makes a clear distinction between foreground and background: the sounds in the foreground, including those of the speaking chorus, tend to be hard-edged, those in the background softer and more ingratiating. What links the two spheres are the reference notes, which can exert their influence over several passages. The B♭ which crops up over and over again at the opening of *Départ* is present for nearly two and a half minutes. After a short period when no one note dominates, G emerges as the note around which all the dissonances revolve. The ending of the piece is curiously ambivalent. By placing mixed chorus and the softer sounds in the background, Rihm invites the listener to succumb to their enchantment. Yet it is these unwanted 'visions and rumours' that Rimbaud wants be rid of. His quest is for a new love to gaze on and other sounds.

Rihm's most ambitious work to date, his opera *The Conquest of Mexico* (1992), is based on the theatrical spectacle which the French stage director and dramatist Antonin Artaud outlined at the end of his 'Second Manifesto on the Theatre of Cruelty' in 1933. Artaud believed that the theatre should abandon narrative and psychological realism and become a place where magic and myth hold sway. 'The Theatre of Cruelty has been created in order to restore to the theatre a passionate and convulsive conception of life,' he wrote, 'and it is this sense of violent rigour and extreme condensation of scenic elements that the cruelty on which it is based should be judged.' He chose the subject of the conquest of Mexico to exemplify this conception because he thought the confrontation of Cortés and Montezuma was of 'vital [relevance] to the problems of modern-day Europe and the world'. Artaud wrote no script as such – his description is entirely devoted to the dramatic spectacle of the clash between the violence and 'moral disorder' of the conquistadors and the peaceful, deeply spiritual nature of Aztec society.

To turn this into an opera, Rihm had to write a text and add one or two characters not mentioned by Artaud. The most important change is that the Aztec leader Montezuma is sung by a woman, so that the relationship between Cortés and Montezuma is charged with love as well as mutual incomprehension. For the Spaniards Rihm writes pungent, abrasive music, for the Aztecs music that is soft-grained and lyrical. The plot's peripeteia takes place in a dream Cortés has after Montezuma's abdication and death. In his dream he becomes Montezuma, and when he wakes he takes over Montezuma's manner of singing; the passage he had earlier sung shrilly and parodistically he now sings lyrically. The death of Cortés's old self is mirrored by the fact that, contrary to history, the Spanish troops also perish. An unusual feature of the opera is Rihm's use of Octavio Paz's poem 'The Roots of Man', one of its four stanzas bringing each of the four parts of the opera to a conclusion. Like Artaud, Paz is a Surrealist, but his poem is not based on dream imagery. It deals with that dark, raging love which has its roots in death as well as life. At the end of the first three parts, the stanzas are sung by female voices (Montezuma and his companions, a soprano, and a contralto singing off stage). The last stanza, on the other hand,

Oliver Knussen conducting the London Sinfonietta in Elliott Carter's Violin Concerto, with the soloist Ole Böhn.

259

is placed after a moving chorus to the words of a text of 1523 lamenting the fate of the Aztecs, and is given to Cortés and Montezuma singing unaccompanied.

This quiet, intimate ending is totally at odds with the one Artaud suggested. For him, the outcome of the confrontation had to be the Aztec uprising after Montezuma's death, in which the Spanish are massacred: 'And the sharp spasms of the battle, the foam of heads of the cornered Spaniards who are squashed like blood against the ramparts that are turning green again.' But no composer writing in the last few decades of the twentieth century could possibly end like that; such melodramatic violence would be considered more suitable for the cinema or television screen than the stage. Nor could he end in the high-spirited manner of the Baroque or Classical composers, the triumph of Beethoven, or the transcendence of Wagner and early Schoenberg. We live in less idealistic, more uncertain times, and even though Cortés and Montezuma appear to be at peace in the final stanza of Paz's poem, Rihm leaves the music hanging on a discord at the end.

There are some composers who never know in advance how a work will end. They argue that the material finds its own solution. There are others for whom the ending is of prime importance. There can be no doubt that when Mark-Anthony Turnage (born 1960) decided to base his orchestral piece *Drowned Out* (1994) on William Golding's novel *Pincher Martin* it was not only the mood of the novel he wanted to capture but also the extraordinary way it concludes. Martin is a naval officer who is blown off his ship by a torpedo in mid-Atlantic but manages to find a barren rock to cling on to. Because his sea boots are weighing him down, his first efforts are devoted to getting them off. The novel then relates the purgatorial experiences he goes through in his fight to survive, his tenacious and ingenious attempts being interspersed with flashbacks to events in his life. That his efforts fail is revealed at the end, when the narrative voice shifts from Martin's inner monologue to a straightforward report of the discovery of his body by two naval officers. The casual remark of one of them discloses that Martin must have lost his grip on the rock almost immediately: 'He didn't even have time to kick off his sea boots.' The reader must consequently reassess the whole of the novel. In the light of the ending, the narrative must be interpreted as the thoughts that rush through Martin's mind in the seconds before he drowns. By devoting his narrative to the story of his survival, he has attempted to defy the judgment of God.

This peripeteia is a literary device that no composer could possibly cope with in purely musical terms. All Turnage can do is to capture something of the novel's mood and one or two of its most important gestures: Martin's failure to maintain his grip on the rock, the sense of falling, the few seconds' gap between life and death. Although he was born and bred in Essex, Turnage's music is much closer to American twentieth-century music than European. It is difficult to think of any score of his that does not bring to mind at least the trumpet and flugelhorn playing of Miles Davis. Most of his music contains passages of great violence, though what tends to prevail are long, lyrical melodies that he himself frequently calls 'bluesy'. And just as blues singers can take their sadness too seriously, and need to be gently mocked from time to time by those who accompany them, so Turnage has to make sure that his lyrical ideas are eventually dismissed by some peremptory gesture or put-down. In *Drowned Out* most of the long opening section is dominated by a sorrowful, lyrical melody. After the second of the work's two violent climaxes, a variant of the melody comes back on a solo clarinet; in the unfolding of this version of the melody, more and more attention is given to a falling semitone (the gesture traditionally associated with anguish and grief). Turnage then focuses on this gesture by repeating it plaintively on two high oboes, only to cut through it with two abrupt chords of dismissal. With them it is obvious the story has come to an end and God's judgment has been executed.

An even more dramatic put-down occurs at the end of Turnage's opera *Greek*, which his teacher, Henze, commissioned for the 1988 Munich Biennale. Based on Steven Berkoff's version of the Oedipus myth, this is a black comedy set in the East End of London in the seventies. The plague

A glimpse into the future, through the crumbled Berlin Wall into the Potsdamer Platz, site of energetic reconstruction.

of the myth is the racism, violence and mass unemployment that afflict the area; Oedipus is Eddy, who opens the proceedings by telling us in broad cockney that he was spawned 'in a Tufnell Park that's no more than a stone's throw from the Angel, a monkey's fart from Tottenham . . . a cess pit'. Like the operas of Brecht and Weill, the structure consists of numbers separated in the main by spoken dialogue. The first number is a chorus for Arsenal supporters who are getting drunk in a pub. As in Sophocles, the peripeteia occurs when Eddy is told that the couple he thought were his mother and father are not his parents: his father was the café owner he killed in a brawl over a slice of cheesecake, his mother the waitress responsible for the delay in serving it. The most memorable of all the bluesy numbers is the love aria in Act 2, in which the mother reflects on ten years of marriage to Eddy. Equally distinctive is the number in which Mum, Dad and Wife try to comfort Eddy after he learns the truth about his birth: 'We only love, so it doesn't matter Eddy, it doesn't matter.' But Eddy decides that the guilt is too much and half seriously threatens to gouge out his eyes, as Sophocles' hero had done. There is even a mock funeral march for him – mock because this is a comedy not a tragedy. Eddy has taken his guilt too seriously and he is the one who must 'put the mockers on it'. 'Bollocks to all that,' he tells the audience when the lights are switched on and he comes to life. 'Yeah I wanna climb back inside my mum, what's wrong with that, it's better than shoving a stick of dynamite up someone's arse and getting a medal for it!'

Debunking, however, can be achieved in more subtle ways. In the music of Thomas Adès (born 1971), endings often involve the return of the principal idea in a guise that reveals it to be somewhat pathetic. Adès first came to prominence in 1993, when he performed his piano piece *Still Sorrowing* at London's Purcell Room. His penchant for the pathetic ending was already evident in the Chamber Symphony, composed while he was still an undergraduate at Cambridge three years earlier. This is scored for fifteen players and has four movements welded into a single continuous form, which invites comparison with Schoenberg's Chamber Symphony, op. 9. Indeed, its principal idea, a theme announced on alto flute against a jazzy percussion accompaniment, sounds to begin with like a slowed-down version of the theme in Schoenberg's scherzo, but it proceeds quite differently: Schoenberg's symphony starts with a short introduction, and then gets under way with a lusty tune on the horn, based on a series of assertive rising fourths. Whenever a rising fourth occurs in Adès's melody, on the other hand, the music immediately draws back as if unsure of itself. Although the listener is not aware of it at the time, this interval hints at the melody's final destiny. Meanwhile, Adès develops his theme in increasingly brilliant and idiosyncratic ways. In the slow movement, for instance, a muted trombone has to sound as if it were being played by a maudlin jazz musician. Later, at the climax of the piece, woodwind instruments have to scream it out at the top of their ranges. Thereafter the confidence begins to melt away. The last movement, which is really just an expanded coda, begins with chords on a wheezy accordion. When, after a while, it makes its faltering exit, Adès brings in the last version of the melody. But now it is played plaintively and slowly by basset and bass clarinets, low in their registers and without any support to give it vitality. The last word is given to a horn, sounding the three-note call that most people will associate with the opening of Beethoven's 'Les Adieux' sonata. Earlier, in the first movement, this has been presented majestically on horn and trombone. Now, on two low clarinets, it appears to limp away as if defeated.

Still Sorrowing takes as its starting point the Romantic preoccupation with loss which was probably at its most poignant in German lieder. The piece is based on a refrain played in the middle register of the piano, in a hollow tone created by sticking 'Blu-tack' on the relevant strings. Below it, deep chords resonate; above it, brilliant contrapuntal figurations ripple. As the centre of the piece approaches the tempo gets faster; and when maximum brilliance is achieved there is a pause before the musical process goes into reverse, the tempo gradually slowing down. Near the end of the piece an assistant has to remove the 'Blu-tack' mutes, so that when the accompanying resonances and ripples are brought to a conclusion the refrain can be heard without any dampening. What emerges is a series of Romantic chords that might have come out of Schumann or Wolf at their saddest.

Arcadiana, a suite of seven pieces for string quartet, which Adès composed in 1994, reaches a similar conclusion but through a different approach. Here the principal idea is not a melody or refrain but an interval, a falling fifth, which eventually comes into its own in the last piece and is then almost immediately stripped of all support and made to sound as if the two notes were being played by muffled gongs. 'Each of the seven pieces,' says Adès in his preface to the score, 'evokes an image associated with ideas of the idyll, vanishing, vanished or imaginary. The odd-numbered movements are all aquatic, and would be continuous if played consecutively.' The first evokes a tipsy journey on a Venetian gondola at night; the third recalls the accompaniment of Schubert's *Auf dem Wasser zu singen*; the fifth, a gracious scherzo designed to sound as if it were coming from a distance, is meant to conjure up the idyllic view of the bay in Watteau's painting *The Embarkation from the Island of Cythera*; while the seventh portrays the ghostly atmosphere traditionally associated with the River Lethe. The second, fourth and sixth movements, by contrast, 'inhabit pastoral Arcadias'. The second recalls the dazzling brilliance of Mozart's Queen of Night and her supposedly idyllic Kingdom of Night in *The Magic Flute*; the fourth, a strange, dragging piece, relates to Nicolas Poussin's *Et in Arcadia ego*, which depicts a group of shepherds trying to decipher the Latin inscription on a tomb, with a dignified young shepherdess in attendance – the implication being that death is present even in an idyllic dreamland. In the sixth movement, 'O Albion', an evocation of the English pastoral idyll, the falling fifth suddenly takes on a more significant role and begins to come into its own. Until now it has introduced most, if not all, of the melodies and textures, but it has never been prominent. Like 'Nimrod' in Elgar's *Enigma Variations*, the movement is in E♭ major and is preceded by a long pause on a single G; the rising and falling sequences in it are also Elgarian. But Adès avoids any direct quotation: as on all the other occasions when he

The Museum of Modern Art, San Francisco, designed by Mario Botta.

refers to music of the past he does so by hints, by oblique allusions. The Elizabethan idyll, for example, is subtly conjured up by his use of a characteristically English false relation just before the movement's final cadence. It is not until the last movement, the one evoking the River Lethe, that a melody built entirely from falling fifths is finally announced. It comes high up on the cello, the other instruments providing wisps of ghostly figurations in the background. The instruction 'serenissimo' given to the cello, suggests that, for Adès, Lethe may

Thomas Adès's
Powder her Face, 1995.

bear some resemblance to the Venetian lagoon (Britten indicates the same connection in *Death in Venice*). The effect is reinforced by the tolling out of a pattern of four falling fifths (B–E, C–F, D–G, C♯–F♯), played unaccompanied, *ppp*, and without any vibrato to give them life.

Adès's biggest work to date is *Powder her Face* (1994–5), a chamber opera scored, like Turnage's *Greek*, for four singers and a chamber ensemble. But on this occasion the setting is the fashionable West End of London. The publisher describes the work as 'a darkly comic piece inspired by the glittering, brittle figure of Margaret, Duchess of Argyll', who had as her maxim the principle 'go to bed early and often', and consequently attracted 'clouds of gossip and scandal'. Cast in eight scenes, the opera deals with seven incidents in the life of an unnamed duchess during the period 1934 to 1990. They cover her rise to become one of the most sparkling society ladies of her time, quite capable of riding out scandal, malicious rumours and even the humiliating remarks of a divorce judge. By the final scene, however, deserted by her friends and ridiculed by the servants, she can no longer pay her hotel bill and is about to be evicted by the manager after ten years' residence; even her perfume bottle is empty. The opera opens with the events leading up to this scene; but, before the dénouement, the action cuts to 1934. We therefore get an inkling at the start of what the outcome will be. But it is only in the last three scenes that the pathos of the duchess's fate takes over. Until then the emphasis has been on wit and stylization. Adès's music

If anything is important, it is just to remind people to listen, and be patient, and listen again. Samuel Beckett says, 'Ever fail, try again, fail better.' We cannot see everything, we cannot hear everything at once, but we can approach it and attack it with joy and whole-heartedness, and every step is a journey to understanding.

amusingly touches on the idioms of a whole range of twentieth-century composers, including Berg, Britten, Poulenc, Strauss and Stravinsky, in addition to popular music. In scene ii, for instance, the tenor, playing the part of a lounge lizard, sings a brilliant parody of pre-war popular song: 'Who said it mattered what the public will say? . . . I'm in your clutches, duchess.' But, as with *Greek*, the opera cannot end tragically. When the duchess finally vacates her room in the hotel, an electrician and a maid appear to prepare it for the next visitor. No sooner have they stripped the bed than they start making love in time to a tango, which first appeared in the opening scene when, dressed as the duchess and striking a camp Statue of Liberty pose, the electrician entertained the maid. The scene must be performed in a playful but highly stylized manner. In the score it is labelled 'Ghost Epilogue'.

At the turn of the century Adès will still be in his twenties. His career will still lie ahead of him, and future generations may think of him as a composer of the twenty-first rather than the twentieth century. It is possible that his affectionate references in *Powder her Face* to so many twentieth-century styles will be regarded as his valediction to the era. He looks back, of course, as everyone does, from his own personal perspective. No one can deny that the century has been one of the most violent in human history, or that this violence has sometimes been reflected in its music. But everyone has to admit that this century has produced more variety, more choice for the listener than any in the past. One reason why twentieth-century music has not always been well received is that most composers have refused to pamper their listeners. They have hoped for audiences who can listen attentively to their works and be open to new perspectives. In a century when music has so often been treated as a palliative or a means of escape, such listeners have tended not to be numerous. But those prepared to meet the challenges of the new music have found themselves taken into worlds that are exciting and rewarding. Doubtless it will always be so.

**Leaving Home
Orchestral music in the twentieth century:
a conducted tour by Simon Rattle**
was produced by LWT Productions
for Channel Four Television

Music featured in the series

Programme 1: 'Dancing on a Volcano'

Wagner, Prelude to *Tristan and Isolde*
Schoenberg, *Transfigured Night*
Mahler, Symphony no. 7
Strauss, *Elektra*
Schoenberg, Five Orchestral Pieces, op. 16, nos. 1 and 2
Webern, Five Orchestral Pieces, op. 10, nos. 3, 4 and 5
Berg, Violin Concerto

Programme 2: 'Rhythm'

Stravinsky, *The Rite of Spring*
Varèse, *Ionisation*
Mahler, 'Abschied' from *Das Lied von der Erde*
Ligeti, *Atmosphères*
Reich, *Music for Pieces of Wood*
Nancarrow, Piano Roll no. 21
Boulez, *Rituel in Memoriam Bruno Maderna*
Messiaen, *Turangalîla Symphony*

Programme 3: 'Colour'

Debussy, *Prélude à l'après-midi d'un faune*
Stravinsky, *The Firebird*
Ravel, *Daphnis et Chloé*
Debussy, *Jeux*
Schoenberg, Five Orchestral Pieces, op. 16, no. 3 'Farben'
Boulez, *Notations*
Messiaen, *Et exspecto resurrectionem mortuorum*
Takemitsu, *Dream / Window*

Programme 4: 'Three Journeys through Dark Landscapes'

Bartók, *Duke Bluebeard's Castle*
Bartók, *Music for Strings, Percussion and Celesta*
Bartók, *The Miraculous Mandarin*
Bartók, Concerto for Orchestra
Shostakovich, Symphony no. 4
Shostakovich, Symphony no. 5
Shostakovich, Symphony no. 14
Lutosławski, Concerto for Orchestra
Lutosławski, *Venetian Games*
Lutosławski, Symphony no. 3

Programme 5: 'The American Way'

Gershwin, *Rhapsody in Blue*
Ives, *Decoration Day*
Carter, *A Celebration of Some 100 x 150 Notes*
Copland, *Appalachian Spring*
Weill, 'Lonely House' from *Street Scene*
Bernstein, 'Symphonic Dances' from *West Side Story*
Cage, *Sonatas and Interludes*
Cage, *First Construction in Metal*
Feldman, *Madame Press Died Last Week at 90*
Riley, *In C*
Adams, *Harmonium*

Programme 6: 'After the Wake'

Strauss, 'Im Abendrot' from *Four Last Songs*
Schoenberg, *A Survivor from Warsaw*
Boulez, *Le marteau sans maître*
Webern, Five Orchestral Pieces, op. 10, no. 4
Stockhausen, *Gruppen*
Britten, Serenade for tenor, horn and strings
Stravinsky, *Agon*

Programme 7: 'Music Now'

Berio, *Laborintus II*
Henze, *Symphony no. 8*
Gubaidulina, *Zeitgestalten*
Kurtág, *Grabstein für Stefan*
Birtwistle, *Ritual Fragment*
Turnage, *Drowned Out*
Knussen, *Flourish with Fireworks*

Glossary

accidental In musical notation, a symbol indicating the inflection of a note: a flat (♭) indicates that a note is lowered by a semitone, a sharp (♯) that it is raised; a natural (♮) is used to cancel one of the other two symbols on a subsequent occurrence of the note.

additive rhythm Rhythm in Classical music was based on the unit of the bar. A $\frac{4}{4}$ bar, for instance, would have one main stressed beat (*see* **down-beat**) and one or more subsidiary or **up-beats**. Additive rhythm, by contrast, is based on units smaller than the bar, such as the quaver, which may be grouped more freely. There is no higher organizing function of up-beats and down-beats that needs to be accommodated, so that additive rhythms are typically more asymmetrical than in Classical music. Additive rhythm is common in non-Western music.

aleatoric From the Latin word for dice, *alea*, aleatoric refers to music in which some aspects are not determined by the composer, but left to the performer. Aleatoric (or aleatory) music may, for example, require that the performer decide in what order to play given material, what instrument to use, or how to realize in music a composer's verbal instruction.

atonality Literally 'not tonality', but in a more precise sense a musical language in which the notes of the scale are of equal importance and exercise no 'gravitational pull' as they do in the tonal system. The term is used both of all non-tonal music, including twelve-note music, and in a more restricted sense of music that post-dates the tonal system but is not strictly twelve-note or **serial**.

beat *See* **pulse**.

bitonality The simultaneous use of a different key in each of two voices or parts (*see* **polytonality**). For music to be bitonal each of the keys has to be presented unambiguously and audibly, otherwise the music might well sound **atonal**.

cadence ('falling') In tonal music, a melodic or (more characteristically) harmonic device or formula with which a phrase or a section of music ends; the cadence often establishes or confirms beyond doubt the identity of the key. By extension, cadence can refer to any musical motif that gives a sense of resolution or closure.

canon A form of **counterpoint** in which the voices or lines carry the same theme, starting one after another. The theme and entries of the lines are designed so that the parts work together satisfactorily melodically and harmonically. They may announce the theme starting at the same pitch (canon 'at the unison') or at differing pitches (canon at the fifth, third, and so on). In more complex canons the theme may be inverted or played backwards (a 'cancrizans' canon), or both simultaneously. Canon is an important technique in twelve-note music, though the theme is usually referred to as a **note row**.

cantus firmus ('fixed song') An existing melody used as the basis of a new composition. In medieval music the cantus firmus was often taken from a plainsong, set in long, equal notes, and placed in the tenor voice; the original melody was thus effectively disguised and might even be unidentifiable by the listener.

chorale In the German Protestant church (specifically the Lutheran church) a hymn – that is, a text and its associated melody. A chorale is, characteristically, metrical, with a melody in predominantly equal note values, moving mostly by step. As with all hymnody, particular chorales are associated liturgically with certain seasons or days of the church's year, such as Advent, Passiontide, Easter and Pentecost. In twentieth-century music, 'chorale' refers to a musical texture that is mainly slow-moving and chordal.

chromatic ('coloured') In tonal music there are seven primary notes in the **diatonic** scale; the five other notes may be introduced for local effect without causing the music to move out of the home or tonic key (that is, without causing it to modulate). In 'chromatic music' considerable use is made of such local effects, which may be strong enough to affect the clarity of the tonal context. The term 'total chromatic' is used to describe music in which the notes of the scale have ceased to function tonally, and is thus synonymous with **atonality** in the broadest sense, and more specifically twelve-note music.

coda ('tail') The last section of a piece or a movement, often, by implication, an addition to the fundamental form, which would be complete without it.

consonance In tonal harmony, the pleasing sounding together of two or more notes; depending on the context, a consonance may impart a sense of resolution, rest or return after **dissonance**.

counterpoint Music is usually characterized as either based on chords (harmony) or melodies. Counterpoint is music made up of melodic lines which have a harmonic coherence (in tonal music, for instance, they would be in the same key) but which have varying degrees of independence (*see* **polyphony**). In twentieth-century music contrapuntal lines often appear to have a high degree of melodic and harmonic independence.

crescendo *See* **dynamics**.

cycle [circle] **of fifths** The arrangement of the twelve degrees of the chromatic scale as a succession of descending or ascending intervals of a fifth, which, if it is continued will end at the starting point, thus making a complete cycle: C–F–B♭–E♭–A♭–D♭–G♭ = F♯–B–E–A–D–G–(C). The cycle depends on the primacy of the first and fifth (tonic and dominant) notes of the **diatonic** scale, which also define the most closely related keys in the tonal system. The notational principle of the cycle of fifths in tonal music is that for every step the ascending cycle adds an extra sharp to the key signature or removes a flat; a descending cycle subtracts a sharp or adds a flat.

development The procedure of varying and reworking musical material, already announced in a straightforward manner. More specifically, that section in a sonata-form movement, following the **exposition**, in which such variation and reworking take place; it generally leads into the **recapitulation**, where the main thematic material of the exposition is repeated in modified form to bring the movement to an end.

diatonic A term used to describe music written in one of the two most prominent scales in Western tonal music – the major and minor – each of which is made up of tones and semitones (that is, whole steps and half steps) configured in a particular sequence. The major scale on C, for example, contains the notes C–D–E–F–G–A–B–(C), the harmonic minor C–D–E♭–F–G–A♭–B–(C). The tonic and dominant notes (the first and fifth notes, or 'degrees', of the scale) are the two most important. (*See also* **tonality**.)

diminuendo *See* **dynamics**.

dissonance In tonal harmony, a clashing or discordant harmony, which creates tension and demands resolution to a **consonance**. In twentieth-century music the use of dissonance is much freer; indeed, in his writings Arnold Schoenberg discusses the idea of 'emancipating' the dissonance from its obligations to resolve.

dominant The fifth note of the **diatonic** major and minor scales, and, by extension, either the triad build up from that note, or the key of which that note forms the tonic.

dominant seventh A four-note chord built up from the dominant note of a **diatonic** scale: it consists of a major triad with an added note at an interval of a seventh above the bottom note (or 'root') of the chord. In the key of C, for example, the dominant seventh chord is G–B–D–F. A dominant seventh inclines strongly to resolve on to the tonic triad.

down-beat The first beat of a bar, or, more loosely, any strong beat in a bar. In a bar of $\frac{4}{4}$ (that is, four crotchets to the bar) the first beat is the main down-beat, the third a subsidiary down-beat.

dynamics The character of musical sound that has to do with volume. Dynamics are generally graded between intensities of loudness ('forte', abbreviated in notation to *f*) and intensities of softness ('piano', abbreviated to *p*). A 'crescendo' involves a steady increase in volume, a 'diminuendo' a steady decrease.

enharmonic In traditional notation, there are several ways to notate pitches, according to their function in a tonal or modal context. The fourth degree of the scale in F major, for example, would be written B♭, whereas the same note could function as the leading note of B major, where it would be notated as A♯. These two 'spellings' are 'enharmonically equivalent', and the fact that the same note can function in two different ways in two different keys allows the **modulation** that is fundamental to the structural possibilities of Classical music.

exposition The first section of a sonata-form movement, in which the main thematic material of the movement is announced. The **development** and **recapitulation**, and sometimes a **coda**, complete the musical form.

fugue A kind of contrapuntal music (*see* **counterpoint**) that treats several parts or 'voices' according to more or less strict formal principles. In a fugue, the theme (or 'subject') is announced by one voice, and imitated by the others in succession. Against the second voice's presentation of the theme, the first plays a 'countersubject', which again is imitated by the following voices, but this time in a less strict way. After the presentation of the theme by all the voices the imitative procedures become less formulaic and may include overlapping themes (*see* **stretto**) and even a second fugue on a new theme. Bach, the supreme master of the fugue, confirmed the paired form of prelude and fugue for keyboard, notably in his collection of forty-eight such pairs, two in each of the major and minor keys of the chromatic scale, known as *The Well-Tempered Clavier*. This example has been followed by other composers up to this century, including Shostakovich and Lutosławski.

grace note A subsidiary, decorative note, which must be executed within the time allowed for the note to which it is attached. Grace notes are printed as small notes in Western notation.

ground bass A thematic bass line, often four or eight bars long, repeated many times in succession; typically, above the bass, the upper parts announce a melody, which is then subjected to different forms of variation.

hairpin ——— ——— The common term for the notation of crescendo and diminuendo.

heterophony The simultaneous performance of the same melody by several, usually contrasting, voices and/or instruments in unison or octaves. Characteristically, slight variations of performance (rhythm, precise timing of notes, or melody) create interesting effects and inflections. The term is also used of non-Western musics, particularly those in which a solo line is replicated, but with variations or decorations, by an accompaniment.

integral serialism *See* **serialism**.

interval The distance between two pitches. In tonal music intervals are usually given according to the distance between degrees of the scale; the interval between the first and fifth degrees of the scale, or the second and sixth, for instance, is a fifth. Examining the interval structure of **diatonic** scales, though, will show that not all such intervals are equal. The interval between the first and third notes and the second and fourth notes in a major scale are different, though they are both 'thirds'. Hence the distinction between a minor third (between second and fourth) and major third (first to third). For clarity, in twelve-note music intervals are usually given in terms of numbers of semitones, a fifth in this case consisting of seven semitones.

isorhythm In music of the Renaissance an isorhythm is a repeated or recurring rhythmic pattern that can work independently of the pitch content. So, for instance, the rhythmic pattern (*talea*) may have four elements, while the melody (*color*) may ·have five. Each time the rhythmic pattern is repeated it starts on a different melodic note; after five repetitions of the rhythm the cycle will be completed. This independence of pitch and rhythm made the technique attractive to many twentieth-century composers.

leading note The seventh degree of the major, and one form of the minor, scale – that is, the penultimate note of the ascending scale. It is so called because it inclines strongly to lead to the tonic note. In the key of C, the leading note is B.

melisma In vocal music, a melodic phrase consisting of many notes set to a single syllable. Melismatic setting is contrasted with 'syllabic' setting, in which there is a single note for every syllable.

metre The organization of music within time in such a way that it falls into a regular pattern of beats (*see* **down-beat** and **up-beat**), grouped into bars of defined duration. Metre is measured according to a basic note value: music in $\frac{4}{4}$ metre has four crotchets to the bar, music in $\frac{9}{8}$ has nine quavers to the bar, and so on; in notation it is indicated by a 'time signature' appearing as a fraction. In the twentieth century composers have experimented extensively with metre – for example, using metres that cannot be subdivided regularly (such as $\frac{11}{16}$ or $\frac{5}{8}$) and metre that changes constantly; some twentieth-century music consists of, or contains passages of, 'unmeasured music' – that is, music without metre.

metric modulation (or more properly, tempo modulation) A term invented by Richard Franko Goldmann to describe the change to a different tempo by means of an arithmetical relationship. If a crotchet is moving at 120 beats per minute, for example, semiquavers will be equal to 480 beats per minute. If the semiquavers are renotated as quintuplets the crotchet equivalent will now be $480 \div 5 = 96$ beats per minute. The technique is particularly associated with the music of Elliott Carter (see picture on p. 69).

mode A term used to describe any scale in which certain types of non-tonal music are written. As with all scales, different modes are distinguished by the order in which their intervals occur. In the context of Western music the term 'modes' is usually understood to apply to the 'church modes', so called because they provided the musical substance of sacred music before the development of the tonal system; as such they are the pre-tonal equivalents of the **diatonic** scales. The easiest way to identify the different modes is to play scales of an octave on the white notes only of the piano: a scale starting on C will produce the Ionian mode, that on D the Dorian, that on E the Phrygian, that on F the Lydian, that on G the Mixolydian, that on A the Aeolian, and that on B the Locrian. Scales that occur in many forms of non-Western music, which do not conform with the tonal system, are also known as 'modes'.

modulation In tonal theory, modulation is the movement out of one key into another as a continuous musical process.

monody In vocal music of the early Baroque period, a song-like piece for a solo voice with continuo accompaniment. More generally, a term applied to any music consisting of a single line, or such a line with a simple accompaniment.

note row The basic organizational principle of some twelve-note music, particularly serial music. A basic order is devised for the twelve notes of the chromatic scale. The sequence of pitches can then be modified in a limited number of ways, each of which will retain the interval relationships. The basic modifications are transposition (in which all the pitches are moved up or down by the same interval), retro-

grade (in which the order of the pitches is reversed) and inversion (in which the direction of each interval is altered). In most twelve-note music, these modifications are combined.

obbligato ('necessary') An independent instrumental line having the quality of a solo. Generally the term is applied to an ensemble instrument that forms part of, but stands out prominently from, the accompaniment to a vocal or instrumental solo. The term is most commonly used of arias, in which the voice and the obbligato instrument perform a duet, accompanied by continuo or a fuller ensemble.

octatonic scale A scale of eight notes to the octave, used by a number of twentieth-century composers, notably Stravinsky and Messiaen, in which intervals of a tone and a semitone alternate: for example, C–C♯–D♯–E–F♯–G–A–B♭–(C).

passacaglia A musical form which consists of a set of continuous variations built on multiple repetitions of a harmonic or melodic formula in the bass (*see* **ground bass**), or, in some cases, in an upper voice. The form originated in the Baroque period, and many twentieth-century composers have drawn on Baroque precedents, particularly the passacaglias of Bach and other German composers.

pentatonic scale A scale of five notes to the octave. In European music the pentatonic scale usually lacks semitones, consisting of sequences of tones and minor thirds (tone + semitone): for example, C–D–E–G–A–(C).

pitch class The modern term for all notes having the same name. All Cs, for example, regardless of which octave they are in, share the same pitch class.

pizzicato ('plucked') A method of playing a string instrument that would normally be bowed. A different, percussive, effect may be achieved by plucking so hard that the string springs back and hits the fingerboard, technique associated with the string music of Bartók.

polymodality The simultaneous use of a different mode in each of several voices of parts. Its effect depends on the listener's being able to distinguish the defining characteristics of the different modes within the musical texture.

polyphony ('many voices') A general term applied to

music in more than one part, in which the parts move to some extent independently: **canon**, **counterpoint** and **fugue** are all polyphonic forms.

polyrhythm The simultaneous use of two or more metres (and consequently rhythms) in different lines. The most audible effect of polyrhythm is that the down-beats in each metre fall at different points, creating the effect known as 'cross-rhythm'. The term 'polyrhythm' is also used to describe the simultaneous presentation of two or more speeds. These may be notated in relation to a common pulse – for instance, triplets against semiquavers, a four-against-three polyrhythm – or, as in the work of Conlon Nancarrow, according to completely separate metronome markings.

polytonality The simultaneous use of a different key in each of several voices of parts. Its effect depends on the listener's being able to distinguish the defining characteristics of the different keys within the musical texture; certain strong harmonic and melodic progresssions (such as cadences, and the resolution of the leading note to the tonic) are likely to be audible, and reinforce the sense that multiple keys are present concurrently.

pulse The underlying articulation in measured music, usually thought of as its speed. Pulse does not imply **up-beats** or **down-beats** and is therefore to be distinguished from **metre**. One of the functions of the conductor is to mark the pulse, or beat.

recapitulation The last (or, where there is a **coda**, the penultimate) section of a sonata-form movement, in which the main thematic material of the movement is repeated in modified form. *See also* **exposition** and **development**.

recitative A style of solo vocal music, found mostly in dramatic works, in which a dialogue is set to a musical line that follows the inflections and rhythms of speech. The character of recitative varies from the simple **secco recitative** to fully accompanied declamatory passages, but a defining feature is that it is through-composed (that is, contains no regularly repeating material) and generally lacks formal structure. Until the late Romantic period, recitative was the main vehicle for the exposition of the plot in opera, arias for the expression of emotions.

register A term used to describe the general position of a note or melody within the range of an instrument or voice. Register is not usually clearly defined, and the term is often used relatively – 'in a higher register', 'in the bass register'.

resolution In tonal and pre-tonal harmony, the process of releasing the tension and discord of a dissonant combination of notes by moving to a consonant combination (*see* **consonance** and **dissonance**). More broadly, the bringing to a conclusion of a melody or a harmonic sequence, usually by means of a **cadence**.

retrograde [*cancrizans* ('crab-like')] A term (used as a noun or an adjective) indicating that a theme, melody, or other sequence of notes is to be repeated in reverse; it may apply to pitch alone, or to both pitch and rhythm. Retrogrades occur seldom in tonal music, but figure prominently in twelve-note music, forming two of the four versions of the **note row** in the strict Schoenbergian form of the technique. The Latin word 'cancrizans' has this meaning in medieval and Renaissance music, though the reason is obscure, in that crabs move sideways and not backwards.

ritornello A passage of music that returns on a number of occasions more or less unchanged.

rubato ('robbed') A style of performing in which strict tempo is distorted for expressive effect: usually the performer stretches the durations of the notes in an irregular way, thus generally slowing down the tempo. In some cases, but comparatively seldom, there will be a compensatory hurrying over other durations, so that in the long term the tempo of the piece or passage is not affected.

scoring In ensemble music the deployment of instruments (and voices, if they are present) to take particular lines and notes within the texture (in which sense the meaning is close to 'instrumentation' or 'orchestration'); also, in a more detailed sense, the style of writing for particular instruments or voices so as to exploit their particular timbres, modes of attack, and other effects. The word is derived from 'score', the written form of the work, but is commonly applied even to music that exists in no written form.

secco ('dry') **recitative** The most speech-like type of **recitative**, typically delivered at speaking speed;

usually the ostensible metre is undetectable, the beginning of each bar being marked by chords supplied by the keyboard accompaniment.

serialism A term applied to music in which a fixed sequence is determined for some or all of the elements; that sequence may be subjected to various treatments (for example, inversion or reversal) but the relationship between the units will not be corrupted. Most commonly the 'series' governs pitch, but rhythm, attack, dynamics and timbre may also be serialized. Where all elements are controlled in this way the technique is referred to as 'total' or 'integral' serialism. Although much serial music makes use of the twelve notes of the chromatic scale, some does not, and by no means all twelve-note music is strictly serial; thus, despite common usage that equates them, the terms 'serial' and 'twelve-note music' are not synonymous.

spondee A rhythmic pattern consisting of two equal stressed values.

stochastic music A term borrowed from probability theory to describe situations in which the number of elements is very large, so that the behaviour of individuals cannot be determined, though the behaviour of the whole collection can be.

stretto ('narrow', 'constricted') In the strict contrapuntal forms of **canon** and **fugue**, a passage in which entries of the theme occur in quick succession, the interval between entries being shorter than in the preceding sections of the piece. A stretto creates tension and excitement and is thus often introduced to build up a climax and prepare for the final entry of the theme and its resolution.

syncopation The temporary disruption of the metrical organization of a passage of music by placing accents on beats other than the main ones in a bar, making a weak beat sound like a strong beat. Syncopation is most effective when the musical metre itself is regular and predictable, for example in jazz.

timbre In its principle sense timbre is the distinctive acoustic properties of sounds or instruments.

tonality A musical language based on the **diatonic** major and minor scales, which forms the substance of musical composition from about 1600 to about 1900.

The tonal system assumes the central importance of one note in any key (the 'tonic' or 'key note') and depends on the strength of relationships between that note and others (principally the fifth or 'dominant'). The relationship between notes gives rise to relationships between the scales built on those notes, and thus between keys. For example, C major is closely related to G major (its dominant) and A minor (its relative minor) because the scale of C major differs by only one note from the scale of G major and that of A minor. Tonal music continues to be written in the twentieth century, alongside music in which hierarchical relationships have broken down.

tonic In tonal music, the principal note of a key, or the chord based on that note.

total chromatic *See* **chromatic**.

total serialism *See* **serialism**.

tritone The interval of three whole tones, or exactly half an octave. It can be referred to as an augmented fourth or a diminished fifth or even, as it was in the Renaissance, as *diabolus in musica* ('the devil in music') because of its instability. This instability has been exploited in the extension and suspension of tonality, and in this century as an expressive interval in its own right.

trochee A pattern of two notes with a stress on the first. This may be articulated in a number of ways, either by dynamics (accenting the first note of the pair) or by rhythm (lengthening the first).

up-beat The last beat in a bar, or more loosely, any beat that anticipates or implies some sort of resolution.

voice In general, the word refers to any musical line, not just a vocal line, that seems continuous and connected. It differs from 'melody' or 'tune' in as much as it doesn't imply a predominant role.

whole-tone scale A scale that includes only major seconds. Melodies and harmonies based on this scale therefore exclude intervals such as the semitone, fourth and fifth, fundamental to tonal or modal music. Because there are no leading notes, and no harmonic relationship that has priority over others, whole-tone music tends to sound unstable and unfocused compared with tonal music.

Further Reading

This list does not aim to be comprehensive; it lists the most important books in English on each composer, or books that will themselves contain extensive bibliographies. Where possible, it includes also writings by composers, where they exist in print in English.

General Books

Whittall, Arnold, *Music since the First World War*, London, 1977

Morgan, Robert P. *Twentieth-century Music*, New York, 1991

Morgan, Robert P. *Anthology of Twentieth-century Music*, New York, 1992

Lebrecht, Norman, *Companion to Twentieth-century Music*, London, 1992

Griffiths, Paul, *Modern Music and After: Directions since 1945*, Oxford, 1995

Conversations

Dufallo, Paul, *Trackings: Composers Speak*, New York, 1989

Ford, Andrew, *Composer to Composer: Conversations about Contemporary Music*, London, 1994

Smith, Geoff, and Nicola Walker Smith, *American Originals: Interviews with 25 Contemporary Composers*, London, 1993

Chapter 1: Dancing on a Volcano

Berg
Perle, George, *The Operas of Alban Berg*, (two vols), Berkeley, California, 1981–6

Jarman, Douglas, *The Music of Alban Berg*, London, 1983

Mahler
Mitchell, Donald, *Gustav Mahler: the Early Years*, London, 1958

Mitchell, Donald, *Gustav Mahler: the Wunderhorn Years*, London, 1975

Mitchell, Donald, *Gustav Mahler: Songs and Symphonies of Life and Death*, London, 1985

Schoenberg
Macdonald, Malcolm, *Schoenberg*, London, 1976

Schoenberg, Arnold, *Style and Idea*, London, 1975

Strauss
Kennedy, Michael, *Strauss Tone Poems*, London, 1984

Osborne, Charles, *The Complete Operas of Richard Strauss*, London, 1995

Webern
Bailey, Kathryn, *The Twelve-note Music of Webern*, Cambridge, 1991

Hayes, Malcolm, *Anton von Webern*, London, 1995

Webern, Anton, *The Path to the New Music*, London, 1963

Chapter 2: Rhythm

Nancarrow
Gann, Kyle, *The Music of Conlon Nancarrow*, Cambridge, 1995

Messiaen
Hill, Peter (ed.), *The Messiaen Companion*, London, 1995

Messiaen, Olivier, *The Technique of My Musical Language*, Paris, 1957

Reich
Reich, Steve, *Writings about Music*, Halifax, 1974

Stravinsky
van den Toorn, Pieter C., *The Music of Igor Stravinsky*, New Haven, 1983

Walsh, Stephen, *The Music of Stravinsky*, London, 1988

Griffiths, Paul, *Stravinsky*, London, 1992

Stravinsky, Igor, *Poetics of Music in the Form of Six Lessons*, Cambridge, Mass., 1951

Varèse
Bernard, Jonathan W., *The Music of Edgard Varèse*, New Haven, 1987

Chapter 3: Colour

Boulez

Stacey, Peter F., *Boulez and the Modern Concept*, Aldershot, 1987

Boulez, Pierre, *Stocktakings from an Apprenticeship*, Oxford, 1991 (previously translated in English as *Notes from an Apprenticeship*)

Boulez, Pierre and John Cage, *The Boulez–Cage Correspondence*, Cambridge, 1993

Debussy

Parks, Richard S., *The Music of Claude Debussy*, New Haven, 1990

Dietschy, Marcel, *Portrait of Claude Debussy*, Oxford, 1994

Ravel

Myers, Rollo H., *Ravel: Life and Works*, 1960

Takemitsu

Ohtake, Noriko, *Creative Sources for the Music of Toru Takemitsu*, Aldershot, 1993

Chapter 4: Three Journeys through Dark Landscapes

Bartók

Antoloketz, Elliott, *The Music of Béla Bartók*, Berkeley, 1984

Gillies, Malcolm (ed.), *The Bartók Companion*, London, 1993

Bartók, Béla, *Essays*, Lincoln, Nebraska, 1992

Lutosławski

Varga, Bálint András, *Lutoslawski profile*, London 1976

Rae, Charles Bodman, *The Music of Lutoslawski*, London, 1994

Shostakovich

Volkov, Solomon, *Testimony: the Memoirs of Shostakovich*, London, 1979

Wilson, Elizabeth, *Shostakovich: a Life Remembered*, London, 1994

Chapter 5: America

Bernstein

Burton, Humphrey, *Leonard Bernstein*, London, 1994

Bernstein, Leonard, *The Unanswered Question*, Cambridge, Mass., 1976

Cage

Pritchett, James, *The Music of John Cage*, Cambridge, 1993

Cage, John, *Empty Words: Writings '73–'78*, London, 1980

Cage, John, *Themes and Variations*, Barrytown, 1982

Cage, John, *X: Writings '79–'82*, London, 1987

Carter

Schiff, David, *The Music of Elliott Carter*, London, 1983

Carter, Elliott, *The Writings of Elliott Carter*, Woodbridge, 1996

Crawford Seeger

Straus, Joseph N., *The Music of Ruth Crawford Seeger*, Cambridge, 1995

Gershwin

Jablonski, Edward, *Gershwin Remembered*, London, 1992

Ives

Ives, Charles, *Essays before a Sonata*, London, 1969

Ives, Charles, *Memos*, London, 1974

Weill

Taylor, Ronald, *Kurt Weill: Composer in a Divided World*, London, 1993

Weill, Kurt, *Essays on: 'New Orpheus'*, New Haven, 1986

Chapter 6: After the Wake

Berio

Dalmonte, Rosanna and Bálint András Varga, *Luciano Berio; Two Interviews*, London, 1985

Osmond-Smith, David, *Berio*, Oxford, 1991

Birtwistle

Hall, Michael, *Harrison Birtwistle*, London, 1984

Britten

Kennedy, Michael, *Britten*, London, 1981

Carpenter, Humphrey, *Benjamin Britten*, London, 1992

Ligeti

Griffiths, Paul, *György Ligeti*, London, 1983

Ligeti in Conversation, London, 1983

Maxwell Davies

Griffiths, Paul, *Peter Maxwell Davies*, London, 1981

Seabrook, Mike, *Max: The Life and Music of Peter Maxwell Davies*, London, 1994

Stockhausen

Maconie, Robin, *The Works of Karlheinz Stockhausen*, London, 1990

Kurtz, Michael, *Stockhausen: A Biography*, London, 1992

Tannenbaum, Mya, *Conversations with Stockhausen*, Oxford, 1987

Nevill, Tim (ed.), *Towards a Cosmic Music: Texts by Karlheinz Stockhausen*, London, 1989

Tippett

Whittall, Arnold, *The Music of Britten and Tippett*, London, 1990

Tippett, Michael, *Those Twentieth-century Blues: an Autobiography*, London, 1994

Bowen, Meirion (ed.), *Tippett on Music*, Oxford, 1995

Xenakis

Matossian, Nouritza, *Xenakis*, London, 1986

Varga, Bálint András, *Conversations with Iannis Xenakis*, London, 1996

Xenakis, Iannis, *Arts/Sciences: Alloys*, Stuyvesant, NY, 1985

Xenakis, Iannis, *Formalized Music*, Stuyvesant, NY, 1991

Chapter 8: Music Now

Ferneyhough

Ferneyhough, Brian, *Collected Writings*, London, 1996

Henze

Henze, Hans Werner, *Music and Politics*, London, 1982

Kurtág

Spangemacher, Friedrich (ed.), *György Kurtág*, Bonn, 1989

Tavener

Haydon, Geoffrey, *John Tavener: Glimpses of Paradise*, London, 1995

Index

Acknowledgements

The publishers gratefully acknowledge the permission of the following to reproduce pictures:

p. v, Carmel Collins; p. viii, LWT Productions Ltd; p. 1, LWT Productions Ltd; p. 4, Österreichische Galerie, Vienna; photo Bridgeman Art Library; p. 5, Moscow, Pushkin Museum; photo AKG/ Erich Lessing; p. 6, Bibliothèque Nationale, Paris; p. 8, Stephane Couturier/Arcaid; p. 9, Heydt Museum, Wuppertal; photo Bridgeman Art Library; p. 13, AKG; p. 18, Lipnitzki–Viollet; photo Roger-Viollet; p. 20, Richard Bryant/Arcaid; p. 21, Richard Bryant/Arcaid; p. 25, Vienna, Österreichische Galerie; photo AKG/Erich Lessing; p. 29, Munich, Lenbachhaus; photo AKG; p. 32, Photo AKG; p. 33, Vienna, Österreichische Galerie; photo AKG; p. 35, Ullstein Bilderdienst; p. 36, Photo AKG; p. 37, Munich, Lenbachhaus; photo AKG; p. 38, Clive Barda; p. 39, Richard-Strauss-Institut, Landeshauptstadt Munchen; p. 40, Vienna, Historische Museum der Stadt Wien; photo AKG; p. 41, Zurich, Buhrle Collection; photo AKG; p. 44, Photo British Film Institute Stills, Posters and Designs; p. 44, Alfred A. Kalmus Ltd, Universal Edition; p. 45, Bibliothèque Musicale Gustav Mahler; p. 46, LWT Productions Ltd; p. 47, Photo British Film Institute Stills, Posters and Designs; p. 48, Photo Hans van den Bogaard; p. 50, Photo British Film Institute Stills, Posters and Designs; p. 52, Photo Maria Enzersdorf; p. 53, Arnold Schoenberg Institute, Los Angeles; p. 54, Courtesy Universal Edition; p. 57, Ben Johnson/Arcaid; p. 58, Photo AKG; p. 58, Hulton Deutsch; p. 60, Museum of Modern Art, New York; photo AKG; p. 61, Photo AKG; p. 62, Photo British Film Institute Stills, Posters and Designs; p. 63, Photo AKG; p. 64, Science Photo Library; p. 65, Lawrence Berkeley Laboratory/Science Photo Library; p. 67, The Charles Ives Papers, Yale University Music Library; p. 69, Chester Music Ltd; p. 72, Tinguely-Museum, Basel; photo AKG/Roche; p. 73 , Schott & Co Ltd, London; p. 74, Phillip Makanna; photo by kind permission of Eva Soltes & Associates; p. 76, Bill Rafferty; p. 77, Betty Freeman; p. 78, Andrew Pothecary; p. 79, Schott & Co. Ltd, London; p. 80, Schott & Co. Ltd, London; p. 81, Lipnitzki-Viollet; photo Roger Viollet; p. 84–5, United Music Publishers; p. 87, Universal Edition, Vienna; p. 89, John Edward Linden/Arcaid; p. 90, Universal Edition, Vienna; p. 93, Photo AKG; p. 94, Photo AKG; p. 95, Photo AKG; p. 96, LWT Productions Ltd; p. 97, Photo AKG; p. 100, Arnold Schoenberg Institute, Los Angeles; p. 101, Tretyakov Gallery, Moscow; photo Bridgeman Art Library; p. 101, Municipal Gallery in the Lenbachhaus, Munich; p. 102, Photo AKG; p. 104, John Batten; p. 105, Photo AKG; p. 105, Bibliothèque Nationale de France; p. 106, The Board of Trustees of the V&A Museum; p. 107, Malcolm Crowthers; p. 108, Photo AKG; p. 109, Malcolm Crowthers; p. 111, Fondation Le Corbusier; p. 112, LWT Productions Ltd; p. 113, Photo Bill Tingey/Arcaid; p. 114, Stockhausen Verlag; p. 116, Bill Rafferty; p. 117, Arnold Schoenberg Institute, Los Angeles; pp. 118–19, Universal Edition, Vienna; p. 119, John Edward Linden; photo Arcaid; p. 123, Popperfoto; pp. 124–5, Bill Rafferty; p. 126, Popperfoto; p. 128, Interfoto MTI; pp. 129–31, Ullstein; p. 132, Science Photo Library; p. 133, Interfoto MTI; p. 135, Interfoto MTI; p. 136, Range/Bettmann; p. 138, Ullstein; p. 140, Haags Gemeentemuseum; photo Bridgeman Art Library; p. 141, Metro Tartan; p. 143, Novosti Photo Library; p. 144, Alissa Poret; p. 147, Society for Cooperation in Russian & Soviet Studies; p. 148, Novosti Photo Library; p. 150, Chester Music, London; p. 152, Chester Music, London; p. 153, Polska Agencja Informacyjna; p. 155, Chester Music, London; p. 156, Polska Agencja Informacyjna; p. 160, Corbis–Bettmann/UPI; p. 164, Simon Matthews; photo Arcaid; p. 165, Corbis–Bettmann/UPI; p. 166, Archiv Fur Kunst und Geschichte, Berlin; p. 167, Corbis–Bettmann/UPI; p. 168, LWT

Productions Ltd; p. 169, Ralph Titus; p. 169, Alex MacLeod; p. 172, Alex Bartel/Arcaid; p. 173, Richard Waite/Arcaid; p. 175, AKG; p. 176, Richard Bryant/Arcaid; p. 177, Kurt Weill Foundation; p. 178, Range/Bettman ; p. 179, Malcolm Crowthers; p. 180, Natalie Tepper/Arcaid; p. 181, Natalie Tepper/Arcaid; p. 184, Hedrich Blessing/Arcaid; p. 185, Susan Schwartzenberg; photo The Exploratorium; p. 188, Alex MacLeod; p. 189, Alex Bartel/Arcaid; p. 191, Warner Bros; photo British Film Institute Stills, Posters and Designs; p. 192, LWT Productions Ltd; p. 193, Natalie Tepper/Arcaid; p. 195, Ullstein Bilderdienst; p. 196, Corbis–Bettmann; p. 197, Britten-Pears Library; p. 201, Jane Brown; p. 206, Archiv für Kunst und Geschichte, Berlin; photo AKG; p. 207, Camera Press; p. 207, Arnold Schoenberg Institute, Los Angeles; p. 208, Alfred Kalmus Ltd, Universal Edition Ltd, London; p. 209, John Batten; pp. 212–3, Stockhausen Verlag;

p. 214, Editions Salabert, Paris; p. 215, Boosey and Hawkes, London; p. 216, Museo del Prado, Madrid; photo AKG; p. 217, Museo Picasso, Barcelona; photo Bridgeman Art Library; p. 224, Courtesy of György Ligeti; p. 225, Photo AKG; p. 228, Victoria and Albert Museum; photo Bridgeman Art Library; p. 229, Faber and Faber; p. 233, Natalie Tepper/Arcaid, 4287:340:2; p. 233, David Churchill/Arcaid; p. 236, Andrew Pothecary; photo Boosey and Hawkes, London; p. 237, Photocrew; p. 238, AKG/AP; p. 239, AKG; p. 240, British Museum; photo Bridgeman Art Library; p. 241, Peters Edition; p. 244, Malcolm Crowthers, 1993; p. 251, Editio Musica Budapest; p. 252, AKG; p. 253, John Edward Linden/Arcaid; p. 254, Camera Press; p. 259, Lynda Stone; photo Hulton Getty Picture Collection; p. 260, Greenaway; p. 261, AKG; p. 262, Ivan Kyncl; p. 263, John Edward Linden/Arcaid